VICTORY

SAVROLA
THE STORY OF THE MALAKAND FIELD FORCE
THE RIVER WAR
LONDON TO LADYSMITH VIA PRETORIA
IAN HAMILTON'S MARCH
LORD RANDOLPH CHURCHILL
MY AFRICAN JOURNEY
LIBERALISM AND THE SOCIAL PROBLEM
THE WORLD CRISIS :
   1911–1914
   1915
   1916–1918
   AFTERMATH
   THE EASTERN FRONT

MY EARLY LIFE
THOUGHTS AND ADVENTURES
MARLBOROUGH, 4 VOLS.
GREAT CONTEMPORARIES
ARMS AND THE COVENANT
STEP BY STEP : 1936–1939
INTO BATTLE
THE UNRELENTING STRUGGLE
THE END OF THE BEGINNING
ONWARDS TO VICTORY
THE DAWN OF LIBERATION

Mr. Churchill celebrates the triumph of VE-Day on the balcony of Buckingham Palace with their Majesties the King and Queen, and the Princesses

VICTORY

War Speeches by the
RIGHT HON. WINSTON S. CHURCHILL
O.M., C.H., M.P.
1945

Compiled by
CHARLES EADE

CASSELL AND COMPANY LTD.
LONDON, TORONTO, MELBOURNE AND SYDNEY

First Published .. 1946

MADE AND PRINTED IN GREAT BRITAIN
AT THE CHAPEL RIVER PRESS
ANDOVER, HANTS
F. 2.46

CONTENTS

CONTENTS

vi

CONTENTS

THE WAR

LIST OF ILLUSTRATIONS

INTRODUCTION

NEW YEAR'S DAY, 1945, saw the military power of the United Nations deployed in its greatest strength. The year which had just closed had brought a series of Allied victories on land, at sea and in the air, unparalleled in history. The great offensive had been successfully launched against German-occupied France. British and American armies had swept across the Continent to the very gates of Germany, while, in the East, the Soviet forces had torn the heart out of the Nazi armies in Russia and Poland. Air raids of ever-growing strength and devastation had wrought havoc throughout enemy lands. The U-boat menace had been throttled. In Asia and the Pacific the Japanese were slowly but steadily losing their grip on the territories they had seized three years earlier.

But despite these glorious and solid successes, the Allied peoples looked at the war at the beginning of 1945 with mixed feelings. So much had been accomplished, the ultimate triumph had appeared so near a few months earlier, that there was natural disappointment at the year's end that not only had final victory still to be won, but the Germans were hitting back in the West with unexpected power and shaking the optimists who had regarded the end as near and certain.

On the Western Front the dangerous counter-offensive launched by Field-Marshal Rundstedt, Commander-in-Chief of the German armies, was being checked by the Allies, but only by a supreme effort. Rochefort, the German strong-point in the Western tip of the Ardennes salient, had just been recaptured, and General Patton's Third U.S. Army had launched a new offensive against the Southern flank of the German salient between St. Hubert and Bastogne.

The German counter-offensive had come as a great shock to the people of the United Nations. It had been launched, a few weeks before, at a time when optimism ran high and when few people thought that the Germans had the capacity for such a revival. In Britain and America there were critics who were quick to enquire into the reasons why the Germans were able to surprise the Allied Command in this way.

However, at the opening of the year the military situation was becoming stabilized, and the push that at one time looked like threatening vital key-points such as Liége, Namur and even Antwerp, was definitely held.

Allied air forces, flying thousands of sorties a day, were bombing enemy communications, oil plants and war factories, and the R.A.F. celebrated the opening of the New Year with the heaviest Mosquito attack Berlin had ever had. Allied air strength was turning the tide.

On the other sections of the Western Front the Armies on both sides were practically at a stand-still, and parties of British troops were returning to England for leave for the first time since the invasion. Isolated pockets of German troops still held out strongly in some of the Channel and Atlantic ports of France. These forces could have no effect on the campaign in the West, but their stubborn resistance denied the Allies the use of valuable harbours.

On the Russian Front, the Soviet Armies were gathering strength for the next great push, and for the moment the main interest centred on the encirclement of Budapest by Red Army forces and the thrust by other units in the direction of Vienna. The Germans had just killed two Russian officers who had entered Budapest carrying white flags and conveying an ultimatum to the garrison. On other parts of the eastern front there was little movement, but great forces of Russians stood poised ready for an attack at many points in the Spring.

In Italy the Allied Armies were pulling their weight in the struggle, but in a less spectacular way. This campaign progressed slowly through the mountains. The German " Gothic Line " in the Northern Apennines had been breached some months before, but the rugged country and the stern resistance of the Germans under General Kesselring made any swift, decisive advances impossible. Ravenna and Faenza had recently been captured, and the Allied Armies slogged away in hard winter weather. But the limelight had moved to other theatres.

The last few weeks of 1944 had been darkened by civil war in Greece. A personal visit by the Prime Minister had failed to produce immediate peace. But Mr. Churchill had advised the King of Greece to agree to a Regency, and this had just been set up with Archbishop Damaskinos as Regent. Despite this move fighting continued, and the country presented one of the gloomiest pictures of the New Year. American criticism of British policy in Greece was not helping to ease a tense and difficult situation. Many offers and counter-offers had been made and talks had been held, but there was no sign of a peaceful solution, and hostilities continued in Greece on New Year's Day.

In Poland the political situation had been complicated by the decision of the National Council at Lublin to declare itself a Provisional Government, thus setting itself in opposition to the Government in London which still had the support of both Great Britain and America. The Polish question, like the Greek, was one of the many " difficult problems " facing the leaders of the United Nations.

In the Far East splendid progress was being made by Admiral Mountbatten's troops through the jungles of Burma, and some units had reached to within 80 miles of Mandalay. The Japanese had been thrown back across the Chindwin River, and there were signs that they were withdrawing from the whole of North Burma.

In the Philippines, General MacArthur's American troops had just cleared the Island of Leyte, and in the North Pacific the American naval forces under Admiral Nimitz were hurling their air strength at the heart of Japan. Already heavy bombers flying from island bases in the Pacific had hammered at factories in Tokyo. The war was reaching the Japanese homeland.

In China the outlook was grim. Chiang Kai Shek's forces, battered and weary after nine years of war, were growing steadily weaker. It appeared on this first day of January that a great military effort would be needed to drive the powerful Japanese Armies from the mainland of Asia.

In England the V.1 flying bombs, although fewer, were more widespread, and the North of England was just beginning to experience what London and the South had suffered during the previous seven months. The V.2 rockets were growing in numbers, and every day many homes in London and the Southern and Eastern Counties were destroyed or damaged with grievous loss of life. It seemed that to the very end of the war the people of Britain would still have to " take it." Such widespread indiscriminate attacks could have little effect on the course of the main conflict, but they helped the Germans to bolster up the morale of their people with hopes of devastating secret weapons which would destroy their enemies.

In America, the startling counter-offensive by Rundstedt had brought forth a new feeling of resolution and tightening-up of manpower and production effort. Mr. Byrnes, Director of War Mobilization, had just announced that four million young Americans who had failed in the medical test for the Army were being told that they would have to get into war services, and those who were fit enough would be assigned to Army duties for which they would be suitable.

At sea the U-boat menace was no longer a powerful factor in the war. Germany's under-sea attack appeared to have been finally throttled.

Hitler marked the opening of the New Year with a broadcast in which he made yet another call to the German people, assuring them there would be no capitulation and that he and the nation were resolved to go to the limit. But in the Allied countries it was felt that Hitler had now been relegated to the background, and that the active conduct of the war was in the hands of Himmler, as leader of the home-front, and Rundstedt and the German High Command in the military spheres.

All the peoples of the United Nations knew at the opening of the New Year that complete and overwhelming victory over Germany and Japan was certain. But most of them now knew, better than ever, that there was still much hard fighting to be done.

CHARLES EADE.

VICTORY

REVIEW OF THE WAR

A Speech to the House of Commons
January 18, 1945

January 1. *Heavy German counter-attacks against U.S. Seventh Army continued along the Palatinate border. The enemy lost 364 aircraft in attacks on Allied air-fields on the Western Front.*

Indian troops made further advances in Arakan (Burma).

German offensive against the 5th Army in Italy collapsed.

January 2. *U.S. Third Army struck back on the Western Front and penetrated flank of the enemy salient in the Ardennes.*

Admiral Sir Bertram Ramsay, Naval Commander-in-Chief A.E.F., was killed in an air accident.

January 3. *U.S. First Army attacked Northern flank of Ardennes salient.*

Russians pressed into the heart of Budapest.

In Burma, the 14th Army entered Yeo, 70 miles from Mandalay.

General Plastiras formed a new Government in Greece.

January 4. *U.S. First Army advanced farther into the Northern flank of the Ardennes salient.*

There was a dead-lock in the political situation in Athens and fighting continued in the city.

January 5. *German High Command claimed 25-mile breach in U.S. lines between Rhine and Saar.*

Mr. Churchill returned from visiting General Eisenhower and Field-Marshal Montgomery in France.

British troops captured Akyab, chief Japanese base in Arakan and third port in Burma.

Fighting ceased in Athens and E.L.A.S. rebels retreated to the mountains.

Russia recognized the Lublin Committee as Polish Provisional Government.

January 6. *Germans increased their pressure North and South of Strasbourg.*

January 7.	*Field-Marshal Montgomery reported that the Allies had regained the initiative in the Ardennes salient.*
	U.S. troops landed on Luzon in the Philippines.
January 9.	*In Ardennes salient enemy made important withdrawals.*
January 10.	*German thrust towards Strasbourg continued. 1,100 U.S. bombers attacked behind Ardennes salient and the Germans made further withdrawals.*
January 11.	*Enemy defence line in Ardennes crumbled, and Laroche was captured.*
	British troops captured Shwebo, Burma.
January 12.	*British and U.S. troops closed on Houffalize, centre of the Ardennes salient, and the German withdrawal continued.*
	In Athens General Scobie signed truce with E.L.A.S.
	The Russians launched a new attack in South Poland, directed at Cracow and Breslau.
January 13.	*Another major Soviet offensive was launched in East Prussia.*
January 14.	*Allies continued their advance in the Ardennes salient and many enemy planes were destroyed on the ground and in the air.*
January 15.	*Russians captured Kielce, communications centre, and reached 50 miles beyond Vistula.*
January 16.	*Allied troops captured Houffalize in Ardennes salient and British Second Army attacked towards the Roer River.*
	Russians advanced 37 miles in three days in their new offensive South of Warsaw.
January 17.	*Russian advance continued on the Warsaw front and Czestochowa was captured.*
January 18.	*Russian troops crossed the Silesian frontier.*

[*January* 18, 1945.

I GATHERED that it was the desire of the House that there should be a further discussion of the war and foreign situations and policies at this time, before any new important international conferences take place. I will try to survey the whole—I cannot say the whole, but large and selected portions—of this vast scene to the best of my ability. It has fallen to the hard lot of Britain to play a leading part in the Mediterranean, and particularly in the Eastern Mediterranean. We have great responsibilities and we have made great exertions there. In Italy the British, or British-controlled, divisions under Field-Marshal Alexander's command, and still more if the whole area of

2

the Mediterranean is included, outnumber three-fold those of the United States. There is battle along the whole front in Italy, and behind the front, in the hard-stricken peninsula, are many economic and political difficulties. The old structure with its hateful rigours has been destroyed, and in its place we have had to raise a Government of improvisation. We have the Bonomi Government, which has been trying to do its best under extraordinary difficulties, but which, of course, has no electoral authority behind it. But now, at any time, perhaps in a few months, perhaps much sooner—for no one can tell what is proceeding in the minds of the German war leaders—the Germans will be driven out of Italy, or will perhaps withdraw ; and immediately the great populous districts of the North, the cities of Turin, Milan, and other centres of industry and activity, and a large population of all kinds of political views but containing great numbers of vehement or violent politicians, and in touch with brave men who have been fighting and maintaining a guerrilla warfare in the Alps, all these will be thrown—probably at a time when the Northern regions have been stripped bare of food by the retreating Germans—upon the fragile structure of the Italian Government in Rome, with consequences which cannot be accurately foreseen, and certainly not measured.

How necessary it is for Britain and the United States, who bear the chief responsibilities, to maintain the closest and most intimate contact in the solution of all these new problems ! Let me say once and for all that we have no political combinations, in Europe or elsewhere, in respect of which we need Italy as a party. We need Italy no more than we need Spain, because we have no designs which require the support of such Powers. We must take care that all the blame of things going wrong is not thrown on us. This, I have no doubt, can be provided against, and to some extent I am providing against it now.

We have one principle about the liberated countries or the repentant satellite countries which we strive for according to the best of our ability and resources. Here is the principle. I will state it in the broadest and most familiar terms : Government of the people, by the people, for the people, set up on a basis of election by free and universal suffrage, with secrecy of the ballot and no intimidation. That is and has always been the policy of this Government in all countries. That is our only aim, our only interest, and our only care. It is to that goal that we try to make our way across all the difficulties, obstacles and perils of the long road. Trust the people, make sure they have a fair chance to decide their destiny without being terrorized from either quarter or regimented. There is our policy for Italy, for Yugoslavia and for Greece. What other interest have we than that ? For that we shall strive, and for that alone.

3

The general principle which I have enunciated guides us in our relations with Yugoslavia. We have no special interest in the political régime which prevails in Yugoslavia. Few people in Britain, I imagine, are going to be more cheerful or more downcast because of the future Constitution of Yugoslavia. However, because the King and the Royal Yugoslav Government took refuge with us at the time of the German invasion, we have acquired a certain duty towards the Government and peoples on the other side of the Adriatic which can only be discharged in a correct and formal manner such as, for instance, would be provided by a plebiscite. I am the earliest outside supporter of Marshal Tito. It is more than a year since in this House I extolled his guerrilla virtues to the world. Some of my best friends and the hon. and gallant Member for Preston [The Prime Minister's son, Major Churchill] are there with him or his Forces now. I earnestly hope he may prove to be the saviour and the unifier of his country, as he is undoubtedly at this time its undisputed master.

Recently Bulgaria and Rumania have passed under the control of the Soviet military authorities, and Russian-controlled armies are in direct contact with Yugoslavia. As we feared that there might be misunderstandings and contrary policies between us and the Soviet Government about Yugoslavia, which can easily arise when armies enter a country which is in great disorder, the Foreign Secretary and I reached at Moscow an understanding with Marshal Stalin by which our two countries pursue a joint policy in these regions, after constant discussions. This agreement raised no question of divisions of territory or spheres of interest after the war. It was aimed only at the avoidance, during these critical days, of friction between the great Allies. In practice I exchange telegrams on behalf of His Majesty's Government personally with Marshal Stalin about the difficulties which arise, and about what is the best thing to do. We keep President Roosevelt informed constantly.

In pursuance of our joint policy, we encouraged the making of an agreement between the Tito Government, which, with Russian assistance, has now installed itself in Belgrade, and the Royal Government of Yugoslavia, which is seated in London, and recognized by us, as, I believe, by all the Powers of the United Nations. Marshal Stalin and His Majesty's Government consider that agreement on the whole to be wise. We believe that the arrangements of the Tito-Subasitch agreement are the best that can be made for the immediate future of Yugoslavia. They preserve the form and the theme of monarchy pending the taking of a fair and free plebiscite as soon as conditions allow. King Peter II agrees in principle with these arrangements, but he makes certain reservations. The nature and effect of these are, I understand, at present under discussion. I should hesitate to prophesy or to promise how all this will turn out, but in all the circumstances, and having regard to the chaotic conditions arising out of this war, I do not see what else except this Tito-Subasitch agreement could be done by His Majesty's Government and the Union of Soviet Socialist Republics to contribute what they can to bringing about the widest possible measure of agreement among Yugoslavs, and to ensure that these issues shall not become a cause of friction among Allies. It is a matter of days within which a decision must be reached upon this matter, and if we were so unfortunate as not to be able to obtain the consent of King Peter, the matter would have, in fact, to go ahead, his assent being presumed. The King's point of view, as I understood it, was that he was anxious about becoming responsible, while he had no power, for any severities or confiscations which might take place in his country before the plebiscite decided whether it was to be a monarchy or a republic. Such scruples must be respected, but of necessity cannot, in these times, indefinitely prevent the march of events.

From the troubles of Italy and Yugoslavia, we come naturally to those of Greece. Once again, we are guided by our simple policy : Victory against the Germans ; the establishment of and aid to the most coherent and substantial government machine that can be found ; the delivery of such food as we and our Allies can spare and our combined shipping afford ; the maintenance of tolerable conditions of law and order ; and the holding of plebiscites or general elections fairly and squarely—then, exit at the earliest practicable moment. We toil through a mighty maze, but I can assure you it is not without plan. The story of events in Greece has been told so fully in the newspapers that I shall not attempt a chronological or descriptive account, but there is no case in my experience, certainly not in my war-time experience, where a British Government has been so maligned and its motives so traduced in our own country by important organs of the Press or among our own people. That this should be done amid the perils of this war, now at its climax, has filled me with surprise and sorrow. It bodes ill for the future in which the life and strength of Britain compared to other Powers will be tested to the full, not only in the war but in the aftermath of war. How can we wonder at, still more how can we complain of, the attitude of hostile or indifferent newspapers in the United States, when we have, in this country, witnessed such a melancholy exhibition as that provided by some of our most time-honoured and responsible journals—and others to which such epithets would hardly apply ? Only the solid and purposeful strength of the National Coalition Government could have enabled us to pursue, unflinching and unyielding, the course of policy and principle on which we were and are resolved.

But our task, hard as it was, has been and is still being rendered vastly more difficult by a spirit of gay, reckless, unbridled partisanship which has been let loose on the Greek question and has fallen upon those who have to bear the burden of Government in times like these. I have never been connected with any large enterprise of policy about which I was more sure in mind and conscience of the rectitude of our motives, of the clarity of our principles, and of the vigour, precision and success of our action, than what we have done in Greece.

We went to Greece for the second time in this war. We went with the full approval of both our great Allies. We went on the invitation of a Greek Government in which all parties, even the Communists, were represented, and as a result of a military conference at which the generals of E.L.A.S. and of E.D.E.S. were equally present. We came with good gifts in our hands, stability and assistance to the all-party Greek Government which was formed and had to face the confusion left by the flight of the Germans. We brought food, clothing and supplies. We came with a small force of troops. We took up our positions from no military point of view, scattering and spreading our troops in a number of places on the coast and at small points inland where we hoped to be able to pour in the largest quantities of supplies as quickly as possible to a very hungry people. We were received with flowers and cheers and other expressions of rapture, and we British, the wicked British—so denounced by the American correspondents, whose names have, no doubt, been noted by the House, and so hounded by some of our own—busied ourselves in the distribution of supplies throughout those parts of the country to which we had access.

We had made Greece safe for U.N.R.R.A. before the outbreak took place. Meanwhile, for a period of six weeks or so, the Greek Government, representative of all parties, was distracted by internal divisions and street demonstrations, and all the time the Communist-directed forces were drawing down from the North and infiltrating into the city of Athens, in which they had also a strong local faction. We had furnished these men, for several years, with arms in considerable quantities in the hope that they would fight against the Germans. They accepted the arms, and they kept them and other arms they procured from the Italians and the Germans in their retreat—captured or bought, or otherwise obtained—and they kept them with a plan to seize the power of the Greek State in Athens once the Germans cleared out and went away. I cannot guarantee to carry unanimous opinion with me at every stage in the discussion of what is admittedly the most controversial matter of the hour in British policy.

I must speak a little about these Greek Communists, among whom Macedonian and Bulgarian elements are also found, possibly with territorial ideas of their own. They are a very formidable people. They have a theme and a policy which they have pursued by merciless methods while all sorts of other people in these regions have only been trying to keep body and soul together. I have been told that I made a mistake in under-rating the power of the Communist-directed E.L.A.S. I must admit that I judged them on their form against the Germans. I do not wish to do them any military injustice. Of course, it was not against the Germans they were trying to fight to any great extent. They were simply taking our arms, lying low and awaiting the moment when they could seize power in the capital by force or intrigue, and make Greece a Communist State with the totalitarian liquidation of all opponents. I was misled by the little use they were against the Germans, especially once the general victory of the Allies became probable, in spite of the arms we gave to them. I certainly under-rated them as a fighting force. If I am accused of this mistake, I can only say with M. Clemenceau on a celebrated occasion : " Perhaps I have made a number of other mistakes of which you have not heard."

While the British were busy distributing the food and endeavouring to keep things steady, the E.A.M. and Communist Ministers, who were eventually increased to seven in the Papandreou Cabinet, were playing a different game. Throughout, this has been a struggle for power. They were playing the game of the E.L.A.S. bands and of their Communist directors. While sitting in M. Papandreou's Cabinet, they were working in the closest combination with the forces gathering to destroy it and all that he and their other colleagues represented in the everyday life of Greece. E.A.M. and Communist Ministers threw sand in the wheels of the Government at every stage. They did their best to hamper the landing and distribution of food by provoking strikes on some occasions. In addition, they fought over every officer in the Army which it was necessary for the poor State to raise—you cannot have a State without some kind of national army ; I am entirely against private armies, and we are not going to have private armies. Every single appointment was wrangled over in this time of crisis till the last minute.

I have spared no pains to try to learn what I believe are the facts. I consider myself far better informed on this matter than I was a month or six weeks ago, but what I have learned with great pains and patience has led me to a strengthening of my original conclusions, and among them is undoubtedly the conclusion that the E.L.A.S. armed bands, at any rate for the last two years, played very little part against the Germans. I, personally, am not prepared to pay them anything like the tributes which are paid to the heroic French or Belgian Maquis, or to the men in Italy who are in the mountains fighting their desperate battle. It seems to me they took aid from us with their eyes on more important local matters after the general war was over.

Every single appointment was wrangled over, and when the fierce mountaineers had got well into the city and joined up with their confederates inside, then all those seven Ministers of the Government resigned like clockwork, except one, whom I told the House about before, who was a little late, but by running very hard, under the threat of death, managed to keep his appointment. So far, the Allies seemed very content with what had happened in Greece. Our minds rested upon its liberation from the Germans. We expected a certain amount of local ebullition while matters readjusted themselves and till food could come in. After all, there were other things going on at the same time. We rested on the pleasure which our early reception in Athens and in other Greek cities and islands had given to all of us, especially to those who care deeply about Greece and her future.

Now we come to a new phase about which it was not possible to consult our Allies, and upon which action had to be taken immediately. On the night of 4th–5th December I had before me a series of telegrams which showed that the advancing E.L.A.S. forces in Athens, the Communists and all they could gather with them, were within about 1,000 yards of the centre of Greek Government in the Hôtel Grande Bretagne, and also within the same distance, or even less, of the British Embassy, into which all our womenfolk of the cipher department, and others, had been gathered, and it seemed that the overrunning of these places, or at any rate of the seat of Government, by this ferocious and well-armed, well-directed mob, or army if you like, or army of brigands, if the hon. Member [Mr. Gallacher] wishes—was about to take place. Almost all the police stations in Athens and the Piraeus had been occupied or stormed by E.L.A.S. forces, some with the slaughter of every single inmate. Firing was widespread throughout the city—it was growing, it was approaching. General Scobie signalled :

" A general strike has been declared in Athens. All power and utility services have ceased working. Unless full order can be restored the situation of the Government will be critical. All British troops, including the Parachute Brigade, are being held here."

We were about to take some of our troops away when this happened. The Parachute Brigade was needed in Italy. The hour was late, or rather early—two o'clock in the morning. Orders were sent to General Scobie to take over the military command of Athens and restore and maintain order by whatever measures were necessary. If I did wrong, I take the full responsibility, but my colleagues are most desirous to

share it with me.   For three or four days, or more, it was a struggle
to prevent a hideous massacre in the centre of Athens, in which all
forms of government would have been swept away and naked, triumphant Trotskyism installed.   I think "Trotskyists" is a better
definition of these people, and of certain other sects, than the normal
word, and it has the advantage of being equally hated in Russia.
However, by the skin of our teeth and thanks to the resolution of the
handful of British soldiers on the spot, the assailants were hurled back,
and Athens, and, as I firmly believe, Greek freedom were saved.

On Christmas Day I thought it necessary to go to Athens with my
right hon. Friend the Foreign Secretary.   There was a demand from
many quarters for a Regency and for the Archbishop.   I was anxious
to test that on the spot : I was anxious to see what could be done at
the conference of all parties, including, of course, the representatives
of E.A.M. and the Communists, which I asked the Archbishop to
convene in Athens.   At this conference those severed by mortal hatred
—mortal and living hatred—were seated around a table and found
themselves united upon the Regency, and in their minds at that
time there was, obviously, only one man who could fill it.   So the
Foreign Secretary and I, on our return, laboured with the Greek
King in order to procure his assent.   We were successful, and on
31st December Archbishop Damaskinos was invested with the Royal
power pending his Regency, and, I think, with more than the Royal
power.

We did not seek to be consulted about his measures, nor did we
interfere in the choice of his Prime Minister, nor in the character and
composition of his Government.   I did not know when I left, with any
assurance, who would be his Prime Minister or what men would be
chosen by that Prime Minister and approved by him to fill the Government.   I gathered, however, that there was a general desire to avoid
merely getting the leaders of parties together, but rather to pick
strong and real representatives of those parties, the leaders of which
are very numerous and not always free from the danger of being
discredited.   The Archbishop struck me as being a very remarkable
man, with his headgear towering up, morally as well as physically,
above the chaotic scene.   I am sure he would not have undertaken
his responsibilities unless he had been free to exercise his own judgment.

He called upon General Plastiras, who, under his close guidance,
formed a Government of the character I have described—Liberal,
Socialist, Left Wing, Democratic and Republican, in fact, as we are
assured, with all the modern virtues, but, undoubtedly, violently
against the Communists.   People here talk of making a Government
of all parties and of every one being persuaded to fall upon each
other's necks, or, at any rate, to work together in a sensible manner.

9

I must admit that I had had some of these ideas when I flew to Athens on Christmas Day, but the House must not suppose that, in these foreign lands, matters are settled as they would be here in England. Even here it is hard enough to keep a Coalition together, even between men who, although divided by party, have a supreme object and so much else in common. But imagine what the difficulties are in countries racked by civil war, past or impending, and where clusters of petty parties have each their own set of appetites, misdeeds and revenges. If I had driven the wife of the Deputy Prime Minister out to die in the snow, if the Minister of Labour had kept the Foreign Secretary in exile for a great many years, if the Chancellor of the Exchequer had shot at and wounded the Secretary of State for War, or the head of one or other of the great spending Departments, if we, who sit here together, had back-bitten and double-crossed each other while pretending to work together, and had all put our own group or party first and the country nowhere, and had all set ideologies, slogans or labels in front of comprehension, comradeship and duty, we should certainly, to put it at the mildest, have come to a General Election much sooner than is now likely.

When men have wished very much to kill each other, and have feared very much that they would be killed quite soon, it is not possible for them next day to work together as friends with colleagues against whom they have nursed such intentions or from whom they have derived such fears. We must recognize the difference between our affairs and those which prevailed in Athens, especially while the firing was continuous all round us. That cannot possibly be overlooked. We should have been very glad to have seen a united Government set up. We left them to it, with a strong urge and appeal to unite and save their country, no exception being made of Communists or any one at that moment. All next day they struggled. On several occasions, the entire Liberal Party left the room and were with difficulty shepherded back into their places. It was absolutely certain that no agreement to form a united front could be reached, and, since then, far worse things have happened than had happened before.

The days passed. Our reinforcements rapidly and steadily arrived. They were found, without altering the operations on the Italian front, by putting, I am sorry to say, an extra effort on divisions which were resting and which would otherwise have gone to rest camps. But the troops accepted these duties in the most loyal and hearty spirit, and have frequently expressed the opinion that the people they were fighting were even dirtier than the Germans. Street by street, Athens was cleared. Progress was very slow, because of the care taken to disentangle the women and children and innocent civilians who were all intermingled with people in plain clothes who were firing.

The assailants have fled; Attica is free; a truce has been signed, giving a much larger area of peace and order around Athens and the Piraeus, which are the heart of Greece and which have always been the dominant centre of the life of Greece. More than one quarter of the entire population lives there and in the region now liberated. I have not the slightest doubt that, in the opinions they express and in the views they take, they represent at least four-fifths of the whole Greek nation, if it could express its view in conditions of peace and normal tranquillity. Fighting has ceased now, except for skirmishes with parties of E.L.A.S. troops, who probably have not yet heard the news in this primitive country. Now the Greek people can talk things over as they choose under the guidance of Archbishop Damaskinos, who is also ready to receive, and has invited, the representatives of E.A.M., or what is left of E.A.M., in the political structure, and E.L.A.S., to come and meet him.

What do we seek in Greece? Do we want anything from Greece? What part do they play in our so-called power politics? How much does it matter to us, from a national point of view, what form their Government takes? I repeat: we want nothing from Greece but her friendship, and, to earn that and deserve that, we have to do our duty. We cannot disentangle ourselves from Greece immediately after what has happened. We cannot do so until there can be either a free vote, or a guarantee of a free vote, under the most stringent and impartial supervision, a vote of all the Greek people as to what they want in the future. Whatever they decide, Monarchy or Republic, Left or Right, that shall be their law, as far as we are concerned. When I see all the fury expended on this subject, and when we are abused, without one shadow of truth, as if we wanted some islands or bases from Greece, as if we needed their aid to keep ourselves alive, I feel added anxiety for the future, which with all its sombre and infinitely complicated problems is closing rapidly upon us.

However, the " Cease fire " has sounded, and the rejoicings of the people of Athens have once again acclaimed the liberating British troops, this time with an intense, agonized fervour. At any rate, there is a region where about 1,500,000 men and women can earn their daily living without fear of pillage, or of being killed in street fighting. Meanwhile, as a result of these events, and also of the complete clearance of the city, which proceeded for several weeks with heavy fighting night and day, various alphabetical groups like S.K.E. and E.L.D. have, I am informed, speaking by the best available leaders they have—for all is in confusion—subtracted themselves from E.A.M., leaving now only K.K.E., the Communists, in uncomfortable isolation, clinging to their hostages.

Let me now read an extract from a dispatch from our Ambassador,

Mr. Leeper, whom I have seen at close quarters in difficult and dangerous circumstances, and who, I am bound to say, has grown in stature with the tests which have been so severely and increasingly applied to him—a man now labouring with the utmost earnestness for a peace on the broadest possible basis. This is what he says :

" Ever since the Germans left, the small but well-armed Communist Party "—

he wrote this in a dispatch a day or two ago—

" —has been practising a reign of terror all over the country. Nobody can estimate the number of people killed or arrested before the revolt in Athens actually began, but, when the truth can be known, there will be terrible stories to tell. When the fighting began in Athens, the brutalities increased rapidly. Men, women and children were murdered here in large numbers, and thousands of hostages were taken, dragged along the roads, and many left to die. Reports from Salonika show that much the same thing was happening there."

> At this point a member interrupted to ask whether the document from which the Prime Minister was quoting would be laid on the Table of the House. The Prime Minister said he was quite ready to lay the whole document, subject to anything that might be excluded on grounds of public security. He then continued :

There is a good deal more in it than I have read out. Some of the news may not be any more palatable to the hon. Member. I am not accepting it at all as an absolute rule, that in time of war documents can be quoted without the most careful survey by the Government. That is absolutely necessary. In times when Blue Books were given to the House, even in peace, frequent excisions were made and indicated by dots by Ministers responsible for the safety of the country.

There is another tale told by a British officer, Lieut.-Colonel H. G. Morrison, the King's Royal Rifle Corps, who obtained his information by personal cross-questioning of a large number of hostages whom he met at a field dressing station. The Colonel said :

" On Christmas Day "—

I will lay this too—

" a column of hostages composed of men and women dragged from their homes by the insurgents moved northwards from Athens. They were collected in one suburb, and after most had been relieved of their footwear and many of their overcoats, they were driven in dead of winter along the mountain roads covered with snow. Every day some died of exhaustion and others were executed. For food these miserable, bare-footed hostages were left entirely to their own resources. The inhabitants in villages from whom they begged food were mostly too terrorized to do more than look on in impotent sympathy. When their starvation became acute E.L.A.S. proposed to buy them food if they supplied the money. The equivalent of about £100 was raised, but all they received in return was one half loaf of bread each. A favourite trick of the E.L.A.S. guards was to assemble these bewildered people and inform them that after so many hours' march they would find a billet, a hot meal and a bed. After several days of this they fully realized they would be lucky if they found room on the floor of a stable with no promise of food of any description.

"Two characteristic details. A woman discovered to have money was deprived of it and shot. When other hostages protested the guards justified themselves by asserting that she had been working for the British. One man managed to extract a gold tooth from his mouth and barter it for a little food. A few fortunate stragglers from this column were picked up in the last stages of exhaustion, their bare feet in ribbons. Hitherto those no longer able to walk had been executed ; but their guards were in a hurry, and received warning that the British armed patrols were on their tail."

> At this point Mr. Gallacher (Communist) interjected : " Tell me the old, old story." He added : " We have heard all those lies before." The Prime Minister continued :

The hon. Member continues to presume. I am reading the facts, and he does not like the facts. I am telling him the truth, and he fears the truth. These facts reflect on those whom he has so thoughtlessly championed, and I will give him further warning. There is a great deal more to come, and I think that the Committee has a right to hear it. When I quote from the Colonel of the King's Royal Rifle Corps and say he gathered his information from the advanced dressing station, where he examined a number of these victims, the hon. Gentleman opposite immediately tries to suggest it is all some fake propaganda. He did not use those words, but the whole sense of his interruption was to cast doubt on an officer who has not the slightest interest, political or otherwise, to do anything but collect, gather and convey the truth. Mr. Leeper adds :

" This is the story of one column of 800 hostages of whom about 200 were dead within ten days. The total number seized runs into thousands, and includes many reputable men and women well known to the Greek public. A good many survivors have now returned to Athens to tell a similar tale."

The following is an eye-witness report by another British officer. I cannot give his name. I have telegraphed for it, and I will shortly lay it before the Committee. He says :

13

" Whilst at Peristeri (an Athens suburb) interrogating E.L.A.S. prisoners, I was informed by civilians and National Guards that a great many hostages had been executed by E.L.A.S. and buried in ditches on the outskirts. I proceeded to the place where exhumation of bodies had begun, and interrogated the cemetery guardian. According to his statement batches of 15 to 20 hostages were brought to the north-east corner of the cemetery every day by E.L.A.S. and murdered ; their bodies were then buried in some disused trenches. This system of trenches, which covers some 200 yards, is now filled with earth, but trial diggings have uncovered bodies along most of its length. Farther to the north and north-west are more trenches and pits, which, according to the guardian, also contain bodies of hostages who were executed there. He estimates that in all 1,200 to 1,500 people were executed, mostly with knives or axes. The latter testimony was borne out by partially exhumed bodies which I saw, which had deep wounds in the back of the head or neck, probably inflicted by a heavy knife. Apparently they were hostages taken in Athens during the early days of the fighting, and who were systematically exterminated up till the E.L.A.S. withdrawal from Athens."

I am sorry to trespass on the Committee. This is one which only arrived this morning. It is from Consul-General Rapp, who is at Salonika :

" Between 1 p.m. and 2 p.m. yesterday, 16th January, 31 sick civilians, of whom 17 to 20 were in a dying condition, were removed by E.L.A.S. from the Municipal Hospital at Salonika, loaded on to bullock carts in their pyjamas (some had pyjama trousers only) and taken off to Verroia. Facts are verified by Mme. Riadis and M. Zannas of the Greek Red Cross who followed the convoy in a car a few hours later and distributed blankets. It is probable that several have already died from exposure. British military authorities are taking all possible steps to secure their immediate return."

Three days ago the roads leading out of Salonika were crowded with long columns of horse- and bullock-drawn vehicles which had been brought in from the countryside and conveyed much booty and loot, their owners having stripped bare every house, rich or poor, in which they could find anything worth carrying away. I know perfectly well that the hon. Member for Ebbw Vale [Mr. Bevan] would not stand for anything of this kind. I know that he would not, but would rather throw away great advantages in an argument than stand for one moment for inhumanity. I am not trying to suggest that hon. Gentlemen opposite, even those who are most excited, are in any way associating themselves with this sort of thing, and therefore I am taking great pains to show what has been going on, and is going

14

on, in order that they may carefully watch their steps and choose their language in such a way as to keep themselves clear of all taint of approbation.

I give my warning to what I must call the E.L.A.S.-ites in this country and elsewhere. The prisoners are coming home and the truth is coming out. Two horrible stultifications await them. First the revelation and proof of the atrocities committed by those whom they have found it their duty to defend, and secondly, a great surprise is going to come upon them in the vote which the Greek people will give about these matters, when our purpose of free election has been achieved. I would warn the Committee that if we are going to tear ourselves asunder in this Island over all the feuds and passions of the Balkan countries which our arms and those of our Allies have liberated, we shall be found quite incapable of making our influence count in the great settlement which awaits the end of the war. It is, I believe, the intention of the Regent and of General Plastiras to broaden the Government continually, but we really must leave this process to them and not try to interfere with it from day to day.

It is only fair for me to tell the Committee that I do not believe that any of the existing authorities in Athens will ever work as colleagues with the Communist leaders who assailed the city and brought, as they think, all these miseries upon Greece. There is a violent feeling throughout the liberated area that there should be no amnesty. Even when we were there three weeks ago, and when we held only a small part of the city, most of the roads were dangerous. There were bands of men marching about, poorly-clad men, with placards bearing the words, " No amnesty." Passions there are tense, and I am told that they tend to become more tense because of questions and answers in this House. We try to allay those passions as much as we can. The Government have been committed by me to the principle of " no proscription." That means that no person, whether ringleader or otherwise, shall be punished for his part in the recent rebellion unless he is found guilty by a properly constituted court of personal breaches of the laws of war, or of the private crimes for which ordinary felons are punished. This principle has been accepted by the Greek Government, and all statements to the contrary are over-ridden. Any statement which does not conform to it is over-ridden by the quite definite agreement which I made on the spot in respect of these matters, and which I have every reason to believe will be maintained. It is quite possible that General Plastiras, under tremendous pressure of people boiling with rage and bursting for revenge, may have used some sentences which do not correspond or seem not to correspond with the interpretation which I have placed upon it. But the position of His Majesty's Government has been definitely taken up, and our opinion is, I am sure, one which will be treated with respect and consideration by the Greek Government, who are so largely dependent upon our Armed Forces for their existence.

I think there is a great difference between putting people to death for the crime of rebellion, or bringing them to penal processes, and making sure that your Government Departments are not full of people who are working for the other side. I am dealing with the whole question of amnesty, which relates to the penal processes of law, such as imprisonment or sentences of death, and an amnesty certainly does not mean that persons who are not trusted by the Government of the day will immediately be made Cabinet Ministers, or that employees who were found to have left their posts in the crisis and taken part in the fighting on the opposite side to the Government of the day should be reinstated or left in their positions. No one can stand for that, and I want to be very careful not to lead the hon. Gentleman the Member for Ebbw Vale [Mr. Bevan] into any idea that I am promising something that goes beyond the actual words I have used.

As I say, this principle, which I have advised, has been accepted by the Greek Government, and I have no doubt it will be observed while any of our Forces remain in the country; but after that Greece will be completely free and sovereign, and I cannot tell at all by what terrible feuds the wrangle may be carried on. There is, however, one further reservation which I must make. The promise of " no proscription " or amnesty—whichever term you prefer—is dependent, as we see it, upon the treatment and delivery of the hostages, and no amnesty could be declared while hostages were held in the grip of E.L.A.S. We thought it better that the fighting should stop. It is always a good thing for the firing to leave off in a case like this, when you wish to reach a parley. We thought it better for the fighting to stop, and that whatever parley took place about hostages would go on more quickly after firing left off than before. But let there be no mistake, the name of Britain and the honour of our country are deeply engaged in this matter of hostages. We cannot let it be said that we made arrangements for all our people to be saved and left anything from 5,000 to 10,000 Greeks, men, women and children to be carried off to the mountains by E.L.A.S. and its remaining associates, to be used as a weapon of blackmail, not merely to procure their own immunity from the crime of rebellion—for that, as I have said, is open to them if they take the proper course—but to be used to procure for them political advantages.

I tell the House quite plainly that His Majesty's Government will discharge their obligations, however painful, with complete integrity, whether it is popular or not to do so, and that we shall not hesitate to rescue these hostages and punish their slaughter or maltreatment, if we are to continue to hold office under the Crown.

At this point the sitting was suspended for lunch. On resuming the Prime Minister said :

I finished before lunch dealing with the Greek question, and I quoted a statement by a British officer about the bodies which were being dug up. I had not got his name then, but it has since arrived by telegraph, and is Captain R. F. G. Blackler, of the Royal Artillery. He gave an eye-witness account.

Now I turn to a very different theme and story. I turn from the pink and ochre panorama of Athens and the Piraeus, scintillating with delicious life and plumed by the classic glories and endless miseries and triumphs of its history. This must give way to the main battle-front of the war. In this, my chief contribution will be the recital of a number of facts and figures which may or may not be agreeable in different quarters. I have seen it suggested that the terrific battle which has been proceeding since 16th December on the American front is an Anglo-American battle. In fact, however, the United States troops have done almost all the fighting and have suffered almost all the losses. They have suffered losses almost equal to those on both sides in the battle of Gettysburg. Only one British Army Corps has been engaged in this action. All the rest of the 30 or more divisions, which have been fighting continuously for the last month, are United States troops. The Americans have engaged 30 or 40 men for every one we have engaged, and they have lost 60 to 80 men for every one of ours. That is a point I wish to make. Care must be taken in telling our proud tale not to claim for the British Army an undue share of what is undoubtedly the greatest American battle of the war, and will, I believe, be regarded as an ever famous American victory.

I never hesitate, as the Committee, I think, will bear me witness, to stand up for our own soldiers when their achievements have been cold-shouldered or neglected or overshadowed as they sometimes are ; but we must not forget that it is to American homes that the telegrams of personal losses and anxiety have been going during the past month, and that there has been a hard and severe ordeal during these weeks for our brave and cherished Ally. This implies no disparagement of our own exertions, for we ourselves, a month or two earlier, lost 40,000 men in opening the Scheldt. The bulk of our Army on this occasion, when von Rundstedt attacked, was separated by scores of miles from the impact of the new offensive. They could not possibly have been moved into battle in large numbers without criss-crossing the lines of communication and creating utter confusion. The British

Army stood, and stands, in its Northern position between the enemy and Antwerp in a strategic attitude, capable of averting all possibility of a major disaster. Our Armies are under the supreme command of General Eisenhower, and we march with discipline wherever we are told to go.

According to the professional advice which I have at my disposal, what was done to meet von Rundstedt's counter-stroke was resolute, wise, and militarily correct. A gap was torn open, as a gap can always be torn open in a line hundreds of miles long. General Eisenhower at once gave the command to the North of the gap to Field-Marshal Montgomery and to the South of it to General Omar Bradley. Many other consequential movements were made, and rightly made, and in the result both these highly skilled commanders handled the very large forces at their disposal in a manner which, I think I may say without exaggeration, may become the model for military students in the future.

Field-Marshal Montgomery at the earliest moment, acting with extraordinary promptitude, concentrated powerful British reserves at the decisive strategic point. Having been placed in command, as he was by General Eisenhower, of American Forces larger than those he holds from His Majesty's Government or from the Canadians, larger than those he holds in the 21st Army Group, he fell unceasingly on the enemy in the North, and has fought the battle all the time from that part of the assailed front. The United States First Army, which was one of the group of Armies under General Omar Bradley, was severed by the inroad. It was reinforced with extraordinary military efficiency from the Metz area by General Patton's Army, who hurled themselves on the intruders from the South side of Bastogne. But all the movements of the commanders would have been futile but for the bravery of the troops. General Omar Bradley was commanding American troops, and so was Field-Marshal Montgomery. All these troops fought in magnificent fashion, and General Eisenhower, balancing the situation between his two commanders, gave them both the fairest opportunity to realize their full strength and quality. Let no one lend himself to the chatter of mischief-makers when issues of this most momentous consequence are being successfully decided by the sword.

Lest it should be thought that the British Commonwealth and Empire are not playing their part in the battle of the Continent, or in the general war, let me give a few facts and figures. We are maintaining at the present time, in the field and in our garrisons, the equivalent of upwards of 100 divisions, apart from the vast Navy and Air Forces and all the workers in the munitions shops. Many, of course, are not mobile, but 67 of them are at the front and in constant or frequent contact with the enemy. We are fighting incessantly on three separate fronts, in North-West Europe, in Italy and in Burma. Of all the troops landed in France the losses sustained in fighting by the British Army and the United States troops have been very level in proportion to the numbers engaged. Of course, there are over twice as many American troops on the Western front as there are troops of the British Commonwealth. We, in fact, have lost half as many as our American Allies.

If you take killed only, British and Canadians have lost a larger proportion than the United States, heavier though the United States losses are. We have taken measures, which I announced some weeks ago, to keep our Armies up to the full strength, whatever the losses may be, and also to reinforce our divisions—I wish they were more numerous—by supplementary units, brigades and so forth, to add to the strength of the foot who bear the brunt of two-thirds of the losses of war. We therefore felt it necessary to make this demand, for movement towards and into the battle, of about 250,000 additional men, to be drawn from every possible source in the next few months, not only men but women. However, in the combatant sphere of the Anti-Aircraft batteries no woman will go but as a volunteer. They have practically all volunteered.

In the United States, also, extreme measures have been taken. Let the Germans dismiss from their minds any idea that any losses or set-backs of the kind we have witnessed will turn us from our purpose. We shall go on to the end, however the storm may beat, and for myself I do not hesitate to-day to give my own opinion, not dissented from by the experts with whom I live in constant contact, that the decisive breaking of the German offensive in the West is more likely to shorten this war than to lengthen it.

We must regard von Rundstedt's attack as an effort to dislocate and, if possible, rupture the tremendous onslaught across the Rhine and Siegfried line for which the Anglo-American Armies have been preparing. The Germans no doubt hoped to throw out of gear, before the on-fall of the Russian Armies from the East, this main stroke from the West. They have certainly lost heavily in their efforts; they have cast away a large proportion of the flower of their last armies; they have made a slight and ineffectual dent on the long front. The question they will be asking themselves is whether they have, at this heavy price, delayed appreciably the general advance of the Armies of the West beyond the period for which it had been planned. That is the question which no doubt to-day the German headquarters are anxiously asking themselves.

I always hesitate to speak at all about the military future, but it is my hope and belief that by this violent attack, in which they have lost perhaps double what they have inflicted, they have in no wise delayed, still less averted, the doom that is closing in upon them from the West. Harsh as it may seem to say, a terrible thing to say in dealing with our own precious flesh and blood, it is our interest and the American interest that the whole Western front, and the air everywhere at all possible flying times, should be in continuous action against the enemy, burning and bleeding his strength away at every opportunity and on all occasions, if we are to bring this horror to an end. I think it was not necessarily a bad thing, indeed it was a good thing, that large parts of the Western front were thrown into counter battles in open country by the enemy, counter battles in the forests, undulations and hills of the Ardennes, rather than that all our troops should be compelled to advance at this season of the year across great rivers and seas of mud against lines of concrete fortifications. It suited the Allies that there should be as much fighting as possible in the open country rather than that the whole front should be crashing up against pillboxes.

In short, as I see it, the Germans have made a violent and costly sortie which has been repulsed with heavy slaughter, and have expended in the endeavour forces which they cannot replace, against an enemy who has already more than replaced every loss he has sustained. These German forces are needed now, not only to support the German front in the West, but even more to fill the awful rents, only now emerging upon our consciousness as the telegrams come in, which have been torn in their Eastern line by the magnificent onslaught of the main Russian Armies along the entire front from the Baltic to Budapest. Marshal Stalin is very punctual. He would rather be before his time than late in the combinations of the Allies. I cannot attempt to set limits to the superb and titanic events which we are now witnessing in the East, or to their reactions in every theatre. I can only say it is certain that the whole of the Eastern and Western fronts, and the long front in Italy, where 27 German divisions are still held by no more than their own numbers, will henceforward be kept in constant flame until the final climax is reached. The advance of the enormous Forces of Soviet Russia across Poland and elsewhere into Germany and German-held territory must produce consequences of a character and degree about which the wisest strategists and the most far-sighted prophets will reserve their opinion until the results are known.

Simultaneously with the battle of the Ardennes another battle, almost as great, has been fought by the United States in the Philippines at the other side of the world. The Philippines and the Ardennes— two vast military episodes—have been proceeding simultaneously. When we think of the distances to be traversed in the Pacific and the vast consumption of ships and war material entailed, of the mighty fleets and air forces engaged as well as the large armies convoyed and supplied in every detail, we must marvel at the triumphant military strength of the United States, now roused from its peaceful free-and-easy life to become, against its desire, the greatest military Power in the world. We can also marvel at the folly of those treacherous schemers in Japan who so wantonly called out against them this incredible manifestation of armed power. General MacArthur's recovery of the Philippines, which is in full progress many months before it was expected, is a fearful warning to the Japanese of their impending defeat and ruin. We offer our congratulations to General MacArthur and Admiral Nimitz on the increasing success and speed of their mighty combined operations.

I cannot pass from this subject without mentioning the loss which we have sustained, and which I personally have sustained, in the death in action of my representative with General MacArthur, Lieut.-General Lumsden, one of our most distinguished and accomplished officers, the man who at the very beginning of the war, in the first contact with the enemy, brought the armoured car back into popularity. He was killed on the port side of the bridge of an American ship approaching Luzon by a bomb which Admiral Fraser himself, the Commander-in-Chief of our gathering Navy, who happened to be there as a spectator, only escaped by the accident of a few seconds. There have been large losses among the high commanders in these campaigns. In Air Chief Marshal Sir Trafford Leigh-Mallory and Admiral Sir Bertram Ramsay we have lost two out of the three British commanders of the expedition across the Channel, General Montgomery being the sole survivor of the three.

There is one other campaign on which we and India have expended immense effort and where good fortune has attended us—the advance of the 14th Army—not forgotten but watched carefully, their movements ever attended by our thoughts. The advance of the 14th Army, in harmony with the Chinese on its Northern flank, has carried them in an attack against the Japanese army in Burma at some points almost 200 miles forward from Imphal, Kohima and Myitkyina. Now is the time when all the fierce fighting at these places last year is reaping its reward. The stuffing was beaten out of the Japanese troops in those terrible conflicts in which we had very heavy losses—40,000 British, Indians and others at least—and in which a far larger toll was taken by disease. I had always dreaded the new campaign in Burma this year on account of the heavy toll of disease which the march through the jungle exacts not only from the British but also from the Indians and the West and East African troops who have been fighting there with great distinction. I dreaded it for that reason, and also because of the unimaginable difficulties of supply from India through all these hundreds of miles of gorges, where every bridge and culvert is swept away by torrential rains, where rivers rise twenty or thirty feet in a few hours, and over which all means of communications are so primitive and scanty.

I had always dreaded the beginning of this new campaign in Burma, which, nevertheless, it was necessary to achieve in order that, having rid Burma of the invader, the large Forces there might acquire mobility to act in the final stages of the war. Moreover, the obstinate prolongation of the war in Europe necessarily delayed the movement to the East of many reinforcements of all kinds. Soldiers, aircraft, vessels of many different kinds used in amphibious operations, were all delayed, although Admiral Mountbatten had been led to count on them. First things have to come first. But in spite of these disappointments, he and his dauntless Army have made greater advances than were required or expected of them up to the present by the Directives of the High Command, and they may well be described as " On the Road to Mandalay," though I think from a different direction. This reference to the 14th Army, moreover, takes no account of the important capture of Akyab, on the coast, with its airfield, a place for which alone a considerable expedition at one time seemed necessary. It has now been picked up out of hand by the troops of the 14th Army.

I have covered as far as I propose to do to-day the different military theatres of the war in which His Majesty's Forces, with all their elements drawn from every part of the British Empire, are contending without a moment's surcease or slackening of effort. So it will go on—great efforts pulsating through the heart of this small Island, arising again all over the vast scope of the Commonwealth and the Empire, and not dying away even with the long fatigues, monotonies and wearisome trials which the war imposes not only on the men who are fighting but on the men and women who stay at home and do all that is in them to back the soldiers at the front.

We have reached the 65th month of the war, and its weight hangs heavy upon us. No one knows what stresses are wrought in these times by this long persistence of strain, quite above the ordinary normal life of human society. Let us be of good cheer. Both in the West and in the East overwhelming forces are ranged on our side. Military victory may be distant, it will certainly be costly, but it is no longer in doubt. The physical and scientific force which our foes hurled upon us in the early years has changed sides, and the British Commonwealth, the United States and the Soviet Union undoubtedly possess the power to beat down to the ground in dust and ashes the prodigious might of the war-making nations and the conspiracies which assailed us. But, as the sense of moral peril has passed from our side to that of our cruel foes, they gain the stimulus of despair, and we tend to lose the bond of combined self-preservation, or are in danger of losing it.

There is therefore demanded of us a moral and intellectual impulse to unity and a clear conception and definition of joint purpose sufficient to overbear the fleeting reinforcement which our enemies will derive from the realization of their forlorn condition. Can we produce that complete unity and that new impulse in time to achieve decisive military victory with the least possible prolongation of the world's misery, or must we fall into jabber, babel and discord while victory is still unattained ? It seems to me to be the supreme question alike of the hour and of the age. This is no new problem in the history of mankind. Very often have great combinations almost attained success and then, at the last moment, cast it away. Very often have the triumphs and sacrifices of armies come to naught at the conference table. Very often the eagles have been squalled down by the parrots. Very often, in particular, the people of this Island, indomitable in adversity, have tasted the hard-won cup of success only to cast it away.

I therefore consider that this is a most grave moment to address the House, and it is one which affects the Members of every party—and all parties have the credit of our war effort ; it is no monopoly to be flung from side to side in some future party dispute—we are all in this for good or ill. We all come through it together. Very often, I say, these troubles have arisen at a moment of success, at a period when no one can doubt what the ultimate result will be ; and it is the duty of all parties to rouse themselves to the highest sense of their obligations and of the services which this House has already rendered to the cause of freedom.

At a time like this it is necessary to concentrate with clarity and command and mental perseverance upon the main practical issues with which we are confronted, and upon which we hope and believe we are in accord with our principal Allies. What, for instance, should be our attitude towards the terrible foes with whom we are grappling ? Should it be unconditional surrender, or should we make some accommodation with them through a negotiated peace, leaving them free to regather their strength for a renewal of the struggle after a few uneasy years ? The principle of unconditional surrender was proclaimed by the President of the United States at Casablanca, and I endorsed it there and then on behalf of this country. I am sure it was right at the time it was used, when many things hung in the balance against us which are all decided in our favour now. Should we then modify this declaration which was made in days of comparative weakness and lack of success, now that we have reached a period of mastery and power ?

I am clear that nothing should induce us to abandon the principle

23

of unconditional surrender, or to enter into any form of negotiation with Germany or Japan, under whatever guise such suggestions may present themselves, until the act of unconditional surrender has been formally executed. But the President of the United States, and I in your name, have repeatedly declared that the enforcement of unconditional surrender upon the enemy in no way relieves the victorious Powers of their obligations to humanity, or of their duties as civilized and Christian nations. I read somewhere that when the ancient Athenians, on one occasion, overpowered a tribe in the Peloponnesus which had wrought them great injury by base, treacherous means, and when they had the hostile army herded on a beach naked for slaughter, they forgave them and set them free, and they said :

" This was not because they were men ; it was done because of the nature of Man."

Similarly, in this temper, we may now say to our foes, " We demand unconditional surrender, but you well know how strict are the moral limits within which our action is confined. We are no extirpators of nations, or butchers of peoples. We make no bargain with you. We accord you nothing as a right. Abandon your resistance unconditionally. We remain bound by our customs and our nature."

There is another reason why any abrogation of the principle of unconditional surrender would be most improvident at the present time, and it is a reason by no means inconsistent with, or contradictory to, that which I have just given. We should have to discuss with the enemy, while they still remained with arms in their hands, all the painful details of the settlement which their indescribable crimes have made necessary for the future safety of Europe and of the world ; and these, when recited in detail, might well become a greater obstacle to the end of the struggle than the broad generalization which the term " unconditional surrender " implies.

The Germans know perfectly well how these matters stand in general. Several countries have already surrendered unconditionally to the victorious Allies, to Russia, to Britain and to the United States. Already there is a tolerable life appointed for their peoples. Take Finland, take Italy : these peoples have not all been massacred and enslaved. On the contrary, so far as Italy is concerned, there are moments when one has almost wondered whether it was they who had unconditionally surrendered to us, or whether we were about to surrender unconditionally to them. This, at least, I can say on behalf of the United Nations to Germany : " If you surrender now, nothing that you will have to endure after the war will be comparable to what you are otherwise going to suffer during the year 1945."

Peace, though based on unconditional surrender, will bring to

Germany and Japan an immense, immediate amelioration of the suffering and agony which now lie before them. We, the Allies, are no monsters, but faithful men trying to carry forward the light of the world, trying to raise, from the bloody welter and confusion in which mankind is now plunged, a structure of peace, of freedom, of justice and of law, which system shall be an abiding and lasting shelter for all. That is how I venture to set before the Committee to-day the grave issue called " unconditional surrender."

I now come to the second of the main questions which lie before us, namely, to the question which I have already dealt with in particular application to Greece, Yugoslavia and Italy, the question what principles should guide us in regard to countries which we and our Allies have liberated, and also in regard to that quite different class, German satellite States which are, in one way or another, working their arduous passage home. Here, of course, I can only speak for Britain and its special responsibility. The expression " power politics " has lately been used in criticism against us in some quarters. I have anxiously asked the question, "What are power politics ? " I know some of our friends across the water so well that I am sure I can always speak frankly without causing offence. Is having a Navy twice as big as any other Navy in the world power politics ? Is having the largest Air Force in the world with bases in every part of the world power politics ? Is having all the gold in the world power politics ? If so, we are certainly not guilty of these offences, I am sorry to say. They are luxuries that have passed away from us.

I am, therefore, greatly indebted to my friend, the illustrious President of the United States, four times summoned by the popular vote to the headship of the most powerful community in the world, for his definition of " power politics." With that marvellous gift which he has of bringing troublesome issues down to earth and reducing them to the calm level of ordinary life, the President declared, in his recent Message to Congress, that power politics were " the misuse of power." I am sure I can say, on behalf of all parties in the House, that we are absolutely in agreement with the President. We go farther ; we define our position with even more precision. We have sacrificed everything in this war. We shall emerge from it, for the time being, more stricken and impoverished than any other victorious country. The United Kingdom and the British Commonwealth are the only unbroken force which declared war on Germany of its own free will. We declared war not for any ambition or material advantage, but for the sake of our obligation to do our best for Poland against German aggression, in which aggression, there or elsewhere, it must also in fairness be stated, our own self-preservation was involved.

After the defeat of France in June, 1940, for more than a year we were alone. We stood alone; we kept nothing back in blood, effort or treasure from what has now become the common cause of more than thirty nations. We seek no territory; we covet no oilfields; we demand no bases for the forces of the air or of the seas. We are an ancient Commonwealth dwelling, and wishing to dwell, at peace within our own habitations. We do not set ourselves up in rivalry of bigness or might with any other community in the world. We stand on our own rights.

We are prepared to defend them, but we do not intrude for our own advantage upon the rights of any friendly country in the world, great or small. We have given, and shall continue to give, everything we have. We ask nothing in return except that consideration and respect which is our due, and even if that were denied us, we should still have a good conscience. Let none, therefore, in our own country and Commonwealth or in the outside world, misname us or traduce our motives. Our actions are no doubt subject to human error, but our motives in small things as in great are disinterested, lofty and true. I repulse those calumnies, wherever they come from, that Britain and the British Empire is a selfish, power-greedy, land-greedy, designing nation obsessed by dark schemes of European intrigue or Colonial expansion. I repulse these aspersions, whether they come from our best friends or our worst foes. Let us all march forward against the enemy, and, for the rest, let all men here and in all countries search their hearts devoutly, as we shall certainly continue to do.

I have tried as well as I could to cover, in a time which is unconscionably long for a speech but ludicrously short for the subject, the more prominent features of the world war. I will just add that we must keep our eye on jet-propelled fighter aircraft, on the V-rockets, and, above all, on the renewed U-boat menace. No doubt there are other dangers, but, taking the position as a whole, I have never at any time been able to present a more confident statement to the House of the ever-growing might and ascendancy of the United Nations or of the military solidarity of the three great Allies. Political misunderstandings and difficulties of an essentially minor rank undoubtedly confront us. That is why I was so glad to hear that the President said in public on Tuesday that he was almost immediately starting to meet me and Marshal Stalin somewhere or other quite soon. The Foreign Secretary and I, with our military and technical advisers, will be present without fail at the rendezvous, and " when the roll is called up yonder, we'll be there."

I have great hopes of this conference because it comes at a moment when a good many moulds can be set out to receive a great deal of molten metal, and also at a moment when direct advance may be made towards the larger problems which will confront the victors and, above all, advance towards that world organization upon which, as we all know, the salvation of our harassed generation and the immediate future of the world depend. We shall enter into all these discussions with your sympathy and with the confidence of your support. Whatever happens, the British Nation and Commonwealth may rest assured that the Union Jack of Freedom will for ever fly from the white cliffs of Dover.

REBUILDING THE HOUSE OF COMMONS

A Speech to the House of Commons
January 25, 1945

[January 25, 1945.

I T is nearly eighteen months since it fell to me to move for a Select Committee upon the rebuilding of the House of Commons, which was destroyed by enemy action. The Committee have now finished their labours, and their Report is before us. We owe a debt to the Committee for the great pains which they have taken and the diligence with which they have received evidence, from, I think, some thirty witnesses, for the thought, knowledge and comprehension they have given to this subject, and we express to them our obligation for the task they have so well discharged. I am, personally, extremely gratified to see that the main principles which I ventured to submit to the House eighteen months ago have been confirmed by the Committee in such emphatic terms : that the Chamber should be oblong and not semi-circular ; that there should not be room for all its Members ; that it should be designed to preserve that intimacy—which is a word frequently used by the Committee—of debate and discussion, that freedom and that sense of urgency and excitement to which our Parliamentary proceedings have owed a great deal in the past—all this is to be preserved. There are several other suggestions which have been made, and which no doubt will be ventilated in this Debate, but His Majesty's Government endorse the views of the Committee, and we submit them to the House with our warmest adhesion.

There are one or two points of procedure which I ought to mention. In the first place, suggestions of a minor character will be made in the Debate, apart from the Amendment which has been put on the Order Paper, to adopt a different architectural style ; and we think that in the light of those suggestions we might call upon the Select Committee again, to be reconstituted with the same membership, and to have a short sitting, not taking more than a few weeks, in order that all the points which come out in the Debate in the House may be reviewed and, if necessary, added to the Report. Therefore, we should give the Committee the following terms of reference :

" To examine the proposals of the Select Committee on the House of Commons (Rebuilding) in the light of suggestions made since the

28

publication of their Report, and to recommend to the House any amendment of detail which may appear desirable."

I hope the Members, who have rendered invaluable service so far, will not be reluctant to undertake this comparatively small addition to their labours.

After the Committee has met again, the Minister of Works will be responsible for carrying out the plans. I think he will naturally require a little latitude for minor changes which may be found necessary during the actual course of building. But if there is any large change, or change of principle, the matter will have to come back to the House. We think that in another Parliament, whenever that may come, it would be advisable to call the Select Committee into being again, in order that it might note the progress of the work and satisfy itself that the purposes are all being carried out. The programme we suggest, assuming the House approves of the plan in principle to-day, is that the architect should be instructed to proceed forthwith with the preparation of drawings, and as soon as the second stage of bomb-raid damage repairs in London is completed, or nearly completed, the work of demolition can start. This would take about six months, during which period the drawings will be going forward.

The proposal is that the building of the new House should be started as soon as the second stage of bomb-raid damage repairs in London is completed. I must, however, say that I consider there is an urgency about this work. I am told that for the first year, for demolitions and the foundations only, while the drawings are proceeding, not more than 100 men would be needed. I am by no means inclined to lend myself to the idea that not one single man may be employed on this work until all danger of the bombardment of London has passed away and until all the damage has been repaired.

This must not be thought to be a private matter for the convenience of Members. We rest upon the Parliamentary institution, and we may have very great need to recur to this matter when the new Parliament, or a still later Parliament, is called into being. The arrangements in this present House for the taking of many Divisions on a single day are very unsatisfactory. There are many ways in which they fall short of the accommodation which we require to conduct heavy party fighting with the conveniences which were available in the other Chamber. We have to look forward to periods when the House will be torn with fury and faction and full vent will be given to the greatest passions, when all the vocabularies may be used to the full. I must say that I feel it to be a matter of high public importance that we should sit as soon as possible in a House of Commons built on the old site, and also that we render up this Chamber to those who have so

kindly made us welcome here—and have not done so badly for themselves in their new and more modest apartment. We ought not to
stay here longer than we need, because the two branches of the
Legislature should both be able to function in their fullest vigour.
Therefore I hope that if the number of men engaged amounts to no
more than 100, and we save a whole year by that process, the Minister
of Works will be given reasonable latitude to fit that in with the
progress of bomb repairs upon which I am told 130,000 men are working.

I have spoken of the procedure and the urgency of this matter, and
I commend this Report to the House. I will venture to add a suggestion of my own to any which may be made in the Debate. I hope
very much that the archway into the Chamber from the Inner Lobby—
where the Bar used to be—which was smitten by the blast of the
explosion, and has acquired an appearance of antiquity that might
not have been achieved by the hand of time in centuries, will be preserved intact, as a monument of the ordeal which Westminster has
passed through in the Great War, and as a reminder to those who will
come centuries after us that they may look back from time to time
upon their forbears who

" kept the bridge
In the brave days of old."

THE CRIMEA DECLARATION

A STATEMENT ISSUED BY THE PRIME MINISTER, PRESIDENT ROOSEVELT
AND MARSHAL STALIN AT THE END OF THEIR CONFERENCE AT YALTA,
IN THE CRIMEA
FEBRUARY 12, 1945

[February 12, 1945.

PLANS FOR THE FINAL DEFEAT OF THE COMMON ENEMY

FOR the past eight days, Mr. Winston S. Churchill, Prime Minister of Great Britain, Mr. Franklin D. Roosevelt, President of the United States, and Marshal J. V. Stalin, Chairman of the Council of People's Commissars of the U.S.S.R., have met, with the Foreign Secretaries, Chiefs of Staff, and other advisers, in the Crimea.

In addition to the three heads of Governments, the following took part in the conference :—

FOR THE UNITED KINGDOM

Mr. Anthony Eden, Secretary of State for Foreign Affairs ; Lord Leathers, Minister of War Transport ; Sir A. Clark Kerr, H.M. Ambassador at Moscow ; Sir Alexander Cadogan, Permanent Under-Secretary of State for Foreign Affairs ; Sir Edward Bridges, Secretary of War Cabinet ; Field-Marshal Sir Alan Brooke, C.I.G.S. ; Marshal of the Royal Air Force Sir Charles Portal, C.A.S. ; Admiral of the Fleet Sir Andrew Cunningham, First Sea Lord ; and General Sir Hastings Ismay, Chief of Staff to the Minister of Defence.

Together with Field-Marshal Alexander, Supreme Allied Commander, Mediterranean Theatre ; Field-Marshal Wilson, Head of the British Joint Staff Mission, Washington ; Admiral Somerville, Joint Staff Mission, Washington ; and diplomatic and military advisers.

FOR THE UNITED STATES

Mr. Edward R. Stettinius, Secretary of State ; Fleet Admiral William D. Leahy, Chief of Staff to the President ; Mr. Harry L. Hopkins, Special Assistant to the President ; Justice James F. Byrnes, Director of Office of War Mobilization ; General of the Army George C. Marshall, Chief of Staff, United States Army ; Fleet Admiral Ernest J. King, Chief of Naval Operations and C.-in-C., United States Fleet ; Lieutenant-General Brehon B. Somervell, Commanding General, Army

31

Service Forces; Vice-Admiral Emery S. Land, War Shipping Administrator; Major-General L. S. Kuter, Staff Committee Commanding
General United States Army Air Forces; Mr. W. Averell Harriman,
Ambassador to the U.S.S.R.; Mr. H. Freeman Matthews, Director
of European Affairs, State Department; Mr. Alger Hiss, Deputy
Director of Office of Special Political Affairs, Department of State;
and Mr. Charles E. Bohlen, Assistant to the Secretary of State; together with political, military, and technical advisers.

FOR THE SOVIET UNION

Mr. V. M. Molotov, People's Commissar for Foreign Affairs of
U.S.S.R.; Admiral Kuznetsov, People's Commissar for the Navy;
Army General Antonov, Deputy Chief of General Staff of the Red
Army; Mr. A. Y. Vyshinski and Mr. I. M. Maisky, Deputy People's
Commissars for Foreign Affairs; Marshal of Aviation Khudyakov;
Mr. F. T. Gusev, Ambassador in Great Britain; and Mr. A. A. Cromyko,
Ambassador in the United States.

The following statement is made by the Prime Minister of Great
Britain, the President of the United States, and the Chairman of the
Council of People's Commissars of the Union of Soviet Socialist
Republics, on the result of the Crimea Conference :—

1.—DEFEAT OF GERMANY

We have considered and determined the military plans of the three
Allied Powers for the final defeat of the common enemy. The Military
Staffs of the three allied nations have met in daily meetings throughout
the Conference. These meetings have been most satisfactory from
every point of view, and have resulted in closer co-ordination of the
military effort of the three allies than ever before.

The fullest information has been interchanged. The timing, scope,
and co-ordination of new and even more powerful blows to be launched
by our armies and air forces into the heart of Germany from the East,
West, North, and South have been fully agreed and planned in detail.

Our combined military plans will be made known only as we execute
them, but we believe that the very close working partnership among
the three Staffs attained at this Conference will result in shortening the
war. Meetings of the three Staffs will be continued in the future
whenever the need arises.

Nazi Germany is doomed. The German people will only make the
cost of their defeat heavier to themselves by attempting to continue a
hopeless resistance.

2.—THE OCCUPATION AND CONTROL OF GERMANY

We have agreed on common policies and plans for enforcing the unconditional surrender terms which we shall impose together on Nazi

Germany after German armed resistance has been finally crushed. These terms will not be made known until the final defeat of Germany has been accomplished.

Under the agreed plan the forces of the three Powers will each occupy a separate zone of Germany. Co-ordinated administration and control has been provided for under the plan through a Central Control Commission consisting of the Supreme Commanders of the three Powers with headquarters in Berlin.

It has been agreed that France should be invited by the three Powers, if she should so desire, to take over a zone of occupation, and to participate as a fourth member of the Control Commission. The limits of the French zone will be agreed by the four Governments concerned through their representatives on the European Advisory Commission.

It is our inflexible purpose to destroy German militarism and Nazism and to ensure that Germany will never again be able to disturb the peace of the world. We are determined to disarm and disband all German armed forces ; break up for all time the German General Staff that has repeatedly contrived the resurgence of German militarism ; remove or destroy all German military equipment ; eliminate or control all German industry that could be used for military production; bring all war criminals to justice and swift punishment and exact reparation in kind for the destruction wrought by the Germans ; wipe out the Nazi Party, Nazi laws, organizations and institutions ; remove all Nazi and militarist influences from public office and from the cultural and economic life of the German people ; and take in harmony such other measures in Germany as may be necessary to the future peace and safety of the world.

It is not our purpose to destroy the people of Germany, but only when Nazism and militarism have been extirpated will there be hope for a decent life for Germans and a place for them in the comity of nations.

3.—REPARATION BY GERMANY

We have considered the question of the damage caused by Germany to the Allied Nations in this war, and recognized it as just that Germany be obliged to make compensation for this damage in kind to the greatest extent possible. A Commission for the Compensation of Damage will be established. The Commission will be instructed to consider the question of the extent and methods for compensating damage caused by Germany to the Allied countries. The Commission will work in Moscow.

4.—UNITED NATIONS' CONFERENCE

We are resolved upon the earliest possible establishment with our Allies of a general international organization to maintain peace and security. We believe that this is essential both to prevent aggression and to remove the political, economic, and social causes of war through the close and continuing collaboration of all peace-loving peoples. The foundations were laid at Dumbarton Oaks.

On the important question of voting procedure, however, agreement was not there reached. The present Conference has been able to resolve this difficulty.

We have agreed that a Conference of United Nations should be called to meet at San Francisco, in the United States, on April 25th, 1945, to prepare the Charter of such an organization along the lines proposed in the informal conversations at Dumbarton Oaks. The Government of China and the Provisional Government of France will be immediately consulted and invited to sponsor invitations to the Conference jointly with the Governments of the United States, Great Britain, and the Union of Soviet Socialist Republics. As soon as the consultation with China and France has been completed the text of the proposals on voting procedure will be made public.

5.—DECLARATION ON LIBERATED EUROPE

We have drawn up and subscribed to a Declaration on Liberated Europe. This Declaration provides for concerting the policies of the three Powers and for joint action by them in meeting the political and economic problems of Liberated Europe in accordance with democratic principles. The text of the Declaration is as follows—

The Premier of the Union of Soviet Socialist Republics, the Prime Minister of the United Kingdom, and the President of the United States of America have consulted with each other in the common interests of the peoples of their countries and those of Liberated Europe. They jointly declare their mutual agreement to concert during the temporary period of instability in Liberated Europe the policies of their three Governments in assisting the peoples liberated from the domination of Nazi Germany, and the peoples of the former Axis satellite States of Europe, to solve by democratic means their pressing political and economic problems.

The establishment of order in Europe and the rebuilding of national economic life must be achieved by processes which will enable the liberated peoples to destroy the last vestiges of Nazism and Fascism and to create democratic institutions of their own choice.

This is a principle of the Atlantic Charter—the right of all peoples to choose the form of government under which they will live—the restoration of sovereign rights and self-government to those peoples who have been forcibly deprived of them by the aggressor nations.

To foster the conditions in which the liberated peoples may exercise these rights, the three Governments will jointly assist the people in any European liberated State or former Axis satellite State in Europe where, in their judgment, conditions require :—

(*a*) to establish conditions of peace ;

(*b*) to carry out emergency measures for the relief of distressed people ;

(*c*) to form interim Governmental authorities broadly representative of all democratic elements in the population and pledged to the earliest possible establishment through free elections of Governments responsive to the will of the people ; and

(*d*) to facilitate where necessary the holding of such elections.

The three Governments will consult the other United Nations and provisional authorities or other Governments in Europe when matters of direct interest to them are under consideration.

When, in the opinion of the three Governments, conditions in any European liberated State or any former Axis satellite State in Europe make such action necessary, they will immediately consult together on the measures necessary to discharge the joint responsibilities set forth in this Declaration.

By this Declaration we re-affirm our faith in the principles of the Atlantic Charter, our pledge in the Declaration by the United Nations, and our determination to build in co-operation with other peace-loving nations a world order under law, dedicated to peace, security, freedom, and the general well-being of all mankind.

In issuing this Declaration the three Powers express the hope that the Provisional Government of the French Republic may be associated with them in the procedure suggested.

6.—POLAND

We came to the Crimea Conference resolved to settle our differences about Poland. We discussed fully all aspects of the question. We re-affirm our common desire to see established a strong, free, independent, and democratic Poland. As a result of our discussions we have agreed on the conditions in which a new Polish Provisional Government of National Unity may be formed in such a manner as to command recognition by the three major Powers. The agreement reached is as follows :—

A new situation has been created in Poland as a result of her complete liberation by the Red Army.

This calls for the establishment of a Polish Provisional Government which can be more broadly based than was possible before the recent liberation of Western Poland. The Provisional Government which is now functioning in Poland should, therefore, be reorganized on a broader democratic basis with the inclusion of democratic leaders from

Poland itself and from Poles abroad. This new Government should then be called the Polish Provisional Government of National Unity.

Mr. Molotov, Mr. Harriman, and Sir A. Clark Kerr are authorized as a Commission to consult in the first instance in Moscow with members of the present Provisional Government and with other Polish democratic leaders from within Poland and from abroad, with a view to the reorganization of the present Government along the above lines.

This Polish Provisional Government of National Unity shall be pledged to the holding of free and unfettered elections as soon as possible on the basis of universal suffrage and secret ballot. In these elections all democratic and anti-Nazi parties shall have the right to take part and to put forward candidates.

When a Polish Provisional Government of National Unity has been properly formed in conformity with the above, the Government of the Union of Soviet Socialist Republics, which now maintains diplomatic relations with the present Provisional Government of Poland, and the Government of the United Kingdom and the Government of the United States will establish diplomatic relations with the new Polish Provisional Government of National Unity, and will exchange Ambassadors by whose reports the respective Governments will be kept informed about the situation in Poland.

The three heads of Government consider that the Eastern frontier of Poland should follow the Curzon Line, with digressions from it in some regions of five to eight kilometres in favour of Poland. They recognize that Poland must receive substantial accessions of territory in the North and West. They feel that the opinion of the new Polish Provisional Government of National Unity should be sought in due course on the extent of these accessions, and that the final delimitation of the Western frontier of Poland should thereafter await the Peace Conference.

7.—YUGOSLAVIA

We have agreed to recommend to Marshal Tito and Dr. Subasitch that the agreement between them should be put into effect immediately, and that a new Government should be formed on the basis of that agreement. We also recommend that as soon as the new Government has been formed it should declare that :—

(1) The Anti-Fascist Assembly of National Liberation (*Avnoj*) should be extended to include members of the last Yugoslav Parliament (*Skupshtina*) who have not compromised themselves by collaboration with the enemy, thus forming a body to be known as a temporary Parliament, and

(2) Legislative Acts passed by the Assembly of National Liberation will be subject to subsequent ratification by a Constituent Assembly.

There was also a general review of other Balkan questions.

8.—MEETINGS OF FOREIGN SECRETARIES

Throughout the Conference, besides the daily meetings of the Heads of Governments and the Foreign Secretaries, separate meetings of the three Foreign Secretaries and their advisers have also been held daily.

These meetings have proved of the utmost value, and the Conference agreed that permanent machinery should be set up for regular consultation between the three Foreign Secretaries. They will, therefore, meet as often as may be necessary, probably about every three or four months. These meetings will be held in rotation in the three capitals, the first meeting being held in London after the United Nations Conference on World Organizations.

9.—UNITY FOR PEACE AS FOR WAR

Our meeting here in the Crimea has reaffirmed our common determination to maintain and strengthen in the peace to come that unity of purpose and of action which has made victory possible and certain for the United Nations in this war. We believe that this is a sacred obligation which our Governments owe to our peoples and to all the peoples of the world.

Only with continuing and growing co-operation and understanding among our three countries and among all the peace-loving nations can the highest aspiration of humanity be realized—a secure and lasting peace which will, in the words of the Atlantic Charter, " afford assurance that all the men in all the lands may live out their lives in freedom from fear and want."

Victory in this war and establishment of the proposed International Organization will provide the greatest opportunity in all history to create in the years to come the essential conditions of such a peace.

(Signed) Winston S. Churchill ;
Franklin D. Roosevelt ;
J. V. Stalin.

TRIBUTE TO RUSSIA

A SPEECH TO TROOPS GATHERED ON THE AIRFIELD IN THE CRIMEA WHEN
THE PRIME MINISTER LEFT FOR HOME AT THE CONCLUSION OF THE
CONFERENCE AT YALTA WITH MARSHAL STALIN AND PRESIDENT
ROOSEVELT
FEBRUARY 14, 1945

January 19. *British troops made steady progress in their attack East of Maeseyck, Holland.*
Russian forces captured Lodz.

January 20. *Hungary and the United Nations signed an Armistice in Moscow.*

January 21. *British made a big advance North of the Ardennes salient, and in the East the Russians made progress in many sectors of the Eastern Front.*
Troops of the 15th Indian Corps landed on Ramree Island, off Burma.

January 22. *British troops continued their progress towards the River Roer.*
Soviet forces captured Allenstein and Insterburg.

January 23. *Russians continued their advance and reached the River Oder, 20 miles from Breslau.*

January 24. *British Second Army entered Heinsberg.*

January 25. *Russians captured Gleiwitz, in Upper Silesia, and Oels and Ostrow.*

January 26. *Ardennes salient was cleared. British troops advanced farther towards the Roer.*
Red Army crossed the Oder at several points and Zhukov's armoured forces reached to within 100 miles of Berlin.

January 27. *U.S. Third Army were back at the German frontier.*
Red Army captured Memel and liberated Lithuania.
Tokio was bombed by U.S. Super-fortresses.

January 28. *U.S. troops captured four towns North-East of St. Vith.*
Russians cleared the industrial area of Upper Silesia.

January 29. *Russians invaded Pomerania and captured a town 95 miles from Berlin.*
U.S. forces advanced to within 30 miles of Manila, capital of the Philippines.

January 30. *Red Army reached the German frontier, 30 miles East of the Oder.*

Colmar Canal, in Alsace, was crossed by French troops.
New U.S. landing on the West coast of Luzon (Philippines).

January 31. U.S. First and Third Armies advanced to within three miles of the main defences of the Siegfried Line.

Russian troops captured Landsberg, 68 miles from Berlin, Heilsberg and Friedland in East Prussia also fell to the Red Army.

February 1. U.S. Third Army troops captured five German towns and established a front of 4½ miles inside Germany. Heavy air attacks on Berlin and railway centres in Germany.

February 2. French troops entered Colmar and U.S. Armies massed along the Siegfried Line from Aachen to the Saar.

Germans concentrated for the defence of Berlin on the Eastern front following new advances by the Russians.

British forces attacked heavily on the North bank of the Irrawaddy.

February 3. Berlin was bombed in a great daylight attack by U.S. forces, Government buildings and railway stations being badly damaged.

U.S. troops entered Manila and rescued 3,700 Allied internees.

February 4. U.S. troops penetrated the main belt of the Siegfried Line defences.

Russians reached to within 38 miles of Berlin, capturing many important enemy strongholds.

February 5. Zhukov's troops reached the Oder on both sides of Kustrin and Koniev's forces crossed the Oder farther to the South.

U.S. First and Third Armies continued their penetration of the Siegfried defences.

R.A.F. Balloon Command was closed down, having served its purpose in the war.

February 6. Heavy air attacks on vital German communication centres were increased.

February 7. It was announced that Mr. Churchill, President Roosevelt and Marshal Stalin had met in the Crimea.

German border crossed in ten places by U.S. Third Army.
The Russians crossed the Breslau-Berlin motor highway.

February 8. Big Allied offensive launched at Nijmegen by Canadian troops and further advances were made by the Americans in the South.

In Burma, British troops opened their attack on Mandalay.

39

February 9. *Allied forces in the West made advances all along the front and heavy air blows were continued against Germany. Russians resumed their advance towards the mouth of the Oder.*

February 10. *Canadian troops captured Donsbruggen, near Cleves.*

   In the East Koniev's troops breached the Oder North-West of Breslau.

   In Burma, British troops extended their bridgehead on the East bank of the Irrawaddy River.

February 11. *Russians captured Liegnitz, one of the largest towns in Silesia, and almost surrounded Breslau.*

   An agreement was signed in Athens between the Greek Government and the E.A.M. Central Committee.

February 12. *Plans for the final defeat of Germany, agreed to by Mr. Churchill, President Roosevelt and Marshal Stalin at the Crimea Conference, were announced.*

February 13. *British troops penetrated the second belt of the Siegfried Line.*

   Russians completed the capture of Budapest and took 110,000 prisoners.

   The Polish Government in London refused to agree with the Crimea Conference plan for Poland.

February 14. *British and U.S. bombers increased heavy day and night attacks on Dresden.*

   Mr. Churchill left the Crimea on his journey home.

[*February* 14, 1945.

COLONEL-GENERAL YERMASHENKOV, officers and soldiers of the Russian Army and Air Force, and officers and men of the Royal Air Force gathered here.

Since we landed twelve days ago upon this airfield in war-torn Crimea great events have happened in the world. The permanent friendship and association of the Three Great Powers has been proclaimed in a manner more precise and more authoritative than ever before. We now look forward to marching into the heart of the enemy's country and crushing down for ever the vile Nazi tyranny which threatened to bar the onward march, the onward progress of mankind. They placed their barriers in the way, and all together our peoples—our three peoples and many other nations of the world—have crashed those barriers down. And in the van of all this struggle the Soviet armies have gained immortal honour.

And after the war is over we have all bound ourselves to work together to make sure that there is increasing happiness and prosperity for the broad masses of the people in every land, and that the nations shall be entitled to live at peace—no longer in fear of vile aggression, no longer subject to the hard straits of war.

There is the prospect which has now opened before us. Let us make sure we devote our united efforts, our unswerving purpose, our unexhausted life-energies to its achievement.

I am so glad that we are all here together to-day, and that the Royal Air Force detachments who have lived here with you have had the chance of knowing what true Russian hospitality is. These are seeds of a harvest which in the future will be gathered in by other generations, who will rejoice in what their fathers are doing now.

I thank you all—and on leaving the soil of Russia, the redeemed Crimea cleansed by Russian valour from the foul taint of the Huns—on leaving Soviet territory I express to you all and to your leaders, and particularly to your great leader the Supreme Commander-in-Chief Marshal Stalin, the gratitude and admiration of the British race, spread as they are all over the world, on the oceans, and in every quarter of the globe, for the Russians and their Army and their valiant people. We pray that they may never again be subjected to the cruel ordeals from which they have emerged with so much glory.

FUTURE OF GREECE

A Speech to a crowd of 50,000 Greeks in Constitution Square, Athens, during a stop on the journey from the Crimea to England
February 14, 1945

[February 14, 1945.

YOUR Beatitude, Soldiers and Citizens of Athens, and of Greece. These are great days. These are days when dawn is bright, when darkness rolls away. A great future lies before your great country.

There has been much misunderstanding and ignorance of our common cause in many parts of the world, and there have been misrepresentations of issues fought out here in Athens. But now these matters are clearing, and there is an understanding of the part Greece has played and will play in the world.

Speaking as an Englishman, I am very proud of the part which the British Army played in protecting this great and immortal city against violence and anarchy. Our two countries have for long marched together along hard dusty roads in friendship and in loyalty.

Freedom and prosperity and happiness are dear to all nations of the British Commonwealth and Empire. We who have been associated with you in the very long struggle for Greek liberty, we will march with you till we reach the end of the dark valley, and we will march with you till we reach the broad highlands of justice and peace.

Let no one fail in his duty towards his country. Let no one swerve off the high road of truth and honour. Let no one fail to rise to the occasion of this great moment and of these splendid days. Let the Greek Nation stand first in every heart. Let it stand first in every man and woman. Let the future of Greece shine brightly in their eyes.

From the bottom of my heart I wish you prosperity. From the bottom of my heart I hope that Greece will take her proper place in the circle of victorious nations—of nations who have suffered terribly in war. Let right prevail. Let party hatreds die. Let there be unity, let there be resolute comradeship.

Greece forever. Greece for all.

42

A MESSAGE OF HOPE

On his return to England the Prime Minister sent the following message to the Regent, Archbishop Damaskinos :—

I should like to thank you on my own behalf and that of the Foreign Secretary for the reception accorded to us by your Beatitude and by the whole Greek people on the occasion of our visit to Athens. The Foreign Secretary and I could not fail to be impressed by the warmth of the welcome which we received. I take this welcome as proof of the friendship which is felt in Greece for Great Britain, and I assure you that these sentiments are fully shared by the British people.

It is our earnest desire that the wounds which political rivalry and dissension have inflicted on Greece should now be healed, and you may count upon all the assistance which we can give to this end. I am confident that under your wise leadership Greece will regain that peace and prosperity which her valour and sufferings in this war have fully merited.

RESULTS OF THE THREE POWER CONFERENCE

A SPEECH TO THE HOUSE OF COMMONS
FEBRUARY 27, 1945

February 15. British and Canadian troops lined West bank of the Rhine on a ten-mile front and out-flanked the second belt of the Siegfried Line defences.

U.S. Pacific planes bombed Tokio.

February 16. German counter attacks in the East were repulsed with heavy losses and Allied bombers continued to smash German oil plants.

Bataan (Philippines) was recaptured by the Americans.

February 17. Canadian First Army executed a flank operation which threatened the towns of Goch and Calcar.

In Burma, British troops made a landing on the Arakan coast 65 miles South East of Akyab, and troops of the 14th Army expanded their bridgehead along the Irrawaddy.

February 18. Russian infantry advanced towards enemy defence line on the Neisse protecting Saxony and South Brandenburg.

February 19. U.S. troops broke through Siegfried defences North West of Echternach.

U.S. Marines landed on Iwo Jima, 750 miles from Japan.

February 20. U.S. Third Army made good progress in the Saar-Moselle Area.

Russians advanced towards Danzig.

February 21. Widespread Allied air raids over Germany, particularly on Berchtesgaden, Nuremberg and Berlin.

Russians captured Czersk, 45 miles from Danzig.

February 22. Allied bombers made a terrific raid in an attempt to put the German railway system out of action. More than 3,000 planes were employed. U.S. Third Army crossed the River Saar.

Russians captured three suburbs of Breslau.

February 23. U.S. troops made further crossings of the Saar and in the East the Russians captured the fortress town of Poznan after a month's siege.

Turkey declared war on the Axis powers.

February 24. Ten towns were captured by the U.S. Third Army in their Eastward advance.

44

February 25.   *Allied troops reached Steinstrass, 18 miles from Cologne, and Allied bombers continued the great assault on German railways and oil supplies.*

           Tokio and Yokohama were bombed by super-fortresses and U.S. carrier aircraft.

February 26.   *Berlin had its biggest daylight air attack of the war.*

February 27.   *British, American and Canadian troops made advances in many sectors of the Western Front and cut farther into the Siegfried Line.*

           Mr. Churchill addressed the House of Commons on the results of the Crimea Conference.

[*February 27, 1945.*

THE recent Conference of the three Powers in the Crimea faced realities and difficulties in so exceptional a manner that the result constituted an act of State, on which Parliament should formally express their opinion. His Majesty's Government feel they have the right to know where they stand with the House of Commons. A strong expression of support by the House will strengthen our position among our Allies. The intimate and sensitive connections between the Executive Government and the House of Commons will thereby also be made plain, thus showing the liveliness of our democratic institutions, and the subordination of Ministers to Parliamentary authority. The House will not shrink from its duty of pronouncing. We live in a time when equality of decision is required from all who take part in our public affairs. In this way also, the firm and tenacious character of the present Parliament, and, generally, of our Parliamentary institutions, emerging as they do fortified from the storms of the war, will be made manifest. We have therefore thought it right and necessary to place a positive Motion on the Paper, in support of which I should like to submit some facts and arguments to the House at the opening of this three days' Debate.

The difficulties of bringing about a Conference of the three heads of the Governments of the principal Allies are only too obvious. The fact that, in spite of all modern methods of communication, fourteen months elapsed between Teheran and Yalta is a measure of those difficulties. It is well known that His Majesty's Government greatly desired a triple meeting in the Autumn. We rejoiced when, at last, Yalta was fixed. On the way there, the British and United States delegations met at Malta to discuss the wide range of our joint military and political affairs. The combined Chiefs of Staff of the two countries were for three days in conference upon the great operations now developing on the Western Front, and upon the war plans against Japan, which it was appropriate for us to discuss together. The Foreign Secretary, accompanied by high officials and assistants, some of whom unhappily perished on the way, also met Mr. Stettinius there. On the morning of 2nd February the cruiser which bore the President steamed majestically into the battle-scarred harbour. A plenary meeting of the combined Chiefs of Staff was held in the afternoon, at which the President and I approved the proposals which had been so carefully worked out in the preceding days for carrying our joint war effort to the highest pitch, and for the shaping and timing of the military operations. Meanwhile the Minister of War Transport and the American authorities concerned had been labouring on a vessel all to themselves at the problems of shipping, which govern our affairs at present and which affect the movement and the reserves of oil, food, munitions and troops. On all these matters, complete agreement was reached—very difficult and complicated matters—like making an international Bradshaw in which the times of all the express trains may have to be varied, if half a dozen unforeseen contingencies arise. No hard-and-fast agreements were made on any political issues. These, naturally, were to form the subject of the triple Conference, and they were carefully kept open for the full meeting.

The reason why shipping is so tight at present is that the peak period of the war in Europe has been prolonged for a good many months beyond what was hoped for last Autumn, and meanwhile the peak period against Japan has been brought forward by the American victories in the Pacific. Thus, instead of one peak period fading out or dovetailing into the other, there is an overlap, or double peak period, in the two wars which we are waging together on opposite sides of the globe. Although for a couple of years past our joint losses by U-boats have ceased to be an appreciable factor in our main business, and although the shipbuilding output of the United States flows on gigantically, and although the Allies have to-day far more shipping than they ever had at any time previously during the war, we are, in fact, more hard-pressed by shipping shortage than ever before. The same double peak of war effort, of course, affects all our preparations for the turn-over to peace, including housing and the much-needed supplies for civilians. All these facts call for the most strenuous and searching economy on the military side, where indulgence in mis-calculation or extravagance of any kind is a grave injury to the common cause. They also lamentably hamper our power to provide for the dire needs of the liberated territories. I am not prepared to have this Island cut below its minimum safety reserves of food and oil, except in cases where sure and speedy replacement can be made. Subject to this, we shall do everything in our power to help the liberated countries. It is easy to see the rigorous character of the discussions which Lord Leathers—who is highly competent in these matters and is admitted to be a magnificent authority on all this aspect, and who holds it all in his head—has conducted on our behalf, and we may be satisfied to-day with the fair and friendly distribution of burden and hardship which has been agreed upon between Great Britain and the United States over the whole inter-Allied shipping pool.

There was the diplomatic conference proceeding on one cruiser ; there was the military discussion proceeding on another, and the discussions on shipping going forward on a third vessel. Then, at the end, the President arrived, and the results were submitted to him and to me. I kept in touch with what was going on, and we jointly approved all these matters, on which action was immediately taken.

After that, we all flew safely from Malta to the airfield in the Crimea, and motored over the mountains—about which very alarming accounts had been given, but these proved to be greatly exaggerated—until we found shelter on the Southern shore of the Crimea. This is protected by the mountains, and forms a beautiful Black Sea Riviera, where there still remain undestroyed by the Nazis a few villas and palaces of the vanished Imperial and aristocratic regime. By extreme exertions and every form of thoughtfulness and ingenuity, our Russian hosts had restored these dwellings to good order, and had provided for our accommodation and comfort in the true style of Russian hospitality. In the background were the precipices and the mountains ; beyond them, the devastated fields and shattered dwellings of the Crimea, across which the armies have twice surged in deadly combat. Here on this shore, we laboured for nine days and grappled with many problems of war and policy while friendship grew.

I have seen a criticism in this country that France was not invited to participate in the Conference at Yalta. The first principle of British policy in Western Europe is a strong France, and a strong French army. It was, however, felt by all three Great Powers assembled in the Crimea that, while they are responsible for bearing to an over-whelming degree the main brunt and burden of the conduct of the war and the policy intimately connected with the operations, they could not allow any restrictions to be placed upon their right to meet together as they deemed necessary, in order that they might effectively dis-charge their duties to the common cause. This view, of course, does not exclude meetings on the highest level, to which other Powers will be invited.

France may however find many reasons for contentment with the Crimea decisions. Under these decisions France is to be invited to take over a zone of occupation in Germany, which we shall immediately proceed to delimit with her, and to sit on the Allied Control Commission in Germany, which regulates the whole affairs of that country after the unconditional surrender has been obtained. France is to be invited to join the United States, the United Kingdom, the Union of Soviet Socialist Republics and China in sponsoring the invitations to the San Francisco Conference, which has been arranged for 25th April this year. She is invited to join the United States, the United Kingdom and the Soviet Union in operating the procedure laid down in the Declaration on Liberated Europe. She is also a member of the European Advisory Commission, to which most important tasks have been relegated, including advice to the Governments upon most important matters connected with the treatment of Germany. This Commission, with French assistance, has already completed in great detail all the terms upon which unconditional surrender will be received and accepted. Everything is provided for in that sphere. If we were confronted to-morrow with a collapse of the German power, there is nothing that has not been foreseen and arranged beforehand by this important European Advisory Commission consisting of Mr. Winant, Ambassador Gusev, and Sir William Strang, of the Foreign Office. This applies to the arrangements for the occupation as far as they can be foreseen, and the Commission is also to advise us on various matters connected with Germany apart from the actual taking-over by our military authorities. All these arrangements show clearly the importance of the role which France is called upon to play in the settlement of Europe, and how fully it is recognized that she must be intimately associated with the other great Powers in this task. In order to give further explanations of the proceedings of the Conference, we invited M. Bidault, the French Minister of Foreign Affairs, to visit London at the earliest opportunity. He was good enough to come, and during the last few days we have had the pleasure of a series of clarifying talks with him, in which he has been able to become fully informed of the whole position, and to express in the most effective manner the views and wishes of France upon it.

On world organization, there is little that I can say beyond what is contained in the Report of the Conference, and, of course, in the earlier reports which emanated from Dumbarton Oaks. In the Crimea, the three Great Powers agreed on a solution of the difficult question of voting procedure, to which no answer had been found at Dumbarton Oaks. Agreement on this vital matter has enabled us to take the next step forward in the setting-up of the new world organization, and the arrangements are in hand for the issue of invitations to the United Nations Conference which, as I have said, will meet in a couple of months at San Francisco. I wish I could give to the House full particulars of the solution of this question of the voting procedure, to which representatives of the three Great Powers, formerly in disagreement, have now whole-heartedly agreed. We thought it right, however, that we should consult both France and China, and should endeavour to secure their acceptance before the formula was published. For the moment, therefore, I can only deal with the matter in general terms.

Here is the difficulty which has to be faced. It is on the Great Powers that the chief burden of maintaining peace and security will fall. The new world organization must take into account this special responsibility of the Great Powers, and must be so framed as not to compromise their unity, or their capacity for effective action if it is called for at short notice. At the same time, the world organization cannot be based upon a dictatorship of the Great Powers. It is their duty to serve the world and not to rule it. We trust the voting procedure on which we agreed at Yalta meets these two essential points, and provides a system which is fair and acceptable, having regard to the evident difficulties, which will meet anyone who gives prolonged thought to the subject.

The Conference at San Francisco will bring together, upon the invitation of the United States, Great Britain, the British Commonwealth, the Union of Soviet Socialist Republics, the provisional Government of the French Republic, and the Republic of China, all those members of the United Nations who have declared war on Germany or Japan by 1st March, 1945, and who have signed the United Nations Conference declaration. Many are declaring war or have done so since Yalta, and their action should be treated with respect and satisfaction by those who have borne the burden and heat of the day. Our future will be consolidated and enriched by the participation of these Powers, who, together with the founder members, will take the opening steps to form the world organization to which it is hoped that ultimately and in due course all States will belong. It is to this strongly-armed body that we look to prevent wars of aggression, or the preparation for such wars, and to enable disputes between States, both great and small, to be adjusted by peaceful and lawful means, by persuasion, by the pressure of public opinion, by legal method, and eventually by another category of method which constitutes the principle of this new organization.

The former League of Nations, so hardly used and found to be inadequate for the tasks it attempted, will be replaced by a far stronger body in which the United States will play a vitally important part. It will embody much of the structure and characteristics of its predecessor. All the work that was done in the past, all the experience that has been gathered by the working of the League of Nations, will not be cast away; but the new body will differ from it in the essential point that it will not shrink from establishing its will against the evildoer, or evil-planner, in good time and by force of arms. This organization, which is capable of continuous progress and development, is at any rate appropriate to the phase upon which the world will enter after our present enemies have been beaten down, and we may have good hopes, and, more than hopes, a resolute determination that it shall shield humanity from a third renewal of its agonies. We have all been made aware in the interval between the two world wars of the weaknesses of international bodies, whose work is seriously complicated by the misfortune which occurred in the building of the Tower of Babel. Taught by bitter experience, we hope now to make the world conscious of the strength of the new instrument, and of the protection which it will be able to afford to all who wish to dwell in peace within their habitations.

This new world structure will, from the outset and in all parts of its work, be aided to the utmost by the ordinary channels of friendly diplomatic intercourse, which it in no way supersedes. For our part, we are determined to do all in our power to ensure the success of the Conference. On such an occasion it is clearly right that the two leading parties in His Majesty's Government and in the British nation should be represented, and all parties bound for the future in these decisions. I am glad to inform the House that His Majesty's chief representatives at this Conference will be my right hon. Friend the Secretary of State for Foreign Affairs (Mr. Eden), and the Lord President of the Council, the leader of the Labour Party (Mr. Attlee). I am most anxious that this principle should be established, even in what are perhaps the closing stages of this memorable coalition. I am anxious that all parties should be united in this new instrument, so that these supreme affairs shall be, in Mr. Gladstone's words, " high and dry above the ebb and flow of party politics." I confess that I have not verified that quotation, and I ask for all indulgence if I should be proved to have made any slip.

The Crimea Conference leaves the Allies more closely united than ever before, both in the military and in the political sphere. Let Germany recognize that it is futile to hope for division among the Allies, and that nothing can avert her utter defeat. Further resistance will only be the cause of needless suffering. The Allies are resolved that Germany shall be totally disarmed, that Nazism and militarism in Germany shall be destroyed, that war criminals shall be justly and swiftly punished, that all German industry capable of military production shall be eliminated or controlled, and that Germany shall make compensation in kind to the utmost of her ability for damage done to Allied nations. On the other hand, it is not the purpose of the Allies to destroy the people of Germany, or leave them without the necessary means of subsistence. Our policy is not revenge ; it is to take such measures as may be necessary to secure the future peace and safety of the world. There will be a place one day for Germans in the comity of nations, but only when all traces of Nazism and militarism have been effectively and finally extirpated.

On the general plan, there is complete agreement. As to the measures to give effect to it, much still remains to be done. The plans for the Allied Control Commission will come into operation immediately on the defeat of Germany ; indeed, they are far advanced—advanced, as I have said, to the point where they could be instantly made effective. On the longer-term measures, there are many points of great importance on which detailed plans have yet to be worked out between the Allies. It would be a great mistake to suppose that questions of this kind can be thrashed out, and solutions found for all the many intractable and complex problems involved, while the Armies are still on the march. To hurry and press matters of this kind might well be to risk causing disunity between the Allies. Many of these matters must await the time when the leaders of the Allies, freed from the burden of the direction of the war, can turn their whole or main attention to the making of a wise and far-seeing peace which will, I trust, become a foundation greatly facilitating the work of the World Organization.

I now come to the most difficult and agitating part of the statement which I have to make to the House—the question of Poland. For more than a year past, and since the tide of war has turned so strongly against Germany, the Polish problem has been divided into two main issues—the frontiers of Poland and the freedom of Poland.

The House is well aware from the speeches I have made to them that the freedom, independence, integrity and sovereignty of Poland have always seemed to His Majesty's Government more important than the actual frontiers. To establish a free Polish nation with a good home to live in has always far outweighed, in my mind, the actual tracing of the frontier line, or whether these boundaries should be shifted on both sides of Poland farther to the West. The Russian claim, first advanced at Teheran in November, 1943, has always been unchanged for the Curzon Line in the East, and the Russian offer has always been that ample compensation should be gained for Poland at the expense of Germany in the North and in the West. All these matters are tolerably well known now. The Foreign Secretary explained in detail last December the story of the Curzon Line. I have never concealed from the House that, personally, I think the Russian claim is just and right. If I champion this frontier for Russia, it is not because I bow to force. It is because I believe it is the fairest division of territory that can, in all the circumstances, be made between the two countries whose history has been so chequered and intermingled.

The Curzon Line was drawn in 1919 by an expert Commission, of which one of our most distinguished Foreign Office representatives of those days, Sir Eyre Crowe, was a member. It was drawn at a time when Russia had few friends among the Allies. In fact, I may say that she was extremely unpopular. One cannot feel that either the circumstances or the personalities concerned would have given undue favour to Soviet Russia. They just tried to find out what was the right and proper line to draw. The British Government in those days approved this Line, including, of course, the exclusion of Lvov from Poland. Apart from all that has happened since, I cannot conceive that we should not regard it as a well-informed and fair proposal.

There are two things to be remembered in justice to our great Ally. I can look back to August, 1914, when Germany first declared war against Russia under the Tsar. In those days, the Russian frontiers on the West were far more spacious than those for which Russia is now asking after all her sufferings and victories. The Tsarist frontiers included all Finland and the whole of the vast Warsaw salient stretching to within 60 miles of Breslau. Russia is, in fact, accepting a frontier which over immense distances is 200 or 300 miles farther to the East than what was Russian territory and had been Russian territory for many generations under the Tsarist regime. Marshal Stalin told me one day that Lenin objected to the Curzon Line because Bialystok and the region round it were taken from Russia. Marshal Stalin and the modern Soviet Government make no such claim, and freely agree with the view taken by the Allied Commission of 1919 that the Bialystok region should go to Poland because of the Polish population predominating there.

We speak of the Curzon Line. A line is not a frontier. A frontier has to be surveyed and traced on the ground and not merely put in on a map with a pencil and ruler. When the Foreign Secretary and I were at Moscow in October Marshal Stalin made this point to me, and at that time he said that there might be deviations of 8 to 10 kilometres in either direction in order to follow the courses of streams and hills or the actual sites of particular villages. It seems to me that this was an eminently sensible way of looking at the problem. However, when we met at Yalta the Russian proposal was changed. It was made clear that all such minor alterations would be at the expense of Russia and not at the expense of Poland, in order that the Poles might have their minds set at rest once and for all and there should be no further discussion about that part of the business. We welcomed this Soviet proposal. One must regard these thirty years or more of strife, turmoil and suffering in Europe as part of one story. I have lived through the whole story since 1911, when I was sent to the Admiralty to prepare the Fleet for an impending German war. In its main essentials it seems to me to be one story of a thirty years' war, or more than a thirty years' war, in which British, Russians, Americans and French have struggled to their utmost to resist German aggression at a cost most grievous to all of them, but to none more frightful than to the Russian people, whose country has twice been ravaged over vast areas, and whose blood has been poured out in tens of millions of lives in a common cause now reaching final accomplishment.

There is a second reason which appeals to me, apart from this sense of continuity which I personally feel. But for the prodigious exertions and sacrifices of Russia, Poland was doomed to utter destruction at the hands of the Germans. Not only Poland as a State and as a nation, but the Poles as a race were doomed by Hitler to be destroyed or reduced to a servile station. Three and a half million Polish Jews are said to have been actually slaughtered. It is certain that enormous numbers have perished in one of the most horrifying acts of cruelty, probably the most horrifying act of cruelty, which has ever darkened the passage of man on the earth. When the Germans had clearly avowed their intention of making the Poles a subject and inferior race under the Herrenvolk, suddenly, by a superb effort of military force and skill, the Russian Armies, in little more than three weeks, since, in fact, we spoke on these matters here, have advanced from the Vistula to the Oder, driving the Germans in ruin before them and freeing the whole of Poland from the awful cruelty and oppression under which the Poles were writhing.

In supporting the Russian claim to the Curzon Line, I repudiate and repulse any suggestion that we are making a questionable compromise or yielding to force or fear, and I assert with the utmost conviction the broad justice of the policy upon which, for the first time, all the three great Allies have now taken their stand. Moreover, the three Powers have now agreed that Poland shall receive substantial accessions of territory both in the North and in the West. In the North she will certainly receive, in the place of a precarious Corridor, the great city of Danzig, the greater part of East Prussia west and south of Koenigsberg, and a long, wide sea front on the Baltic. In the West she will receive the important industrial province of Upper Silesia and, in addition, such other territories to the east of the Oder as it may be decided at the peace settlement to detach from Germany after the views of a broadly based Polish Government have been ascertained.

Thus, it seems to me that this talk of cutting half of Poland off is very misleading. In fact, the part which is to be east of the Curzon Line cannot in any case be measured by its size. It includes the enormous, dismal region of the Pripet Marshes, which Poland held between the two wars, and it exchanges for that the far more fruitful and developed land in the West, from which a very large portion of the German population has already departed. We need not fear that the

E

task of holding these new lines will be too heavy for Poland, or that it will bring about another German revenge, or that it will, to use a conventional phrase, sow the seeds of future wars. We intend to take steps far more drastic and effective than those which followed the last war, because we know much more about this business, so as to render all offensive action by Germany utterly impossible for generations to come.

Finally, under the world organization of nations great and small, victors and vanquished will be secured against aggression by indisputable law and by overwhelming international force. The published Crimea Agreement is not a ready-made plan, imposed by the great Powers on the Polish people. It sets out the agreed views of the three major Allies on the means whereby their common desire to see established a strong, free, independent Poland may be fulfilled in cooperation with the Poles themselves, and whereby a Polish Government which all the United Nations can recognize may be set up in Poland. This has become for the first time a possibility now that practically the whole country has been liberated by the Soviet Army. The fulfilment of the plan will depend upon the willingness of all sections of democratic Polish opinion in Poland or abroad to work together in giving it effect. The plan should be studied as a whole, and with the main common objective always in view. The three Powers are agreed that acceptance by the Poles of the provisions on the Eastern Frontiers and, so far as they can now be ascertained, on the Western Frontiers, is an essential condition of the establishment and future welfare and security of a strong, independent, homogeneous Polish State.

The proposals on frontiers are in complete accordance, as the House will remember, with the views expressed by me in Parliament on behalf of His Majesty's Government many times during the past year. I ventured to make pronouncements upon this subject at a time when a great measure of agreement was not expressed by the other important parties to the affair. The Eastern frontier must be settled now, if the new Polish administration is to be able to carry on its work in its own territory, and to do this in amity with the Russians and behind their fighting fronts. The Western frontiers, which will involve a substantial accession of Germany territory to Poland, cannot be fixed except as part of the whole German settlement until after the Allies have occupied German territory and after a fully representative Polish Government has been able to make its wishes known. It would be a great mistake to press Poland to take a larger portion of these lands than is considered by her and by her friends and Allies to be within her compass to man, to develop, and, with the aid of the Allies and the world organization, to maintain.

I have now dealt with the frontiers of Poland. I must say I think it is a case which I can outline with great confidence to the House. An impartial line traced long ago by a British commission in which Britain took a leading part; the moderation with which the Russians have strictly confined themselves to that line; the enormous sacrifices they have made and the sufferings they have undergone; the contributions they have made to our present victory; the great interest, the vital interest, which Poland has in having complete agreement with her powerful neighbour to the East—when you consider all those matters and the way they have been put forward, the temperate, patient manner in which they have been put forward and discussed, I say that I have rarely seen a case in this House which I could commend with more confidence to the good sense of Members of all sides.

But even more important than the frontiers of Poland, within the limits now disclosed, is the freedom of Poland. The home of the Poles is settled. Are they to be masters in their own house? Are they to be free, as we in Britain and the United States or France are free? Is their sovereignty and their independence to be untrammelled, or are they to become a mere projection of the Soviet State, forced against their will, by an armed minority, to adopt a Communist or totalitarian system? Well, I am putting the case in all its bluntness. It is a touchstone far more sensitive and vital than the drawing of frontier lines. Where does Poland stand? Where do we all stand on this?

Most solemn declarations have been made by Marshal Stalin and the Soviet Union that the sovereign independence of Poland is to be maintained, and this decision is now joined-in both by Great Britain and the United States. Here also, the world organization will in due course assume a measure of responsibility. The Poles will have their future in their own hands, with the single limitation that they must honestly follow, in harmony with their Allies, a policy friendly to Russia. That is surely reasonable.

The procedure which the three Great Powers have unitedly adopted to achieve this vital aim is set forth in unmistakable terms in the Crimea declaration. The agreement provides for consultations, with a view to the establishment in Poland of a new Polish Provisional Government of National Unity, with which the three major Powers can all enter into diplomatic relations, instead of some recognizing one Polish Government and the rest another, a situation which, if it had survived the Yalta Conference, would have proclaimed to the world disunity and confusion. We had to settle it, and we settled it there. No binding restrictions have been imposed upon the scope and method of those consultations. His Majesty's Government intend to do all in their power to ensure that they shall be as wide as possible, and that representative Poles of all democratic parties are given full freedom to come and make their views known. Arrangements for this are now being made in Moscow by the Commission of three, comprising M. Molotov, and Mr. Harriman and Sir Archibald Clark Kerr, representing the United States and Great Britain respectively. It will be for the Poles themselves, with such assistance as the Allies are able to give them, to agree upon the composition and constitution of the new Polish Government of National Unity. Thereafter, His Majesty's Government, through their representative in Poland, will use all their influence to ensure that the free elections to which the new Polish Government will be pledged shall be fairly carried out under all proper democratic safeguards.

Our two guiding principles in dealing with all these problems of the Continent and of liberated countries, have been clear : While the war is on, we give help to anyone who can kill a Hun ; when the war is over, we look to the solution of a free, unfettered, democratic election. Those are the two principles which this Coalition Government have applied, to the best of their ability, to the circumstances and situations in this entangled and infinitely varied development.

The agreement does not affect the continued recognition by His Majesty's Government of the Polish Government in London. This will be maintained until such time as His Majesty's Government consider that a new Provisional Government has been properly formed in Poland in accordance with the agreed provisions ; nor does it involve the previous or immediate recognition by His Majesty's Government of the present Provisional Government which is now functioning in Poland. Let me remind the House, and those who have undertaken what I regard as the honourable duty of being very careful that our affairs in Poland are regulated in accordance with the dignity and honour of this country, that there would have been no Lublin Committee or Lublin Provisional Government in Poland if the Polish Government in London had accepted our faithful counsel given to them a year ago. They would have entered into Poland as its active Government, with the liberating Armies of Russia. Even in October, when the Foreign Secretary and I toiled night and day in Moscow, M. Mikolajczyk could have gone from Moscow to Lublin with every assurance of Marshal Stalin's friendship, and become the Prime Minister of a more broadly constructed Government, which would now be seated at Warsaw, or wherever, in view of the ruin of Warsaw, the centre of Government is placed.

But these opportunities were cast aside. Meanwhile, the expulsion of the Germans from Poland has taken place, and of course the new Government, the Lublin Government, advanced with the victorious

Russian Armies, who were received with great joy in very great areas in Poland, many great cities changing hands without a shot fired, and with none of that terrible business of underground armies being shot by both sides, and so forth, which we feared so much, having actually taken place during the great forward advance. The Russians, who are executing and preparing military operations on the largest scale against the heart of Germany, have the right to have the communications of their armies protected by an orderly countryside, under a government acting in accordance with their needs. It was not therefore possible, so far as recognition was concerned, to procure the dissolution of the Lublin Government as well as of the London Government simultaneously, and start from a swept table. To do that would be to endanger the success of the Russian offensive, and consequently to prolong the war, with increased loss of Russian, British and American blood.

The House should read carefully again and again—those Members who have doubts—the words and the terms of the Declaration, every word of which was the subject of the most profound and searching attention by the Heads of the three Governments, and by the Foreign Secretaries and all their experts. How will this Declaration be carried out ? How will phrases like

" Free and unfettered elections on the basis of universal suffrage and secret ballot "

be interpreted ? Will the " new " Government be " properly " constituted, with a fair representation of the Polish people, as far as can be made practicable at the moment, and as soon as possible ? Will the elections be free and unfettered ? Will the candidates of all democratic parties be able to present themselves to the electors, and to conduct their campaigns ? What are democratic parties ? People always take different views. Even in our own country there has been from time to time an effort by one party or the other to claim that they are the true democratic party, and the rest are either Bolsheviks or Tory landlords. What are democratic parties ? Obviously this is capable of being settled. Will the election be what we should say was fair and free in this country, making some allowance for the great confusion and disorder which prevails ? There are a great number of parties in Poland. We have agreed that all those that are democratic parties—not Nazi or Fascist parties or parties of collaborators with the enemy—all these will be able to take their part.

These are questions upon which we have the clearest views, in accordance with the principles of the Declaration on liberated Europe, to which all three Governments have duly subscribed. It is on that basis that the Moscow Commission of three was intended to work, and on that basis it has already begun to work.

The impression I brought back from the Crimea, and from all my other contacts, is that Marshal Stalin and the Soviet leaders wish to live in honourable friendship and equality with the Western democracies. I feel also that their word is their bond. I know of no Government which stands to its obligations, even in its own despite, more solidly than the Russian Soviet Government. I decline absolutely to embark here on a discussion about Russian good faith. It is quite evident that these matters touch the whole future of the world. Sombre indeed would be the fortunes of mankind if some awful schism arose between the Western democracies and the Russian Soviet Union, if the future world organization were rent asunder, and if new cataclysms of inconceivable violence destroyed all that is left of the treasures and liberties of mankind.

Finally, on this subject, His Majesty's Government recognize that the large forces of Polish troops, soldiers, sailors and airmen, now fighting gallantly, as they have fought during the whole war, under British command, owe allegiance to the Polish Government in London. We have every confidence that once the new Government, more fully representative of the will of the Polish people than either the present Government in London or the Provisional Administration in Poland, has been established, and recognized by the Great Powers, means will be found of overcoming these formal difficulties in the wider interest of Poland. Above all, His Majesty's Government are resolved that as many as possible of the Polish troops shall be enabled to return in due course to Poland, of their own free will, and under every safeguard, to play their part in the future life of their country.

In any event, His Majesty's Government will never forget the debt they owe to the Polish troops who have served them so valiantly, and to all those who have fought under our command I earnestly hope it may be possible to offer the citizenship and freedom of the British Empire, if they so desire. I am not able to make a declaration on that subject to-day, because all matters affecting citizenship require to be discussed between this country and the Dominions, and that takes time. But so far as we are concerned we should think it an honour to have such faithful and valiant warriors dwelling among us as if they were men of our own blood.

We leave the Crimean shores, and travel southwards to warmer climes, in which also we find many matters where British interests are important, and where we are involved. President Roosevelt invited the Emperor of Ethiopia, King Farouk of Egypt, and the King of Saudi Arabia, to meet him at Ismailia before sailing for home, and conferences upon his cruiser were accordingly arranged by him. I myself took leave of the President on the 15th of this month in Alexandria Harbour, after long and most agreeable talks about the state of our affairs in the light of the Crimea Conference, and also talks about our special business in the Far East, in which, as the Japanese are aware, we both take some interest.

We also spoke of our joint occupation of Italy and of our policy there. Upon this, the House is aware, there was a great deal of mis-understanding in large sections of the American Press some weeks ago. During our recent talks I repeatedly asked both the President and Mr. Stettinius to state whether there were any, and if so what, com-plaints by the United States Government against us for any steps we have taken or have not taken in Italy ; and I received categorical assurances that there were none. Moreover, I must place it on record that when I visited Italy in August last I made a series of proposals to His Majesty's Government, of which I informed the President, for mitigating the severity of the Allied occupation in Italy, and generally for alleviating the hard lot of the Italian people. These matters were discussed at our second Quebec Conference, and it was at Hyde Park, the President's private country home, that he and I drafted the declaration of 28th September, which was, and is, intended to make a very definite mitigation in the attitude of the victorious Powers towards the Italian people, and to show our desire to help them in due course to resume their place among the leading nations of Europe. Last Saturday the right hon. Member for Stockton-on-Tees [Mr. Harold Macmillan], who is acting President of the Allied Commission, and Admiral Stone of the United States Navy, who is its Chief Commissioner, were received by the Prime Minister and the Foreign Secretary of Italy, and announced to them the new measures decided upon in favour of the Italian Government in fulfilment of this September declaration.

As I myself have taken the lead in bringing these proposals forward and eventually securing their adoption, I am not prepared to accept suggestions from any quarter—although we suffered injury and ill-usage at Italy's hands in the days of Mussolini's power—that Great Britain has fallen behind other victorious Powers in taking a generous view towards Italy, or that we nourish any design of " power politics " which involve Italy. The sentence I used was that we had no need of Italy for any of our designs, and that was wrested from its context ; but as a matter of fact, it was a mere reply which I was bound to make to suggestions in some quarters of the United States Press that we were embarking on some power politics—whatever they may be— in the Mediterranean. I am glad to say that the facts I am now setting forth have been explicitly accepted by the United States, or at any rate in all responsible quarters, and that this view was thoroughly endorsed by the President and Mr. Stettinius ; and I have received quite definite assurances that no complaints of any kind were or are preferred against us which would call for any reply on my part, such as would certainly be forthcoming.

Our two nations can, therefore, proceed on their joint task in Italy—which in future will be burdened with many new complications and difficulties—in the closest confidence and unity. We look forward to Italy's return under a truly democratic regime to the community of industrious and peace-loving nations. In her efforts to help herself, Italy can count upon British good will, and upon Allied good will. She can count also on such material aid as is at our disposal, and she will continually receive her fair share. I said some time ago that Italy would have to work her passage home. She has some way to go yet, but it would be less than just if I did not pay a tribute to the invaluable services, the full tale of which cannot yet be told, of Italian men and women in the Armed Forces, on the seas, in the countryside, and behind the enemy lines in the North, which are being rendered steadily and steadfastly to the common cause. New difficulties may be cast upon us when the great districts in the North are cleared, and when the problem of feeding the great masses for whom we shall then become responsible is thrown upon us and upon the provisional Italian Government, which Government may itself be called upon to undergo changes as a consequence of the greatly increased constituency for which it will become responsible through the liberation of the Northern districts.

The Foreign Secretary and I thought it would be becoming, as well as convenient and agreeable, that we should also see the two rulers who had made long journeys to Egypt at the President's invitation, and that we should pass in friendly review with them the many matters in which we have common concern. It was our duty also to pay our respects to King Farouk of Egypt, and we thought it right to seek a talk with President Shukri of Syria, in order to calm things down as much as possible in the Levant. It should not, however, be supposed that anything in the nature of a general conference on Middle East affairs took place. The mere fact that the Regent of Iraq and the Emir Abdulla of Transjordania were not on the spot should make this perfectly clear. Any conference would naturally include authorities of that sort. There was no question of shaping new policies for the Middle East, but rather of making those friendly personal contacts by which public business between various States is often helped. I must at once express our grief and horror at the assassination of the Egyptian Prime Minister, Ahmed Maher Pasha, with whom the Foreign Secretary had a long and cordial interview only a few days, almost hours, before he fell a victim to foul play. His death is a serious loss to his King and to his country. The sympathy of Great Britain for the widow and family of the late Prime Minister of

Egypt has of course been expressed, not only in telegrams from the Foreign Office, but also by various personal visits of our Ambassador, Lord Killearn, and I am sure the House will associate itself with these expressions. There is little doubt that security measures in Egypt require considerable tightening, and above all that the execution of justice upon men proved guilty of political murder should be swift and exemplary.

The Egyptian Government have, we feel, acted rightly and wisely in deciding to declare war on Germany and Japan, and to sign the United Nations Declaration. We did not press the Egyptian Government at any time to come into the war, and indeed upon more than one occasion in the past our advice has been to the contrary. There were evident advantages in sparing the populous and famous city of Cairo from wholesale bombardment, and we have been content with the attitude of Egypt as a co-belligerent. Egyptian troops have, during the war, played an important part. They have maintained order throughout the Delta, they have guarded many strong-points and depots, and in all kinds of ways they have been of assistance to our war effort, which has once again proved successful in shielding the fertile lands of the Delta from the shock of the foreign invader. We have had every facility from Egypt under our Treaty of Alliance, and successive Egyptian Prime Ministers and Governments have given us support in the manner which we deemed to be the most effective. Egypt is an Associated Power, and she should take her rightful place as a future member of the world organization and as one of its founders, when the occasion is reached at San Francisco at the end of April.

We are also very glad to welcome Turkey into the ranks of the United Nations. Turkey declared herself most firmly on our side by the Treaty of Alliance in 1939, at a time when the gathering dangers were only too apparent. As I explained to the House on a former occasion, Turkey became conscious of unexpected military weakness after the war had started in earnest on account of the influence—the decisive influence—of new weapons with which she was quite unprovided and which we were not in a position to supply. As these weapons exercise a decisive effect on the modern battlefield, the Turks felt that they could no longer confide their safety to their renowned infantry and to the artillery of the last war. We did not, therefore, for a long time press them for a declaration of war. It was not until after the Teheran Conference that we considered that the moment had come when Turkey could enter the struggle without grave imprudence. The Turkish Government did not feel able to do so at that time, but they have aided us in various ways which it would not be profitable to recount, and we have never had the slightest doubt where their hearts lay. They, also, will be welcomed by Great Britain into the ranks of the United Nations, and I do not consider that the ties renewed between our two countries after the miserable disasters of the last war have been in any way impaired.

I was greatly interested in meeting King Ibn Saud, the famous ruler of Saudi Arabia. I had the honour of entertaining this most remarkable man to luncheon in the Fayoum Oasis, and of expressing to him the thanks of Great Britain for his steadfast, unswerving and unflinching loyalty to our country and the common cause, which never shone more brightly than in the darkest days and in the hours of mortal peril. His aid will be needed at the close of the war in reaching a solution of the problems of the Arab world and of the Jewish people in Palestine. I have hopes that when the war is over good arrangements can be made for securing the peace and progress of the Arab world, and generally of the Middle East, and that Great Britain and the United States, which is taking an increasing interest in these regions, will be able to play a valuable part in proving that well-known maxim of the old Free Trader, " All legitimate interests are in harmony."

My discussions with the Emperor of Ethiopia raised no serious difficulties, because an agreement for the next two years had already been reached as the result of the Mission to Ethiopia which Lord De La Warr had just completed with much patience and address. It was a satisfaction for me to see for the first-time in the flesh Haile Selassie, that historical figure who pleaded the cause of his country amid the storms of the League of Nations, who was the first victim of Mussolini's lust for power and conquest, and who was also the first to be restored to his ancient throne by the heavy exertions of our British and Indian armies in the far-off days of 1940 and 1941.

Finally, we had the pleasure of a long discussion with President Shukri, of Syria, in which we did our utmost to enjoin a friendly attitude towards the French and to encourage negotiations for a suitable settlement with the French, affecting not only Syria but also the Lebanon. I must make clear, once and for all, the position of His Majesty's Government in respect of Syria and the Lebanon, and in relation to our French Allies. That position is governed by the statements made in 1941, in which the independence of these Levant states was definitely declared by Great Britain and France. At that time, and ever since, His Majesty's Government have made it clear that they would never seek to supplant French influence by British influence in the Levant States. We are determined also to respect the independence of these States and to use our best endeavours to preserve a special position for France, in view of the many cultural and historic connections which France has so long established with Syria. We hope that it may be possible for the French to preserve that special position. We trust that these States will be firmly established by the authority of the world organization, and that French privilege will also be recognized.

However, I must make it clear that it is not for us alone to defend by force either Syrian or Lebanese independence or French privilege. We seek both, and we do not believe that they are incompatible. Too much must not be placed, therefore, upon the shoulders of Great Britain alone. We have to take note of the fact that Russia and the United States have recognized and favour Syrian and Lebanese independence, but do not favour any special position for any other foreign country. All these and many other matters affecting the Middle East are fitting and necessary subjects for the Peace Conference, at which we must resolutely strive for final settlements of lasting peace between all the States and races comprised in the Middle East, and in the Eastern basin of the Mediterranean.

On the way back from the Crimea to say good-bye to the President at Alexandria, the Foreign Secretary and I stopped in Athens. I must say that from my point of view this was the high spot of the whole journey. I could not help recalling the grim conditions of our visit only seven weeks before, when the cannon were firing close at hand, and bullets continually struck the walls and people were killed and wounded in the streets not far away. The contrast between those violent scenes and the really rapturous welcome we received from vast crowds of delighted citizens was one of the most vivid, impressive and agreeable experiences of my life. Peace reigned over the beautiful, immortal city. Its citizens were wild with joy. His Beatitude the Archbishop was seated in the Regency, firmly grasping the reins of power. Together we drove through the crowded streets, lined by the first instalment of the new national Greek Army, until I found myself called upon to address what was, incomparably, the largest and most enthusiastic gathering that in a very long experience of such demonstrations I have ever seen. There is no subject in my recollection on which the policy of His Majesty's Government has received more complete vindication than in regard to Greece, nor has there been any on which greater prejudice and misrepresentation has been poured out against them in the United States—not without some assistance from these shores. All this was done with a gay, and, as I said, a wanton disregard of the ill-effects produced on the spot, and the encouragement given to the resistance of the terrorists in Greece. I am sure we rescued Athens from a horrible fate. I believe that the Greek people will long acclaim our action, both military and political. Peace without vengeance has been achieved. A great mass of arms has been surrendered. Most of the prisoners and hostages have been restored. The great work of bringing in food supplies has resumed its former activity. Public order and security are so established that

63

U.N.R.R.A. is about to resume its functions. The popularity of British troops and of those who have guided the course of policy, such as Mr. Leeper and General Scobie, is unbounded in these regions, and their conduct continues to receive the approbation of His Majesty's Coalition Government.

I should by no means lead the House to suppose that our difficulties are over. The Greek National Army has still to be formed, and to be effective in maintaining impartial order. The Greek Budget has to be balanced in some way. The drachma has to be restrained within reasonable limits. The raw materials have to be provided to enable industries of various kinds to get to work in Athens, where there are considerably more than a million people. The sense of unity and responsibility has to grow stronger with the Greek people. And here I must remark that the future of Greece is in the Greeks' own hands. The Greeks must not expect that the whole process of their restoration can be accomplished by British labours or American assistance. The Foreign Secretary remained a day longer in Athens than I did, and he was at pains to bring home to the Greek authorities the fact that, now that political stability has been achieved, financial and economic problems must take first place, that the burden and responsibility are upon the Greek nation, and that they must on no account sit back and leave these tasks to foreigners.

I trust that these remarks will in no way detract from the great kindness and enthusiasm with which I was received a little while ago, but if my words should cause pain I am not entirely sorry for it. The intense political activity of the Greek mind must continue to give way to practical problems. As soon as possible, they must reach that election, fair, free, unfettered, with secret ballot and on a basis of universal suffrage, to which everyone is looking forward, and which can alone regulate and adjust everything that has been done. I look forward to it with the greatest confidence. I particularly welcome the wish of the Greek Government that Russian, British and American observers shall be free, on the spot, to make sure that the will of the people finds complete and sincere expression. So much for that episode, upon which we have had several exciting and even momentarily heated Debates in recent times.

I thank the House very much for their courtesy and attention. I would refer, for a moment or two before sitting down, to the Conference as a whole, and in relation to the grave matters which I mentioned before the interval with which the House indulged me. It was the custom of the Conference at Yalta to hold its meetings of the three Heads of Governments and Foreign Secretaries late in the afternoon, and to sit for several hours each day. Here the main issues were deployed, and the measures both of agreement and of difference were clearly revealed. I remember particularly one moment when a prolonged silence fell upon our small body, maintained for two or three minutes. It was immediately found very convenient to remit the measures of agreement or of difference, wherever our discussion had carried us, to the morning meetings of the Foreign Secretaries. Each Foreign Secretary presided over these meetings in rotation. So excellent was the combined work of the Foreign Secretaries that our problems were returned to us nearly every day, in time for the full meeting, in a form on which final agreement could be reached, and lasting decisions taken.

There was a proposal on the agenda for the institution during the present anxious period of regular meetings of the Foreign Secretaries, an improvement on the system of collective work which has often been asked for here, in order to prevent avoidable divergence of views, and to concert the actions of the three Great Powers. This was to meet a felt want, and to serve to bridge the unavoidable gap in the meetings of the three Heads of Government. There was, however, no need to argue this matter at Yalta, because the work of the three Foreign Secretaries proved itself so invaluable, efficient and indispensable that its continuing collective activity was acclaimed by all. It is, of course, only a temporary arrangement, appropriate to these times of special stress, when so heavy a military burden is resting on the three Great Powers. We may expect it eventually to merge in the larger and permanent organization which will be set up at San Francisco, once that organization is in full working order, and the Peace Conference has finished its labours. In the intervening period these meetings of the three Foreign Secretaries, to whom, from time to time, the Foreign Secretaries of other countries may be added, will prove of undoubted advantage.

Here is the moment when the House should pay its tribute to the work of my right hon. Friend the Foreign Secretary. I cannot describe to the House the aid and comfort he has been to me in all our difficulties. His hard life when quite young in the infantry in the last war, his constant self-preparation for the tasks which have fallen to him, his unequalled experience as a Minister at the Foreign Office, his knowledge of foreign affairs and their past history, his experience of conferences of all kinds, his breadth of view, his powers of exposition, his moral courage, have gained for him a position second to none among the Foreign Secretaries of the Grand Alliance. It is not only my own personal debt, but even more that of the House to him, which I now acknowledge.

I suppose that during these last three winter months the human race all the world over has undergone more physical agony and misery than at any other period through which this planet has passed. In the Stone Age the numbers were fewer, and the primitive creatures, little removed from their animal origin, knew no better. We suffer more, and we feel more. I must admit that in all this war I never felt so grave a sense of responsibility as I did at Yalta. In 1940 and 1941, when we in this Island were all alone, and invasion was so near, the actual steps one ought to take and our attitude towards them seemed plain and simple. If a man is coming across the sea to kill you, you do everything in your power to make sure he dies before finishing his journey. That may be difficult, it may be painful, but at least it is simple. Now we are entering a world of imponderables, and at every stage occasions for self-questioning arise. It is a mistake to look too far ahead. Only one link in the chain of destiny can be handled at a time.

I trust the House will feel that hope has been powerfully strengthened by our meeting in the Crimea. The ties that bind the three great Powers together, and their mutual comprehension of each other, have grown. The United States has entered deeply and constructively into the life and salvation of Europe. We have all three set our hands to far-reaching engagements at once practical and solemn. United, we have the unchallengeable power to lead the world to prosperity, freedom and happiness. The Great Powers must seek to serve and not to rule. Joined with other States, both large and small, we may found a world organization which, armed with ample power, will guard the rights of all States, great or small, from aggression, or from the gathering of the means of aggression. I am sure that a fairer choice is open to mankind than they have known in recorded ages. The lights burn brighter and shine more broadly than before. Let us walk forward together.

SELECT COMMITTEES

A Speech to the House of Commons
March 7, 1945

In a Debate on the Adjournment, questions were raised concerning the administration of the Air Ministry and the British Overseas Airways Corporation, and Lord Winterton called for a Select Committee to investigate the allegations. The Prime Minister then explained the procedure in regard to the appointment of Select Committees.

[March 7, 1945.

THIS brief discussion on the Adjournment is certainly not a time to go into merits, and although both the speakers who have addressed the House have recited certain charges that have been made, there has been no attempt to go into merits. I certainly do not propose to do so. The Noble Lord [Lord Winterton] has not attempted to go into merits. In fact I gather that his position is that he takes no responsibility for the charges. They may be true, they may be false they may be exaggerated ; but however it may be, he raises only the issue of principle, of Parliamentary usage and custom. As that is an important issue, I feel it my duty to deal with it myself, because although I am not the Father of the House I have been here a good deal longer than the Father [Lord Winterton].

I am a little astonished that there does not seem to be more general realization of what the Parliamentary usage is about Select Committees in respect of personal charges made against Ministers. Nothing could be more clear than the Parliamentary usage. I will reduce it to the simplest terms.

The Government advise the House, and the House decides. The Government advise the House whether there should or should not be a Select Committee, and the House decides. The idea that there is any automatic procedure or bounden duty to take a particular course is utterly devoid of foundation. The three last cases of charges against Ministers which were made the subject of debate as to whether there should be a Select Committee or not were the Marconi case in 1912, where the Government proposed a Committee and the House accepted it, without a Division, after prolonged agitation and consideration on both sides ; the Maurice case in 1918, where the Opposition proposed a Motion for a Select Committee and the House rejected it on the advice of the Government ; and the Campbell case in 1924, where the Opposition proposed, and the House accepted, the Motion for a Select Committee. The Government then resigned.

In all these cases it is clear that the Government took their view and had the right to take their view, and the Opposition took, and had the right to take, their view, and the House decided what was to happen.

All these were in the days of party Government, when responsible bodies of men, working together in all the long-established groupings of a party, considered most maturely the merits and the proportions of the charges and took a collective decision. The Government of the day either accepted this decision or rejected it. Now the party system is in abeyance, and the Noble Lord asks us to lay down a new rule to the effect that when any charge is made by any Member against any Minister's honour and integrity, the Government of the day are bound automatically to use their powers to appoint a Select Committee.

No contention could be more absurd. It would be most injurious to the House, and absolutely contrary to its traditions, if such a rule were made. So far as His Majesty's Government are concerned, we refuse to countenance it. We have not only to think of this Debate, of this particular case or occasion; we have to think of the future. If this principle were adopted, it would be open in future for any single Member, however irresponsible, however mischievous, however malignant, to bring any charge, however ill-founded, however worthless, however trivial, against any Minister; and thereupon, automatically, the whole ponderous machinery of a Select Committee would be set in motion.

I can imagine even that in days of party strife and faction, when feelings run high and a score against the Government is a good thing to bring off, there might be a regular racket among half a dozen Members to bring charges against half a dozen Ministers, or to fling insults against them; and then, automatically, there would be half a dozen Select Committees sitting upstairs, investigating the charges and insults which had been made. Such a procedure would bring the whole principle of Select Committees into contempt, and might tend to rob Parliament of an invaluable weapon in its armoury. The fact is, that the Government remains master of its own conduct, and the House itself, the master of the Government, must decide for itself what action to take.

In this case, I have myself personally looked into the charges made both in what is called the " Farm Case " or the " Regent's Park Case ", and also about the general management of the British Overseas Airways Corporation, and with the full agreement of the Cabinet I have told the House that in our opinion there are no grounds for appointing a Select Committee. That is our position, and that is our advice to the House.

I shall be asked " Will you give the House an opportunity to debate on a Motion the position which the Government have taken up ? Will you give them the opportunity ? " If it were the general desire of the House to discuss any matter under the sun, I should take pains to meet their wishes, but proof must be furnished—adequate proof must be furnished—of this general desire.

In the days of party strife the Leader of the Opposition, in consultation with his colleages, would usually express it, but, now, there is no Leader of the Opposition. The Government is a Government of all three parties at the present time, and consequently we have to ascertain whether a substantial body of Members desire, and think it sufficiently important, that this matter of the Select Committee should be debated and that time should be given for the Motion.

I say that if any substantial body of Members wish for time to be given, or if there is a general desire made known through the usual channels, or if the larger parties in the House take it up as a matter on which they wish that an opportunity should be given, certainly we shall agree to find the time. I hope that the House will feel that this is a right and sensible way of dealing with the matter. The Government have the responsibility of advising the House, and if there is a substantial desire to challenge the Government's view, then a Debate can take place and the matter will be carried to its proper conclusion in a Division.

In this case I am quite certain, and take upon myself the full responsibility of advising the House, that there is no sufficient case, no case worthy of investigation at all, and that it would be injurious to the House if the machinery of the Select Committee were invoked. I take it upon myself to say that, so far as we are concerned, we shall oppose that course; but if the House in great body feels alarmed and feels that grave derelictions of duty have taken place on the part of the Secretary of State for Air, and that I, as Prime Minister, and my colleagues, are all condoning and conniving at some guilty act—

Hon Members : No, no.

But that is the proposition. How can the hon. Members say, " No no ? " If we are challenged, if we advise against a Select Committee and we are challenged, the reason is because our solemn statement, given in all honesty and good faith, is challenged and doubted by the House. I am not blaming the Noble Lord ; I should not hesitate to express my view contrary to the Government if I were free to do so; but to pretend that there have been deployed any sufficient grounds or any sufficient evidence, or that there is at the present time any great body of Parliamentary opinion in favour of a Select Committee, is in my view quite incorrect.

I have only two more minutes to speak, and I will devote them to my Noble Friend the Father of the House. There are two aspects of his conduct in this matter which surprise me. The first I have already touched upon—the foolishness of the rule which he seeks to establish, of the automatic reference of any charge to a Select Committee. Such a lack of Parliamentary comprehension is lamentable in one who possesses unique claims to be our guide and mentor. The second is the levity which has allowed my Noble Friend to lend his weight to a demand for a Select Committee on the outpourings of the hon. Member for Mossley [Mr. A. Hopkinson] without ever having taken the slightest trouble to find out for himself whether any substance lies behind them. On both those grounds, his action is to be deplored.

He is a comparatively young Father of the House; he has many years of life before him. We still hope they may be years of useful life in this House, but unless in the future his sagacity and knowledge of the House are found to be markedly superior to what he has exhibited to-day, I must warn him that he will run a very grave risk of falling into senility before he is over-taken by old age.

CIVIL DEFENCE GRATUITIES

A Statement to the House of Commons
March 8, 1945

February 28. *U.S. First Army troops crossed the River Erft, on the way to Cologne, and U.S. 9th Army reached to within 6 miles of Cologne.*

Marshal Rokossovsky captured Neu Stettin in his drive towards the Baltic.

March 1. *München-Gladbach captured by U.S. 9th Army, and tanks of the Third Army reached the outskirts of Trier.*

March 2. *U.S. 9th Army reached the Rhine at Neuss and advances were made at many points on the Western Front.*

March 3. *U.S. 9th Army and British troops of the Canadian First Army joined forces in the East between the Maas and the Rhine.*

March 4. *Germans were in full retreat across the Rhine. Armour of the U.S. First Army reached a line between Düsseldorf and Cologne.*

Two Russian forces under Zhukov and Rokossovsky reached the Baltic at two places.

March 5. *U.S. tanks and infantry entered the suburbs of Cologne.*

March 6. *Cologne was captured by U.S. troops.*

Mr. Churchill returned to London after a visit to the Western Front.

British troops crossed the Irrawaddy 30 miles West of Mandalay.

March 7. *General Hodges's U.S. First Army troops crossed the Rhine at Remagen. General Patton's Third Army reached the Rhine North West of Coblenz.*

March 8. *U.S. First Army established a solid bridgehead on the East bank of the Rhine at Remagen. Big enemy munition dumps were captured in a speedy Allied advance to the Rhine.*

Russian troops reached the outskirts of Stettin.

All the Burma Road from Lashio to Kunming in Allied hands.

[*March* 8, 1945.

SINCE the announcement that the Chancellor of the Exchequer made on 6th February, on the subject of gratuities and other release benefits for members of the Forces, the Government have been examining the claims of other classes to similar benefits. The House will realize that in the case of the Armed Forces a gratuity was given after the last war, and that there was a natural expectation that a similar gratuity would be given after the present war. The Government accordingly felt that their scheme for the resettlement of members of the Forces would not be complete without the provision for the payment of a gratuity.

The Government have had to consider all the analogous classes of the community to whom a gratuity should also be given. They have come to the conclusion that this benefit should be extended, though on a reduced scale, to certain members of the Civil Defence Services where remuneration throughout the war has been related to Army rates of pay, and where, therefore, the basis adopted for the settlement of remuneration, and the facilities available for negotiation, are not comparable with those normally existing in industry.

The Government have accordingly decided that a war gratuity shall be paid to whole-time members who have served under Civil Defence conditions for not less than six months from 3rd September, 1939, in the Civil Defence Services, the local authority Fire Guards, the Auxiliary Police, the Auxiliary Fire Service, and the National Fire Service, excluding, of course, those who were whole-time members of the former local authority or police fire brigades. A gratuity will also be paid to other ranks of the Royal Observer Corps and to the Auxiliary Coastguards. Special considerations apply to officers of the Royal Observer Corps, and this question must be separately examined. The gratuity will be payable on the same general principle as, but at three-fourths the rate of, that payable to the Armed Forces. The basic rate for men will thus be 7s. 6d. for each completed month of whole-time service from 3rd September, 1939, and for women 5s. a month. The gratuity, together with any post-war credits due in respect of Civil Defence service, will be credited to Post Office Savings Bank accounts after a date which will be determined later on the principles applied to the Armed Forces. The Minister of Home Security will notify local authorities shortly of the detailed arrangements. No application need be made at present by those who have left the Civil Defence service, and who may nevertheless be entitled to a gratuity.

The Government have also given careful consideration to claims which have been put forward on behalf of other classes of people. They have felt obliged to consider how far the principles governing their decision to give financial benefits already announced apply to these cases and, after giving the most sympathetic thought to the matter, they have come to the conclusion that they cannot justify the extension of such benefits in any form to classes who are employed under the recognized conditions for the industry or profession to which they belong, and who receive an industrial or professional rate of pay.

The Government are aware that this decision, which they have reached only after the fullest consideration, will cause disappointment in some quarters, and in particular, perhaps, in the case of the Women's Land Army, whose claims have, I know, made a special appeal to a number of hon. Members. I hope, however, that those who are disappointed will recognize the impossibility of making concessions that would open the door to an unending succession of new claims which could not be differentiated on any logical basis.

> Lady Astor said that members of the Women's Land Army were underpaid, overworked, and very often badly housed, and asked the Prime Minister to consider their position. Mr. Churchill replied :

That is one of those sweeping generalizations which we have come to regard as characteristic of the Noble Lady. I hesitate to draw any deductions therefrom, but anyhow, there is no question whatever of our not discussing the merits of the different proposals which have been made. I am clearly of the opinion that the House should find the time to debate this matter, but it is for the Leader of the House to say what is the most convenient way of fitting it in with the already crowded course of Government business.

THE CONSERVATIVE POLICY

A SPEECH TO THE CONSERVATIVE PARTY CONFERENCE AT
CENTRAL HALL, WESTMINSTER
MARCH 15, 1945

[*March* 15, 1945.

THIS is the first time since I became the leader of the party four and a half years ago that I have had the honour of addressing the delegates of the National Union in a full party conference.

That does not mean to say that either you or I have been idle or neglectful of our duties in the interval. We have all worked our hardest in the national cause, and we have been too busy for party politics in any form. We have all abstained from doing or saying anything which would be likely to impair the unity of the British people, or the smooth working of the Coalition Government of all parties which has delivered us from mortal peril, and won for itself a memorable place in our long island story.

We have held in abeyance all party activities, and have allowed our organizations, both local and national, to be devoted entirely to aiding the prosecution of the war. In doing this we have endured patiently and almost silently many provocations from that happily limited class of Left Wing politicians to whom party strife is the breath of their nostrils, and their only means of obtaining influence or notoriety. Many are the insults and slanders which we have allowed to pass, I will not say unnoticed, but unanswered, for the sake of concentration upon the war effort. Even the almost ceaseless series of attacks which have been made upon us in the official Socialist and Liberal newspapers, with their bitter writers, have extorted from us neither protest nor reply.

I am sure I shall carry you all with me in saying that we shall maintain this patriotic restraint as long as the National Coalition, in which Ministers drawn from all parties have distinguished themselves, continues to work together in loyal comradeship.

I must also thank the Conservative Party for the resolute and undivided support which it and its representatives gave to the policy of His Majesty's Government in saving the city of Athens from a hideous massacre, and in preventing an armed Communist minority from shooting their way into place and power. Among all our problems there has not been any which led to so much misunderstanding and misrepresentation at home and abroad as did this Greek trouble ; but the policy of our Coalition Government was sustained by the whole strength of the Conservative Party. They provided five-sixths, or it may be more, of the majorities, and surely never has any episode in these violent days been crowned with more signal vindication.

The nearly continuous and ever more rapid progress of the war against Germany and the Nazi tyranny leads us all to the hope that the giant foe against whom for more than a year we stood alone, unflinching, undismayed, will be forced into unconditional surrender or beaten to the ground in chaos and ruin. It will always be the glory of our island race that in the teeth of what seemed to outsiders overwhelming odds they never swerved from the path of duty, they never lost faith in their mission to fight against tyranny to the death.

Thus we held aloft the flaming torch of freedom when all around the night was black as jet. Thus once again we gained the time for the continental tyrant, for Hitler, that master of wickedness, to make a deadly error. Thus we gained the space for the United States to begin the marshalling of its as yet unmeasured forces of power, of science, and of valour.

But there is another glory in which we may rejoice. In those terrible days the whole of our Empire and Commonwealth of Nations —apart from one melancholy exception, round the corner—stood together with us of their own free will, from the greatest Dominion to the smallest Colony in spontaneous resolve to die or conquer with us in a righteous cause.

This astounding union of communities and races spread round the globe, springing not from legal or physical obligations but from the mysterious, unfathomable uplifting of the soul of man, raises our world-wide association to heights never attained nor even dreamed of by any empire of the past.

Certainly with this unparalleled record we have no need to seek advice even of our most honoured allies as to how we should conduct ourselves with regard to our own affairs. The maxim of Lord Beaconsfield, *Imperium et Libertas*, is still our guide. This truth has already been proved abundantly since those words were spoken. Without freedom there is no foundation for our Empire ; without Empire there is no safeguard for our freedom.

By this we mean freedom for all States and nations within the circle of the Crown, and by this we also mean freedom for individuals within the broad and ever-advancing conception of the British Constitution and the British way of life. We have no use here for totalitarian schemes of government in their various forms. The right of free speech and political opposition has been preserved in hours of national peril to an extent incredible outside the English-speaking world.

" Trust the people," said Lord Randolph Churchill in the last strong revival of Tory democracy. Has not that trust been well repaid ? Has it not stood us in good stead in the hour of need ?

It has often been remarked by bewildered foreign observers that every extension of the franchise in Great Britain has left the Conservative Party in a stronger position. But the reason, or one of the main reasons, which they do not see for this undoubted fact is the steady and ceaseless improvement in the education of the people and in the conditions of their life, and in their growing conscious power to govern their country effectively. Here is the high road along which we march with assured and growing confidence. Here is the course we steer in the full tide of successful experiment.

When I became Prime Minister nearly five years ago I promised nothing but blood, toil, tears, and sweat, and on that I received from the House of Commons a vote of confidence of 397 to 0. From the nation I received such aid and trust as no politician in our history has ever enjoyed before. The other day, after this long period of terrible events, with all their ups and downs, with all their chances and perplexities, that figure of Parliamentary confidence rose to 413 to 0. But the Parliament is nearly ten years old. It has lived almost double its constitutional span, and the Executive Government must refresh itself by direct contact with the electorate.

Should the war in Europe end before the summer ends, or even sooner, as it might well do, we shall have reached a considerable milestone on our journey, and war conditions will no longer prevent, as they have hitherto prevented, the holding of a General Election. And here I regret to say that the public declarations of our Labour and of some of our Liberal colleagues and of the party organizations which they represent leave us in no doubt that they will feel themselves bound to resume their full liberty of action and thus bring this famous Coalition to an end.

We must prepare ourselves for the loss of many loyal and capable fellow-workers in the Administration, and the full clash of party principles and party interests inseparable from an appeal to the judgment of the people.

It will fall to us as the largest party in the existing House of Commons to arrange for a General Election which will be conducted with British fair play and, I trust, with a minimum of party and personal rancour, and above all with the least possible injury to the underlying unity of the nation in serving the national cause.

Nevertheless, we cannot blind ourselves to the fact that the strength of His Majesty's Government which has borne us thus far through the struggle will be seriously weakened. Should we be successful in the election, a very heavy burden will fall upon our shoulders. The gap has to be filled, the job has to be finished; and I am here to tell you that we must brace ourselves and summon all our energies in order that if, as I believe, the nation places its faith in us, we shall not be found unequal to the gigantic toils that lie ahead.

For this purpose we must lay aside every impediment, we must cleanse our hearts of all unworthy feelings, and seek only the faithful discharge of our responsibilities in caring for the long-term welfare of the State. Should it fall to me, as it may do, to form a Government before the Election, I shall seek the aid not only of Conservatives but of men of good will of any party or no party who are willing to serve and thus invest our Administration with a national character.

And if the verdict of the nation should still leave us responsible, that Government after the election will be further re-formed with the sole desire of rallying the strongest forces available to carry our cause to final victory and peace. We must not underrate the enormous tasks that will lie before us if our countrymen accord us their confidence.

Nor must we fear these tasks, nor shrink from them, nor doubt our capacity to surmount all difficulties or make our way through them as we have made our way thus far. There is one thing we shall certainly not do. We shall not bid for votes or popularity by promising what we cannot perform. Nor shall we compete with others in electioneering baits and lures.

It would be very easy for us all to promise or even to give each other presents, bonuses, and gratuities in the most enthusiastic manner; but if we woke up one morning and found that the pound sterling bought only four or five shillings' worth of goods or services, we should have committed a great crime. We should have committed the crime of cheating the soldiers and the workers in this country of the nest-egg, very often amounting to £200 or £300, which millions of people have acquired by their faithful discharge of duty and by their thrift and self-denial during the war.

Great as are the evils of high taxation in clogging the wheels of enterprise and commerce—and that is a fact that must ever be before us—they are not comparable to those which would follow a financial collapse and the destruction of all the standards of value between man and man.

Our Socialist friends have officially committed themselves—much to the disgust of some of their leaders—to a programme for nationalizing all the means of production, distribution, and exchange. Now these are all matters which the British public can consider at their leisure. They can consider them when times are quiet and when our soldiers are home again and settled down in civilian life and employment. Then will be the time to go into all these sweeping proposals, which imply not only the destruction of the whole of our existing system of society, and of life, and of labour, but the creation and enforcement of another system or other systems borrowed from foreign lands and alien minds. But this is not the time.

Now our tasks are severely and precisely defined.

We have to finish the war against Japan and play our part not only as loyal allies of the United States and other nations in that conflict, but also to regain, as we are regaining, the territories which the Japanese have wrested from us.

We have to repay the injuries they have inflicted and the infernal cruelties they have perpetrated upon his Majesty's subjects, British, Australasian, Indian, Burmese, and Malayan alike.

That will require an intense effort, and no mood of war-weariness must prevent us from doing our duty to the last inch and to the last minute. However, the scale of the war against Japan is limited— not by man-power, for that will readily be forthcoming ; it is limited by shipping and other means of transport over the vast ocean spaces and through the steaming jungle.

Although it will be our ceaseless endeavour to hurl our utmost strength into the Japanese war ; although we shall have to provide for the garrisoning of the zone in Germany which has been assigned to us in the discussions with our principal allies ; nevertheless we should have to provide for the return to this country of very large numbers of our soldiers now serving abroad, many of whom have been separated from their families for years. What are the questions that these men are asking now, and what are the questions that are being asked by those they love and those who love them in the cottage homes of Britain ?

Will the warrior return, will the family be reunited, will the shattered houses be restored, will there be a steady job for several years ahead for all who have served their country on the war fronts and for those who were for good reasons deprived of that privilege and ordered by the State to serve it with equal fidelity in the fields and factories at home ?

These are the questions that arise in every breast. How should we answer them ? We have got to answer them in a manner worthy of us, and worthy of our vital strength as a race and as a State.

You hear all this talk by the stay-at-home Left Wing *intelligentsia* that the soldiers will hold us guilty if we do not have a new world waiting for them on their return. The brave new world is to be all ready for them when they disembark at Liverpool, in the Clyde, at Southampton, or at Tilbury Docks.

But that is not what the fighting men are looking forward to. They are not looking forward to a new world constructed behind their backs by politicians who seek their votes. Most of them have lived long enough in uncomfortable proximity to another world to be thinking of that.

Their heart's desire is that after their duty has been done and the job is finished they shall come back home. They do not regard themselves as a slum-bred serf population chased into battle from a land of misery and want. They love their country and the scenes of their youth and manhood, and they have shown themselves ready to die not only in defence of its material satisfactions but for its honour.

They wish to see old England or Scotland or Wales or Northern Ireland playing their part in the forefront of all the nations in battle against tyranny. When they are home and settled down, when our country is again a going concern, paying its way and standing on its own feet in the post-war world, then will be the time for them to settle what form and shape our society should assume. But now our tasks will be precise, sharply and plainly outlined.

Above all they are practical jobs. We have to finish the war. We have to bring the men home. We have to get our dear country on the move again and into its full swing of natural health and life. There will be plenty of time for politics when these grim, fundamental tasks have been discharged. When that time comes we shall not show ourselves incapable of expressing our point of view in the free discussions of our democracy. But there are other tasks which must be added to the stern list. We do not wish to live on the charity or generosity of any nation. We have given our all in the common cause, and many claim assistance to recover our normal economy from those we have helped to victory. But we must never agree to found our economic life on the indulgence or favour even of the allies we most dearly cherish.

Blood, sweat, toil, and tears! There may be less blood and fewer tears; we thank God for that hope. But mental toil and physical sweat, the conscious, united resolve of every man and woman to give all that is in them, will be required from us long after the last bomb or cannon has ceased to thunder.

Let there be no mistake about it; it is no easy, cheap-jack Utopia of airy phrases that lies before us. This is no time for windy platitudes and glittering advertisements. The Conservative Party had far better go down telling the truth and acting in accordance with the verities of our position than gain a span of shabbily-bought office by easy and fickle froth and chatter.

All my experience of the British people, which is a long one, convinces me that never at any moment more than this have they wished and meant to face realities, and woe betide those public men who seek to

slide into power down the slippery slope of vain and profligate under-
takings.

This is no time for humbug and blandishments, but for grim, stark
facts and figures, and for action to meet immediate needs. There is,
however, another note which I must strike on the gong. I have in
mind the resolutions which you proposed at yesterday's session.

If we are to recover from the measureless exertions of the war, it
can only be by a large release from the necessary bonds and controls
which war conditions have imposed upon us. No restriction upon
well-established British liberties that is not proved indispensable to
the prosecution of the war and the transition from war to peace can
be tolerated.

Control for control's sake is senseless. Controls under the pretext
of war or its aftermath which are in fact designed to favour the
accomplishment of quasi-totalitarian systems, however innocently
designed, whatever guise they assume, whatever liveries they wear,
whatever slogans they mouth, are a fraud which should be mercilessly
exposed to the British public.

At the head of our mainmast we, like the United States, fly the
flag of free enterprise. We are determined that the native genius
and spirit of adventure, of risk-taking in peace as in war, shall bear
our fortunes forward, finding profitable work and profitable trade for
our people, and also we are determined that good and thrifty house-
keeping, both national and private, shall sustain our economy.

This does not mean that we are likely to run short of necessary
controls. While food is scarce it must be fairly shared. While
thousands of enemy prisoners are in our midst we must still have
identity cards. While extraordinary conditions prevail, special powers,
safeguards, and regulations will be required. But many of these are
evils which will pass away as we recover our natural life and as these
years of sombre crises brighten and broaden into daylight again.

Still, there are other tasks beyond those I have mentioned. Two
years ago I declared that we must have a Four-years Plan for the new
Parliament after the war, and in spite of our struggles abroad immense
toil and preparation have been given to the design of this plan.

We are making steady and encouraging progress with the programme
I then outlined. We have passed into law the greatest Education
Act ever known in these Islands, and we are bringing that Act into
operation in a fortnight's time. We are now discussing in Parliament
the most long-cherished Family Allowances Bill. We have shaped
and prepared a vast scheme of national insurance from the cradle to
the grave. We propose to introduce a new plan for altering the basis
upon which compensation for industrial injury is at present assessed.
We have adopted plans for revolutionizing our health system. I will

not elaborate the list. But many of these are but bits of paper—
white paper—so far. Some have yet to be brought into operation.
The bulk have yet to be passed into law.

The great mass of this immense constructive effort will be among
the principal tasks of the new Parliament. But there is ever with us
the clamant problem of providing sufficient homes after five years of
no building being possible for us, after five years of destruction by
the enemy.

I can assure you we are grappling with the housing shortage to the
utmost that is possible before the builders, who are also the home-
seekers, return from the Rhine, from the Apennines, from Mandalay.
Everything in human power is being and shall be done. Of course,
we must first concentrate, as we are doing, all available building
labour on those parts of our cities which have suffered most, but we
shall not be content even during the progress of hostilities merely to
repair devastation in places which the enemy has found it most easy
to attack.

The same drive and punch and, may I say, genius in organization
which enabled us to triumph over the U-boats, over the flying bombs,
and to land a mighty army on the Continent last June must and will
be applied, as we regather our strength from the war, to the construction and reconstruction of houses both in towns and in the
country.

The Four-years Plan will require our utmost effort, and whatever
Government is in power will not only have to turn White Papers into
Acts of Parliament but to make those Acts of Parliament a living,
active, and harmonious part of our social system. On all this we must
march ahead even while the Japanese war continues, and even while
the process of bringing back the armies and rehabilitating our trade
is incomplete. Never was there a time when so much was planned and
projected and so much remained to be turned from paper into action.

There is one great change also that the war has brought into our
national life which we must never again cast away. Alone among the
great nations of the world we cannot live without an immense im-
portation of foreign food. The war has taught us that we have long
neglected the treasure-house of the British soil. Twice in a generation
we have called upon the farming community, in spite of that neglect,
to keep the wolf from our doors. They have not failed us. The
record of the agricultural industry in increasing food production and
helping to save vital shipping marks a grand contribution to our
survival.

If we look to the future nothing is more clear than that when the
war is over the world will face an acute shortage of food for several
years. We who, even under war-time pressure, grow only two-thirds

of our necessary food—and that is a marvellous expansion—must feel disquieted at living for years in the midst of a hungry world.

It would be madness indeed to cast away the increased food production which has been achieved in the war. Indeed, having regard to the many improvements which have been introduced into British agriculture under the scourge of necessity, we have every reason to hope, as we are bound to plan, for a substantial further increase in home food-production beyond any we have yet accomplished.

There is another reason for making ourselves more independent in food supplies. We have freely sacrificed our foreign investments which brought a large income into this country and helped to redress our trade balance. We paid them away without a moment's hesitation during the time that we were keeping the flag of freedom flying all alone. After the war the revival and expansion of our export trade will be a prime and indispensable factor in our prosperity. Every ton of food produced here not only helps to fill to some extent the gap caused by the loss of our foreign investments, but by this fact definitely sets free more of our export trade to buy not only food but those raw materials without which neither trade nor production is possible.

Agriculture therefore assumes a place in the forefront of post-war policy. A healthy and well-balanced agriculture is one of the main-springs of our national life. I note with interest and sympathy the Resolution which this conference carried yesterday on this subject, supporting, as the Resolution did, a long-term policy which by means of price stability will secure to the efficient producer a fair return for his capital, and for the worker a standard of living comparable with that in other industries.

A prosperous agriculture brings benefits alike to town and country ; it brings health, both physical and moral, to the nation as a whole, and we must cherish it as the first of British industries and nourish all our other industries thereby.

Victory lies before us, certain and perhaps near. But years of cruel torment and destruction have wasted the earth, and victory with all its brilliant trappings appears to our strained and experienced eyes as a deliverance rather than as a triumph.

Our hearts go out in thankfulness that we have been saved from annihilation and from enduring the ruin of our country, and that, after all our long, famous history, we shall come through once again with life and honour, surmounting a convulsion that has ravaged the globe.

We shall best show our gratitude for these mercies by the zeal and faithfulness with which we devote ourselves to our duty, and prove ourselves worthy in strength and in spirit of the place we hold in the hearts of men, and in the vanguard of the modern world.

SAN FRANCISCO DELEGATION

A Statement to the House of Commons on the Composition of the United Kingdom delegation to the Conference at San Francisco

March 22, 1945

March 9. *Allied armour and infantry in great strength flowed across the Rhine at Remagen bridgehead.*

Hitler paid one of his rare visits to the front in the Oder section.

March 10. *U.S. First Army continued to expand their bridgeheads against stiffening enemy resistance.*

March 11. *4,500 tons of bombs dropped on Essen.*

March 12. *U.S. First Army launched new attack from their Remagen bridgehead.*

Marshal Zhukov's troops captured Kustrin on the East bank of the Oder opposite Berlin.

March 13. *U.S. bridgehead across the Rhine at Remagen expanded to 11 miles in length and 6 miles in depth. Pontoon bridges were thrown across the Rhine in some areas.*

March 14. *R.A.F. dropped 10-ton bombs for the first time, their target being the Bielefeld railway viaduct.*

March 15. *U.S. Third Army made new attacks across the Moselle, S.W. of Coblenz, and outflanked Siegfried Line.*

March 16. *U.S. troops from the Remagen bridgehead cut the Cologne-Frankfort motor road in several places.*

March 17. *Remagen bridgehead increased to 14 miles in length and 7½ miles in depth. The bridge by which the original crossing was made collapsed owing to the weight of traffic passing across.*

March 18. *Coblenz, Bad Kreuznach and Merzig were among the places captured by Allied troops on the Western Front.*

Russians captured port of Kolberg on the Baltic.

Berlin had its heaviest daylight raid of the war.

March 19. *U.S. Third Army advance beyond Moselle forced a massed German withdrawal.*

British patrols reached Randwijk, on the Lower Rhine seven miles North West of Nijmegen.

March 20. *German resistance crumbled West of the Rhine before swift Allied advances. Third and Seventh U.S. Armies joined forces and Remagen bridgehead was expanded to 24 miles.*

> *In Burma, British troops completed the capture of Mandalay.*

March 21. *U.S. Third Army captured Ludwigshafen. Berlin was bombed for the 30th night in succession.*

March 22. *British forces threw a 66-miles-long smoke screen on Montgomery's section of the Rhine front, and carried out concentrated bombing of enemy transport.*

> *Kesselring displaced Rundstedt as Commander-in-Chief on the Western Front.*

> *Russian Armies in Silesia made a 25 miles advance. Germans fell back in Hungary.*

[March 22, 1945.

THE four principal United Kingdom delegates will be :

The Secretary of State for Foreign Affairs.
The Lord President of the Council.
The Secretary of State for Dominion Affairs.
Lord Halifax, His Majesty's Ambassador in Washington.
The delegation will also include :
The Hon Member for Farnworth, Joint Parliamentary Secretary to the Ministry of Labour and National Service.
The Parliamentary Secretary to the Ministry of Home Security.
The Parliamentary Secretary to the Ministry of Health.
The Parliamentary Secretary to the Ministry of Food.
The Parliamentary Secretary to the Ministry of Economic Warfare.

Asked why the Foreign Secretary (Mr. Eden) was going to lead the delegation instead of the Lord President of the Council (Mr. Attlee, the Deputy Prime Minister) Mr. Churchill said :

The Foreign Secretary would, in the normal practice, lead such a delegation. The Lord President of the Council would not in ordinary circumstances take the lead of the Foreign Secretary in this matter. The title of Deputy Prime Minister is a courtesy title, and one which has no constitutional authority at the present time. I may say that in this Government, while it lasts—I do not know how long it will last ; some would like it to last very much longer, and some people like to fish in troubled waters—in this Administration, I say Ministers have not been engaged on a meticulous pushing of their personal claims and questions of etiquette. It was discussed with the Deputy Prime Minister and Lord President of the Council, and he entirely

The famous group of the Big Three taken at the Crimea Conference in February, 1945, surrounded by their Chiefs of Staff

Mr. Churchill greets President Truman in Potsdam during the Big Three Conference

agreed with the arrangement that was made. He agreed to it because he is not a self-seeking man and always tries to play the game and do the best he can, which is very much to his honour. I shall always assert that—except at times when we have special questions of difference.

The Secretary of State for Foreign Affairs holds the Seals of State which make him responsible for the conduct of foreign affairs, and the Lord President of the Council—the capacity in which he has elected to go—is not similarly charged under the Constitution.

> Mr. Shinwell suggested that the Conservative Party, having got all they wanted in the way of assistance, were now going to keep everything that was useful in their hands. Mr. Churchill replied:

There could hardly be a more unfair, and, I may say, a more characteristic utterance than that of the hon. Gentleman. He has done everything in his power to break up this Government. He hopes to gain after its dissolution what he would never gain while national affairs dominated men's minds. Any fair-minded man would say that the Labour Party have had fair representation in this Government.

I am the person responsible for nominating this Delegation, and they have a fair representation in this Delegation. A large proportion, three Labour Members, will be there, and I must say that I think it is a churlish manner to receive an announcement of this kind, on which all my colleagues are in full agreement. I do not mean with all I have said just now, but with the statement on the Delegation, on which all my colleagues are agreed.

A LOST AIRCRAFT

[March 28, 1945.

I DEEPLY regret to have to inform the House that my hon. and gallant Friend the Member for Hythe [Commander Brabner], Joint Under-Secretary of State for Air, who was travelling by air to Canada, is reported missing together with the following senior Air Ministry officials and public servants :

Air Marshal Sir Peter Drummond, Air Member for Training ;

Sir John Abraham, Deputy Under-Secretary of State at the Air Ministry ;

Mr. H. A. Jones. Director of Public Relations ;

Mr. Twentyman, a senior official of the Ministry of Food ;

Mr. Robinson, Private Secretary to Commander Brabner ;

Flight-Lieutenant Plum, Personal Assistant to Sir Peter Drummond.

Commander Brabner was to represent His Majesty's Government at the ceremonies attending the formal termination of the British Commonwealth Air Training Plan in the Dominion. The aircraft, a Liberator of Transport Command, manned by a crew of exceptional experience, left England for the Azores on Monday night. It was last heard of when at 6 a.m. on Tuesday morning it sent a routine message to the Azores. At 5 a.m. it had reported its estimated time of arrival in the Azores as 9 a.m. The weather for the flight was favourable. Air-sea rescue searches were promptly initiated from the Azores and reinforced from Coastal Command. A warship is also taking part in the search under Admiralty direction. Wreckage is reported near the aircraft's intended track, but so far no traces of survivors have been found.

I am sure the House will feel deeply the loss of these distinguished officers, and in particular, so far as the House of Commons is concerned, the cutting short of the bright career which was opening before the hon. and gallant Member for Hythe. He had gained the Distinguished Service Order and the Distinguished Service Cross in this war as a Member of the House of Commons, a distinction which I think is unique. Now his abilities, and the hopes that we had, have been cut short. His wife and the other relatives have been informed, and I am sure the House will wish me to express our deep sympathy with them in their great anxiety.

The crew were specially picked. The machine was the " Commando ", the very one in which the Foreign Secretary and myself have made so many journeys. I cannot think that anything short of the most intense care and effort has been taken, but such journeys cannot be wholly free from an element of danger.

THE DEATH OF EARL LLOYD GEORGE

March 23.	*Heavy bombing attacks were launched on the Ruhr and enemy positions on the East bank of the Rhine.*
March 24.	*Three hundred thousand Allied troops including Montgomery's 21st Army Group crossed the Rhine and established bridgeheads. 6,000 aircraft took part in airborne operations. 40,000 troops were landed by air East of the Rhine.*
March 25.	*Several new Rhine crossings were made. General Patton's U.S. Third Army advanced 30 miles East of the Rhine and crossed the River Main South-East of Frankfort. Darmstadt was taken. Montgomery's bridgehead expanded to 7 miles in depth and 30 miles in width.*
	Mr. Churchill visited Allied troops on the banks of the Rhine.
March 26.	*Sweeping advances reported from all Rhine bridgeheads. U.S. Third Army reached Frankfort.*
	Russians advanced through Czechoslovakia and approached Austrian frontier.
March 27.	*General Eisenhower announced that the Germans in the West were " a whipped Army " and that the main German defence line had been broken by the crossing of the Rhine.*
	British and American advances were made in all parts of the Western Front.
	On the Eastern Front the Russians entered Gdynia.
	Argentina declared war on the Axis.
March 28.	*The whole of the German forces in the West were reported in retreat and many important towns were captured. General Patton's forces were 90 miles east of the Rhine.*

[*March* 28, 1945.

SHORTLY after David Lloyd George first took Cabinet office as President of the Board of Trade, the Liberals, who had been in eclipse for twenty years, obtained in January, 1906, an overwhelming majority over all other parties. They were independent of the Irish ; the Labour Party was in its infancy ; the Conservatives were reduced to little more than 100.   But this moment of political triumph occurred in a period when the aspirations of 19th century Liberalism had been largely achieved.   Most of the great movements and principles of Liberalism had become the common property of enlightened men all over the civilized world.   The chains had been struck from the slave ; a free career was open to talent ; the extension of the franchise was moving irresistibly forward ; the advance in education was rapid and continuous, not only in this Island but in many lands.   Thus at the moment when the Liberal Party became supreme, the great and beneficent impulses which had urged them forward were largely assuaged by success.   Some new and potent conception had to be found by those who were called into power.

It was Lloyd George who launched the Liberal and Radical forces of this country effectively into the broad stream of social betterment and social security along which all modern parties now steer.   There was no man so gifted, so eloquent, so forceful, who knew the life of the people so well.   His warm heart was stirred by the many perils which beset the cottage homes : the health of the bread-winner, the fate of his widow, the nourishment and upbringing of his children, the meagre and haphazard provision of medical treatment and sanatoria, and the lack of any organized accessible medical service of a kind worthy of the age, from which the mass of the wage earners and the poor suffered. All this excited his wrath.   Pity and compassion lent their powerful wings.   He knew the terror with which old age threatened the toiler— that after a life of exertion he could be no more than a burden at the fireside and in the family of a struggling son.   When I first became Lloyd George's friend and active associate, now more than forty years ago, this deep love of the people, the profound knowledge of their lives and of the undue and needless pressures under which they lived, impressed itself indelibly upon my mind.

Then there was his dauntless courage, his untiring energy, his oratory, persuasive, provocative, now grave, now gay.   His swift, penetrating, comprehensive mind was always grasping at the root, or what he thought to be the root, of every question.   His eye ranged ahead of the obvious.   He was always hunting in the field beyond.   I have often heard people come to him with a plan, and he would say " That is all right, but what happens when we get over the bridge ? What do we do then ? "

In his prime, his power, his influence, his initiative, were unequalled in the land.   He was the champion of the weak and the poor.   Those were great days.   Nearly two generations have passed.   Most people are unconscious of how much their lives have been shaped by the laws for which Lloyd George was responsible.   Health Insurance and Old Age Pensions were the first large-scale State-conscious efforts to set a balustrade along the crowded causeway of the people's life, and, without pulling down the structures of society, to fasten a lid over the abyss into which vast numbers used to fall, generation after generation, un-cared-for and indeed unnoticed. Now we move forward confidently into larger and more far-reaching applications of these ideas. I was his lieutenant in those bygone days, and shared in a minor way in the work. I have lived to see long strides taken, and being taken, and going to be taken, on this path of insurance by which the vultures of utter ruin are driven from the dwellings of the nation. The stamps we lick, the roads we travel, the system of progressive taxation, the principal remedies that have so far been used against unemployment—all these to a very great extent were part not only of the mission but of the actual achievement of Lloyd George; and I am sure that as time passes his name will not only live but shine on account of the great, laborious, constructive work he did for the social and domestic life of our country.

When the calm, complacent, self-satisfied tranquillities of the Victorian era had exploded into the world convulsions and wars of the terrible Twentieth Century, Lloyd George had another part to play on which his fame will stand with equal or even greater firmness. Although unacquainted with the military arts, although by public repute a pugnacious pacifist, when the life of our country was in peril he rallied to the war effort and cast aside all other thoughts and aims. He was the first to discern the fearful shortages of ammunition and artillery and all the other appliances of war which would so soon affect, and in the case of Imperial Russia mortally affect, the warring nations on both sides. He saw it before anyone. Here I must say that my hon. and gallant Friend the Member for Wycombe [Sir A. Knox] was a truthful and vigilant prophet and guide in all that information which we received. He was our military representative in Russia. But it was Mr. Lloyd George who fixed on these papers, brought them forth before the eyes of the Cabinet, and induced action to be taken with the utmost vigour possible at that late hour.

Lloyd George left the Exchequer, when the Coalition Government was formed, for the Ministry of Munitions. Here he hurled himself into the mobilization of British industry. In 1915 he was building great war factories that could not come into operation for two years. There was the usual talk about the war being over in a few months, but he did not hesitate to plan on a vast scale for two years ahead. It was my fortune to inherit the output of those factories in 1917—the vast, overflowing output which came from them. Presently Lloyd George seized the main power in the State and the leadership of the Government. [HON. MEMBERS: " Seized ? "] Seized. I think it was Carlyle who said of Oliver Cromwell:

"He coveted the place; perhaps the place was his."

He imparted immediately a new surge of strength, of impulse, far stronger than anything that had been known up to that time, and extending over the whole field of war-time Government, every part of which was of equal interest to him.

I have already written about him at this time, when I watched him so closely and enjoyed his confidence and admired him so much, and I have recorded two characteristics of his which seemed to me invaluable in those days : first, his power to live in the present yet without taking short views ; and secondly, his power of drawing from misfortune itself the means of future success. All this was illustrated by the successful development of the war ; by the adoption of the convoy system, which he enforced upon the Admiralty and by which the U-boats were defeated ; by the unified command on the Western Front which gave Marshal Foch the power to lead us all to victory ; and in many other matters which form a part of the story of those sombre and tremendous years, the memory of which for ever abides with me, and to which I have often recurred in thought during our present second heavy struggle against German aggression, now drawing towards its victorious close.

Thus the statesman and guide whose gentle passing in the fullness of his years we mourn to-day served our country, our Island and our age, both faithfully and well in peace and in war. His long life was, from almost the beginning to almost the end, spent in political strife and controversy. He aroused intense and sometimes needless antagonisms. He had fierce and bitter quarrels at various times with all the parties. He faced undismayed the storms of criticism and hostility. In spite of all obstacles, including those he raised himself, he achieved his main purposes. As a man of action, resource and creative energy he stood, when at his zenith, without a rival. His name is a household word throughout our Commonwealth of Nations. He was the greatest Welshman which that unconquerable race has produced since the age of the Tudors. Much of his work abides, some of it will grow greatly in the future, and those who come after us will find the pillars of his life's toil upstanding, massive and indestructible ; and we ourselves, gathered here to-day, may indeed be thankful that he voyaged with us through storm and tumult with so much help and guidance to bestow.

MESSAGES

"THE BEAST IS CORNERED."

A message broadcast to the resistance groups in Denmark on January 1, 1945 :—

AT the beginning of the New Year I cannot promise you that the end is near ; but I can say that the Nazi beast is cornered and that its destruction is inevitable. The wounds inflicted by the armed might of the Grand Alliance are mortal. And when we in Britain speak of the Grand Alliance, we mean not only the armies, navies, and air forces of the United Nations ; we mean also the resistance movements throughout Europe, whose members have played so gallant a part in this total war against a brutal and unscrupulous enemy.

To you in the Danish resistance movement, under the brave leadership of the Freedom Council, I say this : We know what price you have paid and are paying for refusing to be tempted by Nazi blandishments or cowed by Nazi threats ; we know something of your achievements in harrying and wrecking the German war machine which rolled across your defenceless frontiers nearly five years ago. We admire your steadfastness and your skill. Your resistance is a valuable contribution both to the Allied cause and to the future prosperity of a free Denmark.

Now, as the enemy is near defeat and becomes more violent, we must all stand firm. We must strengthen our grip to hasten the end. With cool heads and stout hearts let us march together to the victory which will restore the ancient liberties of the Danish people.

REOPENING OF THE BURMA ROAD

A message to Admiral Mountbatten, Supreme Allied Commander, S.E. Asia, on January 24, 1945 :—

I send you on behalf of His Majesty's Government our most warm congratulations on re-opening the land route to China in fulfilment of the first part of the directive given to you at Quebec.

That this should already have been achieved in spite of the many disappointments you have sustained in the delay of the reinforcements which you were promised reflects the greater credit on yourself, on all your commanders in the field, and, above all, on the well-tried troops of the Fourteenth Army, gallantly sustained as they have been by the R.A.F. and the 15th Corps.

The ready assistance in all possible ways of the United States forces, and also of the Chinese Forces, is as warmly and gratefully recognized by His Majesty's Government as it has been throughout by you.

TRADE UNIONS IN THE WAR

A message to the World Trade Union Conference in London on February 6, 1945 :—

The Trade Unions of this country have made an outstanding contribution to the war effort, and I take this opportunity of paying testimony to their steadfastness and help in the past five hard years.

This co-operation will be no less important in the years that lie before us. I feel sure that the same high principles inspire, and will inspire, the work of Trade Unions in all countries represented at this Conference.

It is a source of pride that London should be made the meeting-place for this important gathering. I hope your deliberations will be fruitful and that your visitors will take away with them happy recollections of this Conference.

GENERAL CHERNIAKOVSKY'S DEATH

A message to Marshal Stalin on February 23, 1945 :—

I read with sorrow of the loss you have sustained by the death from wounds received in action of General Cherniakovsky. The qualities and services of this brilliant and gallant officer were greatly admired by His Majesty's Government and the British Army.

RED ARMY DAY

A message to Marshal Stalin on February 23, 1945 :—

The Red Army celebrates its twenty-seventh anniversary amid triumphs which have won the unstinted applause of their Allies, and have sealed the doom of German militarism. Future generations will acknowledge their debt to the Red Army as unreservedly as do we who have lived to witness these proud achievements. I ask you, the great leader of a great army, to salute them from me to-day, on the threshold of final victory.

A RESIGNATION

A letter to Mr. H. G. Strauss, M.P., who resigned his position as Parliamentary Secretary to the Ministry of Town and Country Planning, because of his disagreement with the Government's policy on Poland on March 1, 1945 :—

My dear Strauss,—I am very sorry to learn from your letter that you felt it necessary on account of your convictions to abstain from the division about Poland last night. In these circumstances you have taken an appropriate and becoming course in tendering your resignation, which I accept.

I earnestly hope that events will convince you, since our words have not succeeded, that the true and real freedom of the Polish people is an essential part of the cause for which His Majesty's Government are faithfully striving.

Yours sincerely,
WINSTON S. CHURCHILL.

DEATH OF EARL LLOYD GEORGE

A message to Countess Lloyd George on March 28, 1945 :—

Pray accept my deepest sympathy and that of my wife in the heart-breaking loss you have sustained. I greatly grieve that the friend of almost my whole political life and leader in the last Great War is gone.

AIR TRAINING IN CANADA

A message to Mr. Mackenzie King, Prime Minister of Canada, on the completion of the Empire Air Training Scheme, on March 30, 1945 :—

At this moment, when the memorable British Commonwealth Air Training Plan is being brought formally to an end, I send you, the Canadian Government, and the Royal Canadian Air Force my warmest congratulations on the successful accomplishment of a spacious task imaginatively conceived and most faithfully carried out.

This master plan has done much to speed us along the road to victory. In Canada alone, trained air crews, of whom more than half were Canadians, have been turned out at an average rate of 25,000 a year over the last five years. Moreover, the quality of the training has been outstanding, and has shown itself triumphantly in the superiority which we have gained over the enemy in every type of air combat.

In witnessing, as we now do, the consummation of a fine achievement, it is fitting that we should recall the training which has been carried out with equal success, though necessarily on not so big a scale, in Australia, New Zealand, South Africa, and Southern Rhodesia, and, of course, the advanced training which has been carried out in this country for all parts of the British Commonwealth. All alike have done magnificently.

I am glad to learn that although the joint training plan is being wound up, the training in Canada of air crews from this country is to be continued, and I thank the Canadian people most warmly for this further help.

ANSWERS IN THE HOUSE OF COMMONS

JANUARY, FEBRUARY, MARCH

UNCONDITIONAL SURRENDER

Asked to modify the policy of Unconditional Surrender, which, said the questioner, had " a tendency to stiffen the people of Germany behind their Nazi leaders and to prolong the war," the Prime Minister said on January 16 :

W E do not take that view at all, and I think the House would be overwhelmingly against our attempting to make peace by negotiation. At any rate, our Allies would be violently opposed to such a course.

I am not of opinion that a demand for unconditional surrender will prolong the war. Anyhow, the war will be prolonged until unconditional surrender has been obtained.

BRITISH WAR MEDAL

Asked to make a statement regarding the awarding of the 1939–1943 Star, the Prime Minister said on January 16 :

If you widen the existing distribution of the 1939–43 Star, you may easily bring in eight or nine million more people, and that would greatly affect the value of the award to those who have gained it. There will be a British war medal which will be given over the whole area, but I cannot attempt to make any pledge in the matter. The question of the issue of this widely-distributed medal will be one we can take up when the war is over.

When an M.P. said that all who served during the period 1939–1943 should have the Star, the Prime Minister replied :

If you go on like that you would give the ribbon to everybody in the country. All did pretty well.

EMPIRE WAR CASUALTIES

In reply to a Parliamentary question on January 16, the Prime Minister circulated the following table showing British Commonwealth and Empire war casualties :

WAR CASUALTIES

*Casualties to all ranks of British Commonwealth and Empire Forces reported from
3rd September, 1939, to 30th November, 1944*
(Excluding deaths from natural causes)

	United Kingdom (1)	Canada	Australia	New Zealand	South Africa	India	Colonies	Total, British Empire
KILLED, including died of wounds or injuries.	199,497	28,040	18,015	8,919	5,783	17,415	4,493	282,16
MISSING	39,383	4,807	6,913	928	599	13,935	14,015	80,58
WOUNDED ..	235,207	39,010	34,336	17,115	11,796	45,224	3,686	386,37
PRISONERS O F WAR, including Service Internees.	161,020	7,128	25,597	7,153	10,765	76,023 (2)	6,752	294,43
TOTAL ..	635,107	78,985	84,861	34,115	28,943	152,597	28,946	1,043,55

(1) Including men from overseas serving in these forces, in particular from Newfoundland and Southern Rhodesia.

(2) Including 22,803 officers and other ranks missing but presumed to be prisoners of war.

NOTES :—(*a*) These figures exclude civilian casualties due to enemy action and casualties to merchant seamen.

(*b*) The figures are net, i.e., they exclude repatriated or escaped prisoners of war and men reported missing who subsequently rejoined.

ATLANTIC CHARTER

When a member suggested that a statement by President Roosevelt had cast doubt on the genuineness of the Atlantic Charter, the Prime Minister replied on January 16 :

Far from any doubt having been cast on the genuineness of the Atlantic Charter, I note that President Roosevelt is reported to have declared on 22nd December last that its objectives " are just as valid to-day as they were in 1941." However, he then went on to indicate that all the objectives of the Charter were not likely to be attained immediately. I am in agreement with these statements.

Directly on returning, I made a statement about the application of the Atlantic Charter to the British Empire and India which was the result of very careful Cabinet discussion, and which has in no way been departed from, to the effect that the object and purpose and the principles of the Atlantic Charter were already being achieved by the process of extending self-government which has long been in operation.

Asked by another member to state which parts of the Charter were valid immediately, Mr. Churchill replied :

I really do not think there is any need to go into that. It has been very well described by the President as a standard of aims and an indication of the direction in which we are proceeding. It is not a law.

In reply to another Parliamentary question on February 21, the Prime Minister said :

The Atlantic Charter is a guide, and not a rule.

GAS WARFARE

Asked what the Government would do if Germany used gas against us, the Prime Minister said on January 25 :

If the contingency indicated were to occur, tenfold retaliation could very swiftly be inflicted on Germany. It is no doubt the realization of this fact, and not any moral scruple on the part of the enemy, that has hitherto procured us immunity from this particular form of warfare.

SHARK-CHASERS

Asked to make a statement regarding a shark-repellent invention in the U.S.A., the Prime Minister said on February 20 :

The Service Departments concerned and the Ministry of War Transport are aware that a device known as the " Shark-Chaser " has been produced in the United States of America and that a high degree of protection is claimed for it. The United States Navy and Army and Air Forces have been, and are still, testing the device, and the interested Departments in this country are being kept informed of the progress of these trials. Meanwhile preliminary steps to obtain supplies have been taken. My hon. and gallant Friend may rest assured that His Majesty's Government are entirely opposed to sharks.

AIR WARFARE

Asked to consider, after the defeat of Germany, the abolition of aerial warfare, the Prime Minister said on February 22 :

No, Sir. I certainly do not think that the victorious Allies should deprive themselves of the defences which are possible from the air.

EMPIRE EMIGRATION

Asked to make a statement regarding post-war emigration to the Empire, the Prime Minister said on February 22 :

The question of post-war migration has been taken up with the Dominion Governments. As at present advised, I see no need for setting up a separate Department to deal with this important issue; but His Majesty's Government are always open to consider any additional machinery, should their consultations with Dominion Governments indicate that such machinery is required.

I do not, however, wish it to be supposed that we have any large reserve of man-power which we can spare from this Island, especially if we have succeeded in making it a home for all its people.

WORLD SECURITY

Asked to clarify the point that the Dumbarton Oaks proposals assume that, if a small Power were guilty of aggression, it would be dealt with, but when a great Power was guilty of aggression there was no method of dealing with it, the Prime Minister said on March 15 :

I am sorry that there should be a high degree of axiomatic truth in the fact stated by the hon. Member. We must always remember that in the world into which we are moving our opinions will not be the only ones which will have to be regarded.

We have made a perfectly voluntary agreement with the other two Great Powers gathered at Yalta, and it prescribes a differentiation between the greatest and the smallest Powers. We may deplore, if we choose, the fact that there is a difference between great and small, between the strong and the weak in the world, but there undoubtedly is such a difference, and it would be foolish to upset good arrangements which are proceeding on a broad front for the sake of trying to obtain immediately what is a hopeless ideal.

FOOD STOCKS

Asked to state the quantity of food stocks under the control of the Ministry of Food, the Prime Minister said on March 21 :

In the earlier years of the war there was very good reason, on security grounds, against disclosing our food-stock figures. In view of the present military position that objection no longer holds. I read in the newspapers that there is an impression in some quarters in the United States that our stocks in Great Britain amount to 700,000,000 tons. Actually they are now rather less than 6,000,000 tons. They are in process of being reduced, by aid to the liberated countries, to about 4,750,000 tons by the end of June. This latter figure is no more than is necessary to maintain a regular flow of distribution under present conditions. I thought it was worth while mentioning these facts about our stocks of food, which have been built up by foresight and self-denial over five years of strict rationing and frequent bombardment.

The American Government have been continually informed. The statement I was quoting did not emanate from the American Government, but I think it is a mistake to get widespread misunderstanding in these matters, which are going to be settled in the most friendly and considerate manner by both sides.

Asked to make available a comparison of the consumption per head of the population in Britain as compared with the United States, in the various categories of foodstuffs, Mr. Churchill said :

No. I should deprecate the Debate being carried-on on the basis of invidious comparisons. I believe that the usual processes of patience, good will and interchange of fair argument will have the effect of enabling us to reach a full agreement about what is best to do in the common cause.

I hope myself that we shall remember the old saying that " comparisons are odious."

Large portions of Europe may be faced with varying degrees of famine—in some cases total famine—in this coming winter. That is a reason for accelerating the military operations to the utmost of our intensity.

M.P.s' POSTS ABROAD

Asked how many M.P.s he had appointed to positions abroad and how many were members of the Labour Party, the Prime Minister said on March 27 :

Excluding members of His Majesty's Forces posted abroad, seventeen Members of this House have been so appointed since the present Government took office. Of these, six have given up their appointments, making a total of eleven at the present time. One of them was, at the time of the appointment, a member of the Labour Party.

These appointments were made without any regard to Party at all.

GERMAN SURRENDER PROPOSALS

Asked to give an assurance that the House of Commons would be informed of any surrender proposals by Germany and that Parliament would have an opportunity of discussing them, the Prime Minister said on March 27 :

No, Sir. Such matters, if they arose at any time, would, first of all, enter immediately into the province of inter-Allied discussions. We should not be in a position at all to disclose any matters of that kind, except purely military surrender at the front. Anything that touched peace negotiations, and so on, we should immediately communicate to our Russian and American Allies, and the House would have to wait, necessarily, until those discussions had taken place. They all lie in the power of the Crown, which is vested in the Executive.

MINISTERIAL DUTIES

Asked to state the Government activities of the Lord Privy Seal and the Chancellor of the Duchy of Lancaster, the Prime Minister said on March 27 :

In addition to discharging the formal duties of his office, the Lord Privy Seal undertakes such other tasks as may be assigned to him, in Cabinet Committee or otherwise.

The Chancellor of the Duchy of Lancaster primarily controls the management of the Duchy estates and revenues, and, within the County Palatine, performs various duties which in other counties devolve upon the Lord Chancellor and the Home Secretary. Besides these duties, he is Chairman of the European Committee of the Council of the United Nations Relief and Rehabilitation Administration. In addition, he is available to perform a variety of pressing and temporary duties which are not assigned to any particular Minister, such as membership of Government Committees and assistance in the work of this House.

It used to be pressed upon me most vigorously in the first two years of the life of the present Government that we should have a War Cabinet entirely composed of persons who had no duties at all except to brood at large over our fortunes. We have followed, in general, the opposite principle, but there is great advantage in having one or two Ministers in an Administration who have no heavy Departmental duties, and are available for all kinds of other tasks, and these two particular offices, which have long traditions behind them, are extremely suitable for those who discharge such functions.

SERVICE VOTERS

Asked what steps he was taking to provide elementary factual political information for men and women in the Services to enable them to judge intelligently between addresses at the General Election, the Prime Minister said on March 27 :

In spite of the unavoidable limitations imposed on members of H.M. Forces from time to time by distance and dispersal and the late arrival of newspapers, they are, in general, probably at least as well informed on these matters as most other classes of the community, and I do not consider any special action by Government Departments is necessary.

I do not think the hon. Gentleman should suppose that soldiers of the British Army do not keep themselves very well informed, and do not have a strong opinion on the course of events.

DEATH OF PRESIDENT ROOSEVELT

A Speech to the House of Commons
April 17, 1945

March 29.   *The great Allied advance in the West continued.*

March 30.   *British tanks entered Münster on the main route to Hanover and Berlin. American Third Army tanks reached Lauterbach 200 miles from Berlin.*

March 31.   *Three thousand tanks formed spearhead of advance into Central Germany.*

April 1.   *100,000 German troops reported trapped in the Ruhr by U.S. 1st and 9th Armies.*

April 2.   *British airborne troops crossed the Dortmund-Ems Canal and reached to within 12 miles of Osnabrück. General Patton's troops reached Cassel.*

        U.S. Pacific forces cut Okinawa in two.

April 3.   *All German supply lines into Holland threatened by Canadian 1st Army's advance.*

        The battle of Central Burma ended in a great British victory.

April 4.   *British armoured troops by-passed Osnabrück. American troops reached the Weser. Cassel, Gotha and Suhl were cleared by the Americans. French troops captured Karlsruhe.*

        Soviet tanks reached to within 12 miles of Vienna.

April 5.   *U.S. 9th Army crossed the Weser. Minden, Osnabrück and Mülhausen were cleared of the enemy.*

        Russia denounced Russo-Japanese neutrality pact.

April 6.   *Allied tanks closed on Hanover and German newspapers admitted that defeat was inevitable.*

        Yugoslav troops captured Sarajevo.

April 7.   *Allied parachute troops landed east of the Zuider Zee. Canadian 1st Army struck North and Hamm was captured and Bremen and Hanover were threatened by British advance.*

        Americans captured Göttingen.

        Japan's biggest battleship and five other warships were sunk in a battle near Okinawa.

        In Burma strong Japanese forces were cut off between Mandalay and Meiktila.

April 8.   American troops captured Germany's gold reserve which
was hidden in a salt mine.
    Russian troops reached the suburbs of Vienna, and the
Soviet Government re-affirmed the independence of Austria.

April 9.   American 1st Army 140 miles from Berlin. British armoured
forces closed on Bremen. The German pocket battleship
Admiral Scheer was sunk at Kiel.

April 10.   U.S. 9th Army captured Hanover and cut the motor road
to Brunswick. Their tanks reached to within 120 miles of
Berlin.
    8th Army launched powerful attack in Adriatic sector of
Italian Front.

April 11.   American forces reached Magdeburg on the Elbe 70 miles
from Berlin. Brunswick, Coburg and Gelsenkirchen were
among the German cities to be captured on this day.
    Russian forces surrounded Vienna and cleared most of the
city.
    In Italy the 8th Army reached the river Santerno.

April 12.   President Roosevelt died. Mr. Harry S. Truman became
President of the United States of America.
    Neustadt, Weimar, Heilbronn and Celle and other German
towns were captured by Allied forces in a sweeping advance.
U.S. 1st Army closed on Leipzig.
    8th Army continued their advance and crossed the river
Santerno. Carrara was captured.

April 13.   British troops entered Arnhem. U.S. 9th Army got to within
48 miles of Berlin. Duisburg was cleared of the enemy.
    The Russians completed the capture of Vienna.

April 14.   Franz von Papen, notorious German diplomat, was captured.
American troops entered Bayreuth.
    Super-fortresses carried out a heavy raid on Tokio.

April 15.   Canadians reached the North Sea near Ems estuary. Leuna
was captured.
    Russians advanced 40 miles West of Vienna.

April 16.   Nuremberg fell to the U.S. 7th Army. British infantry
reached outskirts of Bremen.
    Russians launched great offensive along the Oder front
towards Berlin.
    5th Army opened an assault in Italy south of Bologna.

April 17.   It was announced that in the first 16 days of April 755,573
Germans had been captured on the Western Front, and the
total captured by the Allies since D-Day was 2,055,575.

[*April* 17, 1945.

I BEG to move :

" That an humble Address be presented to His Majesty to convey to His Majesty the deep sorrow with which this House has learned of the death of the President of the United States of America, and to pray His Majesty that in communicating his own sentiments of grief to the United States Government, he will also be generously pleased to express on the part of this House their sense of the loss which the British Commonwealth and Empire and the cause of the Allied Nations have sustained, and their profound sympathy with Mrs. Roosevelt and the late President's family, and with the Government and people of the United States of America."

My friendship with the great man to whose work and fame we pay our tribute to-day began and ripened during this war. I had met him, but only for a few minutes, after the close of the last war, and as soon as I went to the Admiralty in September, 1939, he telegraphed, inviting me to correspond with him direct on naval or other matters if at any time I felt inclined. Having obtained the permission of the Prime Minister, I did so. Knowing President Roosevelt's keen interest in sea warfare, I furnished him with a stream of information about our naval affairs, and about the various actions, including especially the action of the Plate River, which lighted the first gloomy winter of the war.

When I became Prime Minister, and the war broke out in all its hideous fury, when our own life and survival hung in the balance, I was already in a position to telegraph to the President on terms of an association which had become most intimate and, to me, most agreeable. This continued through all the ups and downs of the world struggle until Thursday last, when I received my last messages from him. These messages showed no falling-off in his accustomed clear vision and vigour upon perplexing and complicated matters. I may mention that this correspondence which, of course, was greatly increased after the United States entry into the war, comprises, to and fro between us, over 1,700 messages. Many of these were lengthy messages, and the majority dealt with those more difficult points which come to be discussed upon the level of Heads of Governments only after official solutions have not been reached at other stages. To this correspondence there must be added our nine meetings—at Argentia, three in Washington, at Casablanca, at Teheran, two at Quebec and, last of all, at Yalta, comprising in all about 120 days of close personal contact, during a great part of which I stayed with him at the White

House or at his home at Hyde Park or in his retreat in the Blue Mountains, which he called Shangri-la.

I conceived an admiration for him as a statesman, a man of affairs, and a war leader. I felt the utmost confidence in his upright, inspiring character and outlook, and a personal regard—affection I must say—for him beyond my power to express to-day. His love of his own country, his respect for its constitution, his power of gauging the tides and currents of its mobile public opinion, were always evident, but added to these were the beatings of that generous heart which was always stirred to anger and to action by spectacles of aggression and oppression by the strong against the weak. It is, indeed, a loss, a bitter loss to humanity that those heart-beats are stilled for ever.

President Roosevelt's physical affliction lay heavily upon him. It was a marvel that he bore up against it through all the many years of tumult and storm. Not one man in ten millions, stricken and crippled as he was, would have attempted to plunge into a life of physical and mental exertion and of hard, ceaseless political controversy. Not one in ten millions would have tried, not one in a generation would have succeeded, not only in entering this sphere, not only in acting vehemently in it, but in becoming indisputable master of the scene. In this extraordinary effort of the spirit over the flesh, of will-power over physical infirmity, he was inspired and sustained by that noble woman his devoted wife, whose high ideals marched with his own, and to whom the deep and respectful sympathy of the House of Commons flows out to-day in all fullness.

There is no doubt that the President foresaw the great dangers closing in upon the pre-war world with far more prescience than most well-informed people on either side of the Atlantic, and that he urged forward with all his power such precautionary military preparations as peace-time opinion in the United States could be brought to accept. There never was a moment's doubt, as the quarrel opened, upon which side his sympathies lay. The fall of France, and what seemed to most people outside this Island the impending destruction of Great Britain, were to him an agony, although he never lost faith in us. They were an agony to him not only on account of Europe, but because of the serious perils to which the United States herself would have been exposed had we been overwhelmed or the survivors cast down under the German yoke. The bearing of the British nation at that time of stress, when we were all alone, filled him and vast numbers of his countrymen with the warmest sentiments towards our people. He and they felt the blitz of the stern winter of 1940–41, when Hitler set himself to rub out the cities of our country, as much as any of us did, and perhaps more indeed, for imagination is often more torturing than reality. There is no doubt that the bearing of the British and, above all, of the Londoners, kindled fires in American bosoms far harder to quench than the conflagrations from which we were suffering. There was also at that time, in spite of General Wavell's victories—all the more, indeed, because of the reinforcements which were sent from this country to him—the apprehension widespread in the United States that we should be invaded by Germany after the fullest preparation in the spring of 1941. It was in February that the President sent to England the late Mr. Wendell Willkie, who, although a political rival and an opposing candidate, felt as he did on many important points. Mr. Willkie brought a letter from Mr. Roosevelt, which the President had written in his own hand, and this letter contained the famous lines of Longfellow :

> " . . . *Sail on, O ship of State !*
> *Sail on, O Union, strong and great !*
> *Humanity with all its fears,*
> *With all the hopes of future years,*
> *Is hanging breathless on thy fate !* "

At about that same time he devised the extraordinary measure of assistance called Lend-Lease, which will stand forth as the most unselfish and unsordid financial act of any country in all history. The effect of this was greatly to increase British fighting power, and for all the purposes of the war effort to make us, as it were, a much more numerous community. In that autumn I met the President for the first time during the war at Argentia in Newfoundland, and together we drew up the Declaration which has since been called the Atlantic Charter, and which will, I trust, long remain a guide for both our peoples and for other peoples of the world.

All this time, in deep and dark and deadly secrecy, the Japanese were preparing their act of treachery and greed. When next we met in Washington, Japan, Germany and Italy had declared war upon the United States, and both our countries were in arms, shoulder to shoulder. Since then we have advanced over the land and over the sea through many difficulties and disappointments, but always with a broadening measure of success. I need not dwell upon the series of great operations which have taken place in the Western Hemisphere, to say nothing of that other immense war proceeding on the other side of the world. Nor need I speak of the plans which we made with our great Ally, Russia, at Teheran, for these have now been carried out for all the world to see.

But at Yalta I noticed that the President was ailing. His captivating smile, his gay and charming manner, had not deserted him, but his face had a transparency, an air of purification, and often there was a faraway look in his eyes. When I took my leave of him in Alexandria harbour I must confess that I had an indefinable sense of fear that his health and his strength were on the ebb. But nothing altered his inflexible sense of duty. To the end he faced his innumerable tasks unflinching. One of the tasks of the President is to sign maybe a hundred or two State papers with his own hand every day, commissions and so forth. All this he continued to carry out with the utmost strictness. When death came suddenly upon him " he had finished his mail." That portion of his day's work was done. As the saying goes, he died in harness, and we may well say in battle harness, like his soldiers, sailors, and airmen, who side by side with ours are carrying on their task to the end all over the world. What an enviable death was his ! He had brought his country through the worst of its perils and the heaviest of its toils. Victory had cast its sure and steady beam upon him.

In the days of peace he had broadened and stabilized the foundations of American life and union. In war he had raised the strength, might and glory of the great Republic to a height never attained by any nation in history. With her left hand she was leading the advance of the conquering Allied Armies into the heart of Germany, and with her right, on the other side of the globe, she was irresistibly and swiftly breaking up the power of Japan. And all the time ships, munitions, supplies, and food of every kind were aiding on a gigantic scale her Allies, great and small, in the course of the long struggle.

But all this was no more than wordly power and grandeur, had it not been that the causes of human freedom and of social justice, to which so much of his life had been given, added a lustre to this power and pomp and warlike might, a lustre which will long be discernible among men. He has left behind him a band of resolute and able men handling the numerous inter-related parts of the vast American war machine. He has left a successor who comes forward with firm step and sure conviction to carry on the task to its appointed end. For us, it remains only to say that in Franklin Roosevelt there died the greatest American friend we have ever known, and the greatest champion of freedom who has ever brought help and comfort from the new world to the old.

AN UNSPONSORED M.P.

A Speech to the House of Commons
April 17, 1945

On April 17, 1945, Mr. R. D. McIntyre, newly elected M.P. for Motherwell, attempted to take his seat in the House without being introduced by two other Members. The House then debated a Motion (defeated by 273 to 74) that he should be permitted to depart from the normal custom. In the course of the Debate the Prime Minister said:

[April 17, 1945.

I COULD not advise the House on this occasion to depart from ancient tradition and custom. On the contrary, I think these are the days when Parliament and the British House of Commons are so much under the gaze of the whole world, and the admiring gaze of large parts of it, that we should not in the least shrink from upholding the ancient observances which have added to our dignity and to our power.

The gentleman who is seeking to present himself at this moment speaks, so far as I can judge, in favour of old traditions, older than we have known for many years. But for the hitch which has occurred in the moment of his introduction, we certainly could, I think, have a right to claim him as a supporter with us in the Division which is about to take place.

At any rate, so far as we are concerned, I hope that those who support His Majesty's Government will resist the proposal so very abruptly thrown out to give away customs and traditions of our Island which have lasted since 1688, and I am strongly of opinion that those who feel this way should testify so in the Division Lobby.

FAR EAST TROOPS' WELFARE

A Speech to the House of Commons
April 18, 1945

[*April* 18, 1945.

ON December 20 last I made a statement to the House about the report by Lord Munster on the welfare of troops in India and South-East Asia Command, and I told the House that on the advice of the Secretary of State for War I had appointed Lieut.-General King to be my personal representative in these Commands for welfare matters. Since then, I have kept in close personal touch with progress on these matters in conjunction with the Ministers directly concerned. General King has now returned after a three months' visit, and I think the House may wish to be informed of some of the main points on which he has reported. I am accordingly going to read to the House a statement prepared, under my supervision, by the Ministers directly concerned, which I hope the House will not consider too long.

In the first place, General King has reported, and his report in this respect is fully borne out by many other people in a position to judge, that the morale of British Service men in these theatres is of the highest quality, and is unsurpassed elsewhere. The success of the campaigns in which they are now engaged is itself the best evidence of their spirit, which has enabled them to triumph over a dangerous enemy and over the most difficult natural obstacles.

On the material side, General King's report is on the whole satisfactory, but this is not to suggest that there is not much still to be achieved in improving the physical conditions of men serving in India and the Far East.

As regards accommodation in transit and leave camps and static camps such as R.A.F. and Naval air stations, General King reports that great strides have been made in the past year or so, and, with the exception of some items of special equipment, to which reference is made later, the general standard of comfort is reasonable, and in many of them it bears comparison with camps in this country and with those in India occupied by our American Allies. Deolali camp, which has earned a certain amount of unenviable notoriety, has been greatly improved. Full hutting, including amenity buildings for 5,000 men, is nearing completion, the target date for which is May. Cookhouses, cooking equipment and catering staff are being increased and improved. Similar progress is being effected at another large transit camp at Kalyan and at a number of smaller camps. Eight new leave camps are under construction, and additional accommodation is being provided at a further six existing camps.

No reference to the topic of leave camps could be complete without mention of the serious lack of women workers : where they are available, they help to create that homelike atmosphere which is so much appreciated by men on leave. With the help of the voluntary organizations, every effort is being made to find assistance from this country to supplement the small numbers of women available for this purpose in India.

There are serious difficulties in providing all the equipment needed for these camps, in particular refrigerating equipment, air-conditioning sets, fans and similar stores. Many factories making these things have, during the course of the war, been put on to the manufacture of strictly operational products. It is now becoming possible for those factories to revert to the manufacture of these amenity stores, but the process takes time. The Minister of Labour and National Service and the Minister of Supply are taking every possible step to meet the requirements. It would, however, be wrong to expect that the back of this particular problem will be broken before the end of this year or the early months of next year.

Travelling conditions are still indifferent. Great efforts to improve them are being made, but India's rolling stock is limited, and her railways are being called upon to carry ever-increasing loads to nourish the campaign in Burma. Special coaches for British Servicemen are, however, being provided, canteen coaches are being constructed, and proper arrangements for cleaning are being made, as well as for meals en route. Plans for providing air-conditioning for troop and ambulance trains are at present held up because certain essential components have to come from America, and cannot be immediately provided.

To turn to the question of food and drink. Greater variety is being introduced into the rations, and improvements are being effected in cooking. When refrigerators become available on a large scale, still further improvements will be possible. By the use of mobile refrigerators it will be possible to provide fresh meat for men in areas where this cannot be done at present. Meanwhile, local production of eggs, poultry, fruit and vegetables is being encouraged. The canteen services in India have been improved, and a good range of commodities is now available in most of them. Beer is one of the greatest difficulties. Great efforts are being made to increase the export of beer to India and S.E.A.C., and the quantity allocated to these theatres has been greatly increased. Nevertheless, it is not yet up to the target we are aiming at. When the beer gets to India, it has to be distributed, and this is no easy matter. Indeed, with the very long lines of communication over which we are now operating, it is inevitable that there will be local disparities in the supply of beer, as of other commodities. Everything possible is being done to overcome this. The Government of India have agreed to exempt beer for consumption by Servicemen from import duty. As regards cigarettes, it has just been arranged that a privilege which previously applied only to certain parts of India, by which 50 cigarettes a week were issued free, should now be extended to all parts of India. Cigarettes are now being made in India consisting of 70 per cent. American tobacco and 30 per cent. Indian tobacco. The blend is the choice, after prolonged experiment, of Servicemen themselves. It is hoped that these cigarettes will be available for distribution in the course of the next few months.

The position as regards mails is now very much more satisfactory than previously. Letters up to one ounce in weight are carried all the way by air at the cost of 1½d., and the Government of India and Ceylon have granted one ounce letters free conveyance homewards. These facilities also extend to letters to and from ships. The parcels mail has also been improved. Distribution of mail within India is done by air so far as possible. As a consequence of these measures, delays in mail have been very materially reduced.

The supply of newspapers and books has improved. Sunday newspapers are now being flown out and distributed free, and since 1st January this year over 400,000 books have been distributed to the Army and R.A.F. alone in addition to those for the Royal and Merchant Navies. This is still not enough, and it is hoped the public in this country will continue to hand in books they do not want—or books they do want—to post offices so that the quantity sent out may be still further increased.

E.N.S.A. is still somewhat of a bone of contention, and Mr. Basil Dean's recent report is being carefully studied, here and in India ; but E.N.S.A. parties have been getting well forward, and having regard to the vast distances to be covered, are giving entertainment to a very large number of men. Arrangements have also been made for the transport to India of up to twelve artists a month by air. Home-made concert parties are also flourishing, and efforts are being made to increase the number of bands. Cinema entertainment is improving, but slowly. There is a shortage of projectors and films which we are doing our best to overcome, again with the help of the Minister of Supply. The provision of wireless sets is being very greatly increased, and it is hoped to meet requirements by the end of this year. A special Services transmitter is already in use, and one with much greater range should be in operation in the theatre by the end of the year.

I am sure the House would not wish me to make any apology for giving this account, for every word that is said is watched with the greatest interest by this most gallant and devoted Army, which has achieved, in conditions far less satisfactory than they were led to expect, in so far as the supply of reinforcements is concerned, objectives greater than those which were prescribed on the basis of those large reinforcements. It is a grand and glorious Army, and I know the House would wish me to proceed in laying this matter before them in detail. These men ought to feel that the House is watching their fortunes. I am indebted for the pressure brought to bear by this House in regard to this matter and I am most anxious that it should be thoroughly maintained.

Reference has been made to the need for women workers. They are also wanted to work under the joint auspices of S.S.A.F.A. and the Help Society to assist in sorting out the domestic worries of Service-men separated for long periods from their homes.

We are doing our best to arrange that men repatriated on compassionate grounds should travel all the way by air, at any rate when their presence here is urgently necessary.

Service in India, Burma and the Pacific involves, owing to the climate, long periods when physical activities are limited. For this reason, special efforts are being made to give increased opportunities for education ; and to keep men abreast of developments in the social and political field, the Minister of Reconstruction is producing a pamphlet giving an objective and simple account of the various measures, such as the National Insurance Bill, now before the House— [HON. MEMBERS: " Not before the House "]—I mean before the House in the sense that it is advancing upon it. That is not to say that the House should beat a hasty retreat. Further, the Minister of Labour and National Service has provided several admirably-chosen lecturers to tour India and the Pacific, to tell Servicemen of the plans made for their release and resettlement when their term of service comes to an end. These lecturers, preceded by a pamphlet on the subject, are already on their way.

The above relates mainly to the Army and R.A.F. The Navy and Merchant Service have their own problems, which are being dealt with on similar lines, so far as the differing conditions of service allow. The First Lord made a statement on Naval amenities on 11th April. As regards the Merchant Navy, the Reverend Mervyn Armstrong, a well-known worker in these fields, has been appointed to a post in the Commerce Department of the Government of India in which he will be able to direct and co-ordinate welfare work on behalf of merchant seamen.

Thus it will be seen that every one of the recommendations made in the Munster Report is receiving the earnest attention of the authorities both here and in India. The Prime Minister himself receives monthly reports on each one of them which enable him to see that any obstacles to progress that may arise are overcome as speedily as may be. The Forces serving in India, Burma and the Far East never were a forgotten Army; the valour and endurance they have displayed, and the victories they have won and are winning, keep them ever present in our minds, and in the minds of the general public. There is still much to be done in their interests, but much has already been done, and we hope to do still better in future.

THE ENDURANCE OF BRISTOL

A Speech on Receiving the Freedom of the City
April 21, 1945

[April 21, 1945.

I VALUE enormously the gifts presented to me, and even more the feeling of friendship accompanying them.

You have told me in terms which, if I were not a hardened warrior, would have made me blush, the reasons which have led you to take this most agreeable course of action, but I am sure you and every one here realizes what great advantages I had in the matter of the leadership of this country during the last five years. I had an absolutely united nation behind me, and the support of colleagues as loyal as any Government in Britain has ever had. I have had in the handling of great affairs the united force of all three main parties.

In Mr. Bevin I have found a colleague who has handled most intricate and difficult problems in the maintenance, not only of our armies, but of the vast effort of our factories, and who has laid a heavy, but in many cases not an unwelcome, hand upon every human being in the kingdom.

In the First Lord of the Admiralty I have also found a true colleague and friend, and you will notice that in this Government many of the most important offices have been held already for nearly five years by the men first called upon to occupy them. A sense of continuity comes to the holder of the office, and a sense of loyalty and service to those who carry out his instructions. To be at the Admiralty during a time of war and for so long has been the great experience of one who, like Mr. Bevin, is a true Bristolian. There he is, with all the great problems of the organization and administration of the Navy, and with all the important direction of affairs under the advice of the naval staff at his disposal, carrying on what must still be regarded as Britannia's shield.

I have often looked across from No. 10, Downing Street to the other side of the parade ground to the Admiralty building, to see that building crumbling under the fire of the enemy, where a very hideous gap was made. His own dwelling was pierced with fragments, so that many of the pictures we value will go down to all generations with little marks in them to tell of the brave days of old.

I never could have got through this business if I had not had with

113

me a powerful band of men, representative of the nation, and bound together by a loyalty which rose far above party politics. Now we are coming to the ending of the long journey, so far as Europe is concerned. All our armies are in action, and British armies in Holland and Germany are marching against the enemy and are to-day advancing, sometimes in long strides, on the Elbe. We shall soon be on the Baltic, and we shall soon be at the Zuider Zee, and shall be able to bring relief to the gallant, starving people of Holland.

This is no time to talk of celebrations. We might easily give vent to well-founded rejoicings, and a few days later find that the troops have to go into battle, and find ourselves facing the further losses of war. We have no intention of encouraging any festivities or thanksgiving until we are assured by our military commanders that the task is so far concluded and completed that every one may cheer.

We have the Japanese to finish, and we have to stand absolutely with our great American Ally, paying-off at the other end of the world debts as heavy as ever were inflicted on us. I shall have to ask you, or whoever stands in my place—and whoever it be I shall support him—we shall have to ask you for a new leap forward, for a new lifting of soul and body so that this second war shall also be brought to a conclusion altogether free from any doubt.

When I last came to you the hand of war lay heavily on you. Now the clouds of war have rolled far away, thanks to the skill of our inventors, the bravery of our fighting men, and the audacity of our pilots. You may devote yourselves to rebuilding as soon as sufficient numbers come back from the Forces to help you. I wish you a period of prosperity to refresh the strong life of the city. The merchant adventurers must never lose their daring and ingenuity. In the pages of the history of Bristol your bearing, your fortitude and endurance in this ordeal will not be among the least worthy.

NO TIME TO RELAX

A SPEECH AT BRISTOL UNIVERSITY WHEN, AS CHANCELLOR, THE
PRIME MINISTER CONFERRED DEGREES OF DOCTOR OF LAWS ON
MR. ERNEST BEVIN (MINISTER OF LABOUR) AND MR. A. V.
ALEXANDER (FIRST LORD OF THE ADMIRALTY)
APRIL 21, 1945

[April 21, 1945.

THIS ceremony, in its simplicity, must move all who are present.
We have inscribed upon the honours list of the University two
eminent sons of Somerset and the West Country, both long and
intimately connected with Bristol. Both are among the most distinguished Ministers of the Crown. Both have served for almost five
years in the British Government, and they have rendered remarkable
services to the State. They have never feared the violence of the
enemy, nor the responsibilities which fall heavily on shoulders burdened
with the duties of First Lord of the Admiralty or Minister of Labour.

The opportunity for making serious mistakes has never been lacking
for these two men in these five memorable and glorious years. At
the end, or very nearly the end, of the journey, we find them having
conducted most wide, far-reaching measures of administration and of
executive action.

Both enjoy the confidence of their colleagues, and of the nation at
large, and both are in a position to exercise ever more fully the influence
they have on those with whom they have particularly to deal. Here
they are, and I have greatly enjoyed the honour which my position
gives me to be the expressor of the University's wish to bind them
into the fabric of this great educational institution.

The University of Bristol asked me to become its Chancellor in days
when, as Chancellor of the Exchequer, I could not have been the
most popular man in the country. Afterwards, through nearly eleven
years, I had the opportunity of complete freedom of speech and
action, and felt myself in a position to offer guidance and warning
about the future which, if I had been woven into the texture of Government, I could never have expressed with such clear, and even harsh,
vigour.

The conduct of our affairs in this country during the great period
through which we are passing, and the efficiency of our actions in so
many fields, will, I believe, bring upon this nation the admiration of

those who will follow us. Already in the world we are viewed with great respect. We have our mistakes, our weaknesses and failings, but in the fight which this island race has made, had it not been the toughest of the tough, if the spirit of freedom which burns in the British breast had not been a pure, dazzling, inextinguishable flame, we might not yet have been near the end of this war.

The last time I came here the building was in flames, and the officers of the University who had to participate in the ceremony pulled on their robes over khaki dress blackened and wetted by the night's work they had done. But nothing interrupted the ceremony or diverted its course. We conferred degrees on a distinguished Australian, Mr. Menzies, whose work for the Commonwealth and Empire at the beginning of the war we do not forget, and also on Mr. Winant, the outstanding figure who represents to us here in London and England the expression of those feelings of good will which have surged in a great stream since the days of our lonely struggle. We have a feeling of great sentiment towards our brothers across the ocean, and I am glad to see some of them here to-day.

The world organization which we must build, as we shall build, will be free and open to all the nations of the world, and they must live in peace and justice with one another; but there must be always the necessary force to restrain aggression. Inside this vast structure, from which we hope will come a long and peaceful period, is that open, avowed, and inseparable friendship and affection of the great English-speaking nations of the world.

Now we are reaching a period when the Germans will be conquered completely, and Europe will be entirely liberated from their thrall. The brutal hosts which marched so enthusiastically upon us, their eyes alive with greed and the passion of war and the earnest desire for mastery over others, have reached a time when they will be added to those long, melancholy, and humiliating streams of prisoners who, having done the worst to the world, have no hope but in its mercy.

For my part, I have deprecated any attempt on the part of individuals in this country to forecast the period when official festivities and rejoicings should be embarked upon, as it is, in the main, for the generals in the field, the great commanders of the United States and the great men our Russian allies have produced, to inform their Governments when their task is done. I do not think it need be long delayed. We shall fail in our duty if we allow ourselves anything but a brief pause for thanksgiving, because there lies before us the need for finishing the war started by that wicked and treacherous Power which committed an act of baseless aggression against the United States, and has inflicted the most grievous injuries upon the British Empire in the East.

We may pause for a moment, we may rejoice, but it must only be for the purpose of regathering strength. There may be danger that people will feel after this long struggle, and this great and undisputed victory over a formidable antagonist, that we can relax. I cannot give the word for that. Our unity must be complete. Shoulder to shoulder we must face the task. We must finish the war, bring our men home, and complete the process of unwinding that which has been so tightly wound up in these past years.

I should be failing in my duty if I led you to believe that an easy or quiet time lay before you, but I should also be failing if I did not express the confidence that this nation, welded together as never before, the base of the whole movement of the world, will rouse itself and pool its strength sufficiently, not only to overcome the greatest antagonists, but to place our people in a situation where they may reap the reward of their gallantry in the field, their steadfastness in comprehending the national and world cause ; and where they may enjoy, with their families, a period when we shall really have a peace founded on a rock of security, and when we shall feel there is no friendly country in the world to which we can go without receiving a warm welcome as citizens of the land which has played its part in what we must pray will be a long, lasting liberation of mankind.

WAITING FOR VICTORY

A STATEMENT MADE TO THE HOUSE OF COMMONS REGARDING
PLANS FOR THE ANNOUNCEMENT OF VICTORY IN EUROPE
MAY 1, 1945

[*May* 1, 1945.

I HAVE no special statement to make about the war position in Europe, except that it is definitely more satisfactory than it was this time five years ago.

Should information of importance reach His Majesty's Government during the four days of our Sittings this week, as it might do, I will follow precedents which have occurred in this war, and ask Mr. Speaker's permission to ask the indulgence of the House to interrupt Business and make a brief announcement. But that would only occur if, as I say, information of exceptional importance reached us.

With regard to the conditions and regulations which would obtain if an announcement of decisive consequence justifying celebrations were to be made this week, or at any time in the future, and if what is called VE-Day—Victory in Europe Day—were announced, a number of arrangements have been prepared and will be issued to-night in a Home Office circular; but this is only making reasonable preparations to prevent inconvenience and giving general guidance to the local authorities, as well as to the public, as to the sort of proceedings which would be regarded as not undesirable.

I do not know in what form any message will reach us, or whether it will reach us in a form justifying disturbing the House in its Debates; but should such a message reach us, then we will give the substance of it immediately to the House. We do not consider that the information should be withheld until the exact occupation of particular zones is achieved. The movement of troops and the surrender of enemy troops may well take an appreciable period of time. Moreover, it is not by any means certain at this time that a complete surrender of the enemy's forces will be the subject of a future announcement.

I shall make no statement that is not in accord with statements which will be made by our Allies, and those Governments will not make statements in the making of which they have not considered maturely the advice of their military commanders in the different theatres both on the North-Western Front, and on the Italian Front.

I will certainly not delay the news for a moment. It will break from some authorized or unauthorized channel, and if the House is sitting I will, if the House permits me, take the liberty of coming down and informing them myself.

When a member said bank employees were dissatisfied because they would not be released for VE celebrations, the Prime Minister said :

It will be absolutely impossible, whatever happens, to have a day or more of rejoicing without making provision for minimum staffs in every department of this country—banks and other places—to make sure that great injury is not wrought to the public interest, and that old age pensioners and others having most urgent requirements to be met are properly attended to on a minimum scale. This will affect practically every sphere of our life, but those who are called upon to stay at their posts during such an occasion will, of course, receive their reward later on, in compensatory holidays.

Mr. Aneurin Bevan said the fact that a large number of troops were still engaged in the Far East would exercise a sobering restraint. Mr. Churchill replied :

I hope that soberness and restraint, for which my hon. Friend is renowned, will always be maintained with propriety in all parts of the country ; but soberness and restraint do not necessarily prevent the joyous expression of the human heart.

GERMANS SURRENDER IN ITALY AND AUSTRIA

A STATEMENT TO THE HOUSE OF COMMONS
MAY 2, 1945

April 18. *Nine Russian armies launched a great offensive against Berlin.*

 Germans in Western Holland were cut off by the Canadians who reached the Zuider Zee. U.S. troops captured Magdeburg, Düsseldorf, Brinkum and other German cities. U.S. 3rd Army entered Czechoslovakia.

 8th Army in Italy cleared Argenta and advanced on Ferrara.

April 19. *Goebbels appealed to the Germans to make a last effort. British tanks reached the Elbe, and other British armoured forces got to within six miles of Hamburg. Germans flooded the Hook of Holland.*

April 20. *British troops outflanked Bremen and approached Hamburg suburbs.*

 Russian leading forces reported to be eight miles from Berlin suburbs.

 British M.P.s arrived in Germany to inspect the Nazi concentration camps.

 Germany's last pocket battleship Lützow *was sunk by the R.A.F.*

 In Central Burma the 14th Army reached points 70 miles South of Meiktila.

April 21. *Russian tanks entered Berlin's N.E. suburbs. British launched an offensive against the Germans in Hamburg.*

 In Italy the German defences were breached and Bologna was liberated.

 In Burma the British 14th Army closed in on Pyinmana, 200 miles from Rangoon.

 The Soviet Union and the Polish (Lublin) Provisional Government signed a treaty.

April 22. *Berlin was invested on three sides by the Russians and many suburbs were captured.*

 German Naval Headquarters at Buxtehude with German admiral and 500 German Wrens was captured by the British. French 1st Army captured Stuttgart.

April 23. German defences East of Berlin were smashed and Russians also entered the city from the South. Many other towns, including Potsdam and Frankfort-on-Oder, were taken.

First radio liaison established between U.S. 9th Army on the Elbe and the advancing Russians.

The dim-out in Great Britain was lifted.

April 24. Russians captured 11 more Berlin suburbs and advanced towards the centre of the city. British troops fought their way into Bremen.

Marshal Pétain entered Switzerland to surrender to France.

Allied troops crossed the River Po in Italy, and Spezia, Modena and Ferrara were captured.

April 25. Russian and American troops made a link-up at Torgau on the River Elbe. Berlin was surrounded and the centre of the city was reached by Russian forces. The British took most of Bremen, and five Allied armies moved to attack Hitler's Southern redoubt.

The United Nations Security Conference opened at San Francisco.

April 26. Russian troops continued to pour into Berlin. British forces cleared most of Bremen. American troops crossed the Danube at Ingolstadt.

In Italy the Allies captured Verona and crossed the River Adige. They also took Mantua, Reggio and Parma, and the whole German army in Italy appeared to be on the point of collapsing.

It was reported that Goering had been relieved of his post owing to heart disease.

April 27. Russians continued to strike deeper into Berlin. Potsdam and Spandau were also cleared. American 1st Army thrust farther into Austria.

General Dittmar, German High Command radio commentator, surrendered to the Allies.

In Italy the 5th Army occupied Genoa.

April 28. It was announced that Himmler had offered unconditional surrender to Britain and America but not to Russia, following a report that Hitler was dying.

Mussolini and other leading Fascists were captured near Milan and executed by Italian partisans. Turin and Milan were liberated by Italians.

Russians advanced through the Berlin suburbs and took 27,000 more prisoners.

R.A.F. bombers dropped food to the starving people of Holland.

April 29. Russians neared the centre of Berlin and attacked the Headquarters of the German High Command. U.S. 7th Army
entered Munich. U.S. 5th Army occupied Milan and Como.
British forces entered Venice.

April 30. In Berlin the Red Flag was hoisted on the Reichstag. Russians
massed for a final assault on the centre of the city. British
advanced beyond the Elbe. Dachau concentration camp was
liberated. Americans freed 110,000 Allied prisoners at
Moosburg.

Marshal Tito's Yugoslav troops entered Trieste.

May 1. The death of Hitler was announced by German radio. Admiral
Doenitz declared himself the new Führer. Field-Marshals
List and Ritter von Leeb and Admiral Horthy were captured
by U.S. 7th Army.

Australian troops landed in Borneo.

May 2. Unconditional surrender of the German armies in Italy to
Field-Marshal Alexander. One million men laid down their
arms.

Berlin capitulated to the Russians and 134,000 prisoners
were taken. British captured Wismar and Lubeck.

Field-Marshal von Rundstedt was captured. M. Laval was
arrested at Barcelona.

Dr. Fritsche, Goebbels' deputy, declared that Hitler, Goebbels
and General Krebs had committed suicide.

British airborne and seaborne troops landed 20 miles south
of Rangoon.

I PROMISED that I would come to the House if anything of major
importance occurred, and would ask the leave and the indulgence
of the House to make a short statement.

There has been a considerable amount of matter issuing·continuously
from the tape machine, but I thought that perhaps the House would
like to hear a very short account which I have received from Field-
Marshal Alexander.

Field-Marshal Sir Harold Alexander, the Supreme Allied Commander
in the Mediterranean theatre of operations, has just announced that
the land, sea and air forces commanded by Colonel-General Heinrich
von Wietinghof-Scheel, German Commander-in-Chief, South-West
Command, and Commander-in-Chief of the Army Group " C," have
surrendered unconditionally. This instrument of surrender was signed
on Sunday afternoon, 29th April, at the Allied Forces Headquarters
at Caserta, by two German plenipotentiaries, and by Lieut.-General

W. D. Morgan, Chief of Staff at Allied Forces Headquarters. The terms of surrender provided for the cessation of hostilities at 12 o'clock noon Greenwich mean time on Wednesday, 2nd May, that is to say, 2 o'clock to-day by our time, but as all these matters are accompanied by many elements of uncertainty, it was not until effective confirmation was obtained by the actual orders issued to the troops from the German High Command that Field-Marshal Alexander issued the statement which has now come over the wireless.

The territory under General von Wietinghof-Scheel, South-West Command, includes Northern Italy to the Isonzo River in the North-East, and the Austrian Provinces of Salzburg, Vorarlberg, and the Tyrol and portions of Carinthia and Styria. It is, therefore, geographically, a surrender which puts us into very close touch with the position of the United States' Armies of the North. The total forces of the enemy—the fighting troops of the enemy, including the remnants of 22 German divisions and six Italian Fascist divisions, with the combat and echelon troops upon the lines of communication and throughout this territory, which they have held for so long—who have surrendered to the Allies are estimated to amount to nearly 1,000,000 men. Not only has a vast area of territory, vital in its character, fallen into the hands of the Supreme Commander, Sir Harold Alexander, but the actual surrender which has taken place so far, comprising the numbers it does, constitutes, I believe, a record for the whole of this war, and cannot fail to be helpful to the further events to which we are all looking forward.

This Army in Italy, American and British composed, commanded by our trusted General, having under him General Mark Clark, a most efficient and daring American soldier, has had a marvellous record since they first landed in the Peninsula. The landing at Salerno, the tremendous fighting at Anzio, when we tried a turning movement, the capture of Rome, and the driving of the enemy north-ward placed an enormous effort on the troops, and have been attended by very heavy losses through the stern fighting. What has made it particularly difficult and depressing for this Army is the tremendous inroads which have been made upon it in order to help forward other great operations. In June and July of last year, what nearly amounted to an Army was taken from this Command in Italy, while only a very small corresponding reduction took place on the enemy's side. Recently —a few months ago—feeling that it would probably be beyond the strength of this Army, so weakened, to make a decisive attack, we moved another large addition to the divisions on the Western Front, and some others went to Greece. Thus this Army was an Army stripped of its strength, and facing an enemy force which, for all the purposes of war, must have been considered far stronger, because it

had the duty of defending mountain ranges and, afterwards, plains
flooded by autumn and winter rains, and which certainly, in the
number of divisions, exceeded those which were left to attack. Those
Forces left to attack, as I pointed out in my message of congratulation
to Sir Harold Alexander, were of so many different nations, that only
a personality of commanding qualities could have held them all, and
woven them together.

If we look over the whole list of those men who have fought, we find,
taking first our own contribution, which was the largest, the British
divisions, and a British Indian division of the highest quality. In
addition to the British divisions, we had the Poles, who have always
fought with the greatest loyalty, the New Zealanders, who have marched
all the way from the beginning right up to the very spearpoint of the
advance, the South African Armoured division, which was very forward in the fray, and the great Forces of the United States, second in
numbers only to our own. Then there have been the Brazilian Forces,
which have made their steady advances, a Negro division of United
States troops, which has also distinguished itself, the Jewish Brigade,
which we formed a year or so ago, and which has fought in the front
line with courage, and the Japanese of American birth, who entered
Turin. Finally, there were the Free Italians who have played their
part in clearing their country from the German Fascist yoke. All
these Forces, weakened as they have been, were not discouraged.
Divided as they were by racial differences, they were united and resolved upon their purpose, and now their reward has come. I am very
glad that it has come at a time when it can be singled out. It stands
out and brings to a conclusion the work of as gallant an Army as has
ever marched, and brings to a pitch of fame and military reputation a
Commander who, I may say, has always enjoyed the fullest confidence
of the House of Commons.

For the last two days I have known what was going on, but one was
not certain that it might not be snatched away at the last minute,
and therefore great secrecy was necessary. May I also say that, in
the combination of the forces of the nationalities I mentioned, a
tremendously powerful American Air Force, with a very strong British
Air Force and also a very large detachment of the British Navy, have
throughout been the mainstay and sustenance and shield of the whole
of the land operations.

UNCONDITIONAL SURRENDER

A WORLD BROADCAST
MAY 8, 1945

May 3. *Hamburg surrendered to the British Second Army. Kiel and Flensburg were declared open cities. The whole German defence in the North of the British Front collapsed, and 500,000 prisoners were taken.*

U.S. 9th Army joined forces with the Russians at three new places. U.S. troops also penetrated into Austria.

New Zealand troops occupied Trieste and Yugoslavs took Fiume.

British forces entered Rangoon.

May 4. *Field-Marshal Montgomery received surrender of all enemy forces in Holland, North-West Germany and Denmark, amounting to 1,000,000 men.*

U.S. 7th Army advanced through Brenner Pass and joined 5th Army in Italy.

Admiral Mountbatten announced that the battle of Burma had ended and Allied forces had killed 97,000 Japanese.

May 5. *Two more German Armies surrendered to American troops in the Munich area. In the Western Netherlands the German 25th Army surrendered to Canadians. Cease-fire sounded on the whole of the British Front.*

Danish patriots took over Copenhagen and the King of Denmark broadcast to the Danes the news of the liberation of his country.

May 6. *Admiral Doenitz ordered all German ships to abstain from any act of war.*

May 7. *Unconditional surrender of all German armed forces was signed by General Jodl, German Chief of Staff, at General Eisenhower's Headquarters at Rheims.*

Cease-fire ordered on all Allied fronts in Europe.

All Germans in Norway capitulated and Allied units were at Oslo. Only in Prague was fighting continued by the Germans.

The bodies of Goebbels and his family were found in Berlin, death having been due to poisoning.

VICTORY

*May 8.   VE-Day celebrations throughout the world.   A broadcast to the
Empire by the King followed Mr. Churchill's broadcast announcing that Germany had surrendered unconditionally.*

*Field-Marshal Keitel and commanders of the German Army,
Navy and Air Force signed unconditional surrender in Berlin
in the presence of Marshal Zhukov and Air Chief Marshal
Tedder.   Hostilities ended officially at midnight.*

[*May 8*, 1945.

YESTERDAY morning at 2.41 a.m. at Headquarters, General
Jodl, the representative of the German High Command, and
Grand Admiral Doenitz, the designated head of the German State,
signed the act of unconditional surrender of all German land, sea, and
air forces in Europe to the Allied Expeditionary Force, and simultaneously to the Soviet High Command.

General Bedell Smith, Chief of Staff of the Allied Expeditionary
Force, and General François Sevez signed the document on behalf of
the Supreme Commander of the Allied Expeditionary Force, and
General Susloparov signed on behalf of the Russian High Command.

To-day this agreement will be ratified and confirmed at Berlin, where
Air Chief Marshal Tedder, Deputy Supreme Commander of the Allied
Expeditionary Force, and General de Lattre de Tassigny will sign on
behalf of General Eisenhower.   Marshal Zhukov will sign on behalf of
the Soviet High Command.   The German representatives will be
Field-Marshal Keitel, Chief of the High Command, and the Commanders-
in-Chief of the German Army, Navy, and Air Forces.

Hostilities will end officially at one minute after midnight to-night
(Tuesday, May 8), but in the interests of saving lives the " Cease fire "
began yesterday to be sounded all along the front, and our dear
Channel Islands are also to be freed to-day.

The Germans are still in places resisting the Russian troops, but
should they continue to do so after midnight they will, of course,
deprive themselves of the protection of the laws of war, and will be
attacked from all quarters by the Allied troops.   It is not surprising
that on such long fronts and in the existing disorder of the enemy
the orders of the German High Command should not in every case
be obeyed immediately.   This does not, in our opinion, with the best
military advice at our disposal, constitute any reason for withholding
from the nation the facts communicated to us by General Eisenhower
of the unconditional surrender already signed at Rheims, nor should it
prevent us from celebrating to-day and to-morrow (Wednesday) as
Victory in Europe days.

To-day, perhaps, we shall think mostly of ourselves. To-morrow we shall pay a particular tribute to our Russian comrades, whose prowess in the field has been one of the grand contributions to the general victory.

The German war is therefore at an end. After years of intense preparation, Germany hurled herself on Poland at the beginning of September, 1939 ; and, in pursuance of our guarantee to Poland and in agreement with the French Republic, Great Britain, the British Empire and Commonwealth of Nations, declared war upon this foul aggression. After gallant France had been struck down we, from this Island and from our united Empire, maintained the struggle single-handed for a whole year until we were joined by the military might of Soviet Russia, and later by the overwhelming power and resources of the United States of America.

Finally almost the whole world was combined against the evil-doers, who are now prostrate before us. Our gratitude to our splendid Allies goes forth from all our hearts in this Island and throughout the British Empire.

We may allow ourselves a brief period of rejoicing ; but let us not forget for a moment the toil and efforts that lie ahead. Japan, with all her treachery and greed, remains unsubdued. The injury she has inflicted on Great Britain, the United States, and other countries, and her detestable cruelties, call for justice and retribution. We must now devote all our strength and resources to the completion of our task, both at home and abroad. Advance, Britannia. Long live the cause of freedom. God save the King.

GRATITUDE TO PARLIAMENT

After making his broadcast announcement of Germany's Unconditional Surrender, the Prime Minister read the same statement to the House of Commons a few minutes later, and added :

That is the message which I have been instructed to deliver to the British Nation and Commonwealth. I have only two or three sentences to add. They will convey to the House my deep gratitude to this House of Commons, which has proved itself the strongest foundation for waging war that has ever been seen in the whole of our long history. We have all of us made our mistakes, but the strength of the Parliamentary institution has been shown to enable it at the same moment to preserve all the title-deeds of democracy while waging war in the most stern and protracted form. I wish to give my hearty thanks to men of all Parties, to everyone in every part of the House where they sit, for the way in which the liveliness of Parliamentary institutions has been maintained under the fire of the enemy, and for the way in which we have been able to persevere—and we could have persevered much longer if need had been—till all the objectives which we set before us for the procuring of the unlimited and unconditional surrender of the enemy had been achieved. I recollect well at the end of the last war, more than a quarter of a century ago, that the House, when it heard the long list of the surrender terms, the armistice terms, which had been imposed upon the Germans, did not feel inclined for debate or business, but desired to offer thanks to Almighty God, to the Great Power which seems to shape and design the fortunes of nations and the destiny of man; and I therefore beg, Sir, with your permission to move :

" That this House do now attend at the Church of St. Margaret, Westminster, to give humble and reverent thanks to Almighty God for our deliverance from the threat of German domination."

This is the identical Motion which was moved in former times.

"THIS IS YOUR VICTORY"

DURING THE CELEBRATIONS WHICH FOLLOWED THE ANNOUNCEMENT
OF GERMANY'S UNCONDITIONAL SURRENDER THE PRIME MINISTER
MADE TWO SHORT SPEECHES FROM THE BALCONY OF THE MINISTRY OF
HEALTH BUILDING TO THE CROWDS IN WHITEHALL
MAY 8, 1945

[*May* 8, 1945.

GOD bless you all. This is your victory! It is the victory of
the cause of freedom in every land. In all our long history we
have never seen a greater day than this. Everyone, man or woman,
has done their best. Everyone has tried. Neither the long years, nor
the dangers, nor the fierce attacks of the enemy, have in any way
weakened the independent resolve of the British nation. God bless
you all.

[*May* 9, 1945.

MY dear friends, I hope you have had two happy days. Happy
days are what we have worked for, but happy days are not
easily worked for. By discipline, by moral, by industry, by good laws,
by fair institutions—by those ways we have won through to happy
days for millions and millions of people.

You have been attacked by a monstrous enemy—but you never
flinched or wavered.

Your soldiers were everywhere in the field, your airmen in the skies
—and never let us forget our grand Navy. They dared and they did
all those feats of adventure and audacity which have ever enabled
brave men to wrest victory from obstinate and bestial circumstances.
And you people at home have taken all you had to take—which was
enough, when all is said and done. You never let the men at the front
down. No one ever asked for peace because London was suffering.

London, like a great rhinoceros, a great hippopotamus, saying:
"Let them do their worst. London can take it." London could take
anything.

My heart goes out to the Cockneys. Any visitors we may happen
to have here to-day—and many great nations are represented here, by

129

[*May* 13, 1945.

IT was five years ago on Thursday last that His Majesty the King commissioned me to form a National Government of all parties to carry on our affairs. Five years is a long time in human life, especially when there is no remission for good conduct. However, this National Government was sustained by Parliament and by the entire British nation at home and by all our fighting men abroad, and by the unswerving co-operation of the Dominions far across the oceans and of our Empire in every quarter of the globe. After various episodes had occurred it became clear last week that so far things have worked out pretty well, and that the British Commonwealth and Empire stands more united and more effectively powerful than at any time in its long romantic history. Certainly we are—this is what may well, I think, be admitted by any fair-minded person—in a far better state to cope with the problems and perils of the future than we were five years ago.

For a while our prime enemy, our mighty enemy, Germany, overran almost all Europe. France, who bore such a frightful strain in the last great war, was beaten to the ground and took some time to recover. The Low Countries, fighting to the best of their strength, were subjugated. Norway was overrun. Mussolini's Italy stabbed us in the back when we were, as he thought, at our last gasp. But for ourselves—our lot, I mean—the British Commonwealth and Empire, we were absolutely alone.

In July, August and September, 1940, forty or fifty squadrons of British fighter aircraft in the Battle of Britain broke the teeth of the German air fleet at odds of seven or eight to one. May I repeat again the words I used at that momentous hour : " Never in the field of human conflict was so much owed by so many to so few.' The name of Air Chief Marshal Lord Dowding will always be linked with this splendid event. But conjoined with the Royal Air Force lay the Royal Navy, ever ready to tear to pieces the barges, gathered from the canals of Holland and Belgium, in which a German invading army could alone have been transported. I was never one to believe that the invasion of Britain, with the tackle that the enemy had at that time, was a very easy task to accomplish. With the autumn storms, the immediate danger of invasion in 1940 passed.

Then began the blitz, when Hitler said he would "rub out our cities." That's what he said, "rub out our cities." This blitz was borne without a word of complaint or the slightest sign of flinching, while a very large number of people—honour to them all—proved that London could "take it", and so could our other ravaged centres. But the dawn of 1941 revealed us still in jeopardy. The hostile aircraft could fly across the approaches to our Island, where forty-six millions of people had to import half their daily bread and all the materials they needed for peace or war : these hostile aircraft could fly across the approaches from Brest to Norway and back again in a single flight. They could observe all the movements of our shipping in and out of the Clyde and Mersey, and could direct upon our convoys the large and increasing numbers of U-boats with which the enemy bespattered the Atlantic— the survivors or successors of which U-boats are now being collected in British harbours.

The sense of envelopment, which might at any moment turn to strangulation, lay heavy upon us. We had only the North-Western approach between Ulster and Scotland through which to bring in the means of life and to send out the forces of war. Owing to the action of Mr. de Valera, so much at variance with the temper and instinct of thousands of Southern Irishmen who hastened to the battle-front to prove their ancient valour, the approaches which the Southern Irish ports and airfields could so easily have guarded were closed by the hostile aircraft and U-boats. This was indeed a deadly moment in our life, and if it had not been for the loyalty and friendship of Northern Ireland we should have been forced to come to close quarters with Mr. de Valera or perish for ever from the earth. However, with a restraint and poise to which, I say, history will find few parallels, His Majesty's Government never laid a violent hand upon them, though at times it would have been quite easy and quite natural, and we left the de Valera government to frolic with the Germans and later with the Japanese representatives to their heart's content.

When I think of these days I think also of other episodes and personalities. I think of Lieutenant-Commander Esmonde, V.C., of Lance-Corporal Kenneally, V.C., and Captain Fegen, V.C., and other Irish heroes that I could easily recite, and then I must confess that bitterness by Britain against the Irish race dies in my heart. I can only pray that in years which I shall not see the shame will be forgotten and the glories will endure, and that the peoples of the British Isles as of the British Commonwealth of Nations will walk together in mutual comprehension and forgiveness.

My friends, when our minds turn to the North-Western approaches, we will not forget the devotion of our merchant seamen, and our minesweepers out every night, and so rarely mentioned in the head-lines. Nor will we forget the vast, inventive, adaptive, all-embracing and, in the end, all-controlling power of the Royal Navy, with its ever more potent new ally, the air. These have kept the life-line open. We were able to breathe ; we were able to live ; we were able to strike. Dire deeds we had to do. We had to destroy or capture the French fleet which, had it ever passed undamaged into German hands, would, together with the Italian fleet, have perhaps enabled the German Navy to face us on the high seas. This we did. We had to make the dispatch to General Wavell all round the Cape, at our darkest hour, of the tanks—practically all we had in the Island—and this enabled us as far back as November, 1940, to defend Egypt against invasion and hurl back with the loss of a quarter of a million captives and with heavy slaughter the Italian armies at whose tail Mussolini had already planned to ride into Cairo or Alexandria.

Great anxiety was felt by President Roosevelt, and indeed by thinking men throughout the United States, about what would happen to us in the early part of 1941. The President felt to the depths of his being that the destruction of Britain would not only be an event fearful in itself, but that it would expose to mortal danger the vast and as yet largely unarmed potentialities and the future destiny of the United States. He feared greatly that we should be invaded in that spring of 1941, and no doubt he had behind him military advice as good as any that is known in the world, and he sent his recent Presidential opponent, the late Mr. Wendell Willkie, to me with a letter in which he had written in his own hand the famous lines of Longfellow, which I quoted in the House of Commons the other day.

We were, however, in a fairly tough condition by the early months of 1941, and felt very much better about ourselves than in those months immediately after the collapse of France. Our Dunkirk army and field force troops in Britain, almost a million strong, were nearly all equipped or re-equipped. We had ferried over the Atlantic a million rifles and a thousand cannon from the United States, with all their ammunition, since the previous June. In our munition works, which were becoming very powerful, men and women had worked at their machines till they dropped senseless from fatigue. Nearly one million of men, growing to two millions at the peak, although working all day, had been formed into the Home Guard. They were armed at least with rifles, and armed also with the spirit " Conquer or Die."

Later in 1941, when we were still alone, we sacrificed unwillingly, to some extent unwittingly, our conquests of the winter in Cyrenaica and Libya in order to stand by Greece ; and Greece will never forget how much we gave, albeit unavailingly, of the little we had. We did this for honour. We repressed the German-instigated rising in Iraq. We defended Palestine. With the assistance of General de Gaulle's indomitable Free French we cleared Syria and the Lebanon of Vichyites and of German aviators and intriguers. And then in June, 1941, another tremendous world event occurred.

You have no doubt noticed in your reading of British history— and I hope you will take pains to read it, for it is only from the past that one can judge the future, and it is only from reading the story of the British nation, of the British Empire, that you can feel a well-grounded sense of pride to dwell in these islands—you have sometimes noticed in your reading of British history that we have had to hold out from time to time all alone, or to be the mainspring of coalitions, against a Continental tyrant or dictator, and we have had to hold out for quite a long time : against the Spanish Armada, against the might of Louis XIV, when we led Europe for nearly twenty-five years under William III and Marlborough, and a hundred and fifty years ago, when Nelson, Pitt and Wellington broke Napoleon, not without assistance from the heroic Russians of 1812. In all these world wars our Island kept the lead of Europe or else held out alone.

And if you hold out alone long enough, there always comes a time when the tyrant makes some ghastly mistake which alters the whole balance of the struggle. On June 22, 1941, Hitler, master as he thought himself of all Europe—nay, indeed, soon to be master of the world, so he thought—treacherously, without warning, without the slightest provocation, hurled himself on Russia and came face to face with Marshal Stalin and the numberless millions of the Russian people. And then at the end of the year Japan struck a felon blow at the United States at Pearl Harbour, and at the same time attacked us in Malaya and Singapore. Thereupon Hitler and Mussolini declared war on the Republic of the United States.

Years have passed since then. Indeed every year seems to me almost a decade. But never since the United States entered the war have I had the slightest doubt but that we should be saved, and that we only had to do our duty in order to win. We have played our part in all this process by which the evil-doers have been overthrown, and I hope I do not speak vain or boastful words, but from Alamein in October, 1942, through the Anglo-American invasion of North Africa, of Sicily, of Italy, with the capture of Rome, we marched many miles and never knew defeat. And then last year, after two years' patient preparation and marvellous devices of amphibious warfare—and mark you, our scientists are not surpassed in any nation in the world, especially when their thought is applied to naval matters—last year on June 6 we seized a carefully-selected little toe of German-occupied France and poured millions in from this Island and from across the Atlantic, until the Seine, the Somme, and the Rhine all fell behind the advancing Anglo-American spearheads. France was liberated. She produced a fine army of gallant men to aid her own liberation. Germany lay open.

Now from the other side the mighty military achievements of the Russian people, always holding many more German troops on their front than we could do, rolled forward to meet us in the heart and centre of Germany. At the same time, in Italy, Field-Marshal Alexander's army of so many nations, the largest part of which was

British or British Empire, struck their final blow and compelled more than a million enemy troops to surrender. This Fifteenth Army Group, as we call it, British and Americans joined together in almost equal numbers, are now deep in Austria, joining their right hand with the Russians and their left with the United States armies of General Eisenhower's command. It happened, as you may remember—but memories are short—that in the space of three days we received the news of the unlamented departures of Mussolini and Hitler, and in three days also surrenders were made to Field-Marshal Alexander and Field-Marshal Montgomery of over two million five hundred thousand soldiers of this terrible warlike German army.

I shall make it clear at this moment that we never failed to recognize the immense superiority of the power used by the United States in the rescue of France and the defeat of Germany. For our part, British and Canadians, we have had about one-third as many men over there as the Americans, but we have taken our full share of the fighting, as the scale of our losses shows. Our Navy has borne incomparably the heaviest burden in the Atlantic Ocean, in the narrow seas and the Arctic convoys to Russia, while the United States Navy has had to use its immense strength mainly against Japan. We made a fair division of the labour, and we can each report that our work is either done or going to be done. It is right and natural that we should extol the virtues and glorious services of our own most famous commanders, Alexander and Montgomery, neither of whom was ever defeated since they began together at Alamein. Both of them have conducted in Africa, in Italy, in Normandy and in Germany, battles of the first magnitude and of decisive consequence. At the same time we know how great is our debt to the combining and unifying command and high strategic direction of General Eisenhower.

And here is the moment when I pay my personal tribute to the British Chiefs of the Staff, with whom I worked in the closest intimacy throughout these heavy, stormy years. There have been very few changes in this small, powerful and capable body of men who, sinking all Service differences and judging the problems of the war as a whole, have worked together in perfect harmony with each other. In Field-Marshal Brooke, in Admiral Pound, succeeded after his death by Admiral Andrew Cunningham, and in Marshal of the Air Portal, a team was formed who deserved the highest honour in the direction of the whole British war strategy and in its relations with that of our Allies.

It may well be said that our strategy was conducted so that the best combinations, the closest concert, were imparted into the operations by the combined staffs of Britain and the United States, with whom, from Teheran onwards, the war leaders of Russia were joined. And it may also be said that never have the forces of two nations fought side by side and intermingled in the lines of battle with so much unity, comradeship and brotherhood as in the great Anglo-American Armies. Some people say : Well, what would you expect, if both nations speak the same language, have the same laws, have a great part of their history in common, and have very much the same outlook upon life with all its hope and glory ? Isn't it just the sort of thing that would happen ? And others may say : It would be an ill day for all the world and for the pair of them if they did not go on working together and marching together and sailing together and flying together, whenever something has to be done for the sake of freedom and fair play all over the world. That is the great hope of the future.

There was one final danger from which the collapse of Germany has saved us. In London and the South-Eastern counties we have suffered for a year from various forms of flying-bombs—perhaps you have heard about this—and rockets, and our Air Force and our ack-ack batteries have done wonders against them. In particular the Air Force, turned on in good time on what then seemed very slight and doubtful evidence, hampered and vastly delayed all German preparations. But it was only when our Armies cleaned up the coast and overran all the points of discharge, and when the Americans captured vast stores of rockets of all kinds near Leipzig, which only the other day added to the information we had, and when all the preparations being made on the coasts of France and Holland could be examined in detail, in scientific detail, that we knew how grave had been the peril, not only from rockets and flying-bombs but from multiple long-range artillery which was being prepared against London. Only just in time did the Allied armies blast the viper in his nest. Otherwise the autumn of 1944, to say nothing of 1945, might well have seen London as shattered as Berlin.

For the same period the Germans had prepared a new U-boat fleet and novel tactics which, though we should have eventually destroyed them, might well have carried anti-U-boat warfare back to the high peak days of 1942. Therefore we must rejoice and give thanks, not only for our preservation when we were all alone, but for our timely deliverance from new suffering, new perils not easily to be measured.

I wish I could tell you to-night that all our toils and troubles were over. Then indeed I could end my five years' service happily, and if you thought that you had had enough of me and that I ought to be put out to grass, I tell you I would take it with the best of grace. But, on the contrary, I must warn you, as I did when I began this five years' task—and no one knew then that it would last so long—that there is still a lot to do, and that you must be prepared for further efforts of mind and body and further sacrifices to great causes if you are not to fall back into the rut of inertia, the confusion of aim, and the craven fear of being great. You must not weaken in any way in your alert and vigilant frame of mind. Though holiday rejoicing is necessary to the human spirit, yet it must add to the strength and resilience with which every man and woman turns again to the work they have to do, and also to the outlook and watch they have to keep on public affairs.

On the continent of Europe we have yet to make sure that the simple and honourable purposes for which we entered the war are not brushed aside or overlooked in the months following our success, and that the words " freedom," " democracy," and " liberation " are not distorted from their true meaning as we have understood them. There would be little use in punishing the Hitlerites for their crimes if law and justice did not rule, and if totalitarian or police governments were to take the place of the German invaders. We seek nothing for ourselves. But we must make sure that those causes which we fought for find recognition at the peace table in facts as well as words, and above all we must labour that the world organization which the United Nations are creating at San Francisco does not become an idle name, does not become a shield for the strong and a mockery for the weak. It is the victors who must search their hearts in their glowing hours, and be worthy by their nobility of the immense forces that they wield.

We must never forget that beyond all lurks Japan, harassed and failing but still a people of a hundred millions, for whose warriors death has few terrors. I cannot tell you to-night how much time or what exertions will be required to compel the Japanese to make amends for their odious treachery and cruelty. We—like China, so long undaunted —have received horrible injuries from them ourselves, and we are bound by the ties of honour and fraternal loyalty to the United States to fight this great war at the other end of the world at their side without flagging or failing. We must remember that Australia and New Zealand and Canada were and are all directly menaced by this evil Power. They came to our aid in our dark times, and we must not leave unfinished any task which concerns their safety and their future. I told you hard things at the beginning of these last five years ; you did not shrink, and I should be unworthy of your confidence and generosity if I did not still cry : Forward, unflinching, unswerving, indomitable, till the whole task is done and the whole world is safe and clean.

THE KING IN THE WAR

A SPEECH TO THE HOUSE OF COMMONS
MAY 15, 1945

[May 15, 1945.

I BEG to move,

" That an humble Address be presented to His Majesty as followeth :
    Most Gracious Sovereign,

We, Your Majesty's most dutiful and loyal subjects, the Commons
of the United Kingdom of Great Britain and Northern Ireland in
Parliament assembled, beg leave to convey to Your Majesty our
heartfelt congratulations on the victorious conclusion of the war in
Europe, and to assure Your Majesty of our resolute support in the
continuing war against Japan.

We rejoice with Your Majesty in the deliverance brought both to
this Nation and to the enslaved peoples of Europe by the success of
Your Majesty's Forces fighting in comradeship with those of Your
Majesty's Allies.

We would acknowledge the powerful help given without hesitation
and without stint to the common cause by the peoples of Your Empire
and Commonwealth of Nations overseas.

We would wish to express the deep feeling which exists throughout
the whole country that Your Majesty and Your gracious Consort have
from the beginning contributed in a wonderful manner to the courage
and constancy of the people by your inspiring example, by the extreme
personal exertions you have made year after year, by your willingness
to share all their trials, and your constant sympathy with them in the
losses which they have endured.

It is our earnest prayer that, under God's grace, the glorious victory
won in Europe may be followed by a speedy and successful conclusion
of the struggle against Japan, and that Your Majesty's reign, so many
years of which have been darkened by war and the threats of war, may
long continue in a world at peace."

It is fitting, and in accordance with the precedents, which I have
carefully consulted, that on emerging victorious from a great peril and
calamity, like the German war, we should express our sentiments of
gratitude and loyalty to the Sovereign. The King is the Commander
of all our Armed Forces, and is the symbol of the whole war effort of
the British Nation in the innumerable forms in which it has been

manifested by all his subjects, in their various posts and stations, according to their strength and opportunity. The King is also, since the Statute of Westminster, in a very special sense the constitutional link which joins us to the self-governing Dominions. He embodies a multiple Kingship unique in the world of to-day and, so far as I know, in the history of the past.

Of this multiple Kingship, we in these Islands, the Mother country, are but a single member, namely the United Kingdom of Great Britain and Northern Ireland; but it is a Kingship to which all the other Governments of the Empire feel an equal allegiance and an equal right. Governments so proud and independent that they would not brook the slightest sign of interference from this House, vie with each other, and with us, in their respect for the ancient and glorious institution of the British Monarchy. It is the golden circle of the Crown which alone embraces the loyalties of so many States and races all over the world. It is the symbol which gathers together and expresses those deep emotions and stirrings of the human heart which make men travel far to fight and die together, and cheerfully abandon material possessions and enjoyments for the sake of abstract ideas.

Woeful would it be in this modern age, were such forces to be used in a wrongful cause of greedy aggression, in a lust for conquest, or in a vain conceit of earthly grandeur. Glorious is it when all the mysterious powers of the British Commonwealth and Empire come together by a spontaneous impulse to face unmeasured and immeasurable dangers, when they fight for honour and win the fight. That is glorious indeed. It is at such moments that the House expresses its respect and its loyalty by formal and reasoned Resolution, not only for the institution of the Monarchy but for the person of the Sovereign who occupies the Throne. We are fortunate indeed that an office of such extraordinary significance should be filled by one who combines with an intense love of our country and of all his people a thorough comprehension of our Parliamentary and democratic Constitution. Well may it be said, well was it said, that the prerogatives of the Crown have become the privileges of the people.

Sincere affection, quite apart from constitutional respect, is given to King George VI from all parts of his Empire and Commonwealth. He is well beloved because of his courage, of his simple way of living, and of his tireless attention to duty.

I will give just one instance of many, but one which has been brought much before my eyes in my daily work. In all, 92,000 decorations have been awarded to those who have done brave or arduous service in this war. Of this great number of 92,000, over 37,000 have been personally presented to the recipients by the hands of His Majesty the King.

The continuous discharge of every function helpful to the peace and happiness of the country and to the prosecution of the war by the King and by the Royal Family has been long remarked and admired by people in all parts of the country engaged in all kinds of functions, and most especially those in the areas which have been shattered by the bombing of the enemy. His Majesty's visits to the battlefronts have involved his Royal person in that element of danger which cannot be divorced from travel by air, but we must also remember him as a sailor King who fought as a young officer in the greatest of all naval battles, the battle of Jutland. It would be altogether unfitting if I mentioned these personal aspects of His Majesty's work without referring also to his gracious Consort the Queen, who has been everywhere with him to scenes of suffering and disaster, to hospitals, to places shattered the day before by some devastating explosion, to see the bereaved, the sufferers and the wounded, and I am sure that many an aching heart has found some solace in her gracious smile.

I do not think that any Prime Minister has ever received so much personal kindness and encouragement from his Sovereign as I have. Every week I have my audience, the greater part of which occurs most agreeably at luncheon, and I have seen the King at close quarters in every phase of our formidable experiences. I remember well how in the first months of this administration the King would come in from practising with his rifle and his tommy-gun in the garden at Buckingham Palace, and if it had come to a last stand in London, a matter which had to be considered at one time, I have no doubt that His Majesty would have come very near departing from his usual constitutional rectitude by disregarding the advice of his Ministers.

It is in no perfunctory sense that we sing the National Anthem. We have a King and Queen well fitted to sit at the summit of all that the British nation stands for, and has largely achieved in these tremendous times.

I have only one more observation to make. If it be true, as has been said, that every country gets the form of government it deserves, we may certainly flatter ourselves. The wisdom of our ancestors has led us to an envied and enviable situation. We have the strongest Parliament in the world. We have the oldest, the most famous, the most honoured, the most secure and the most serviceable monarchy in the world. King and Parliament both rest safely and solidly upon the will of the people expressed by free and fair election on the basis of universal suffrage. Thus this system has long worked harmoniously both in peace and war, and I think that this is indeed a fitting occasion when we should give our wholehearted thanks to the Sovereign in the Resolution which has appeared upon the Paper and which I now, Mr. Speaker, have the honour to move.

CAMPAIGN STARS

A Speech to the House of Commons
May 18, 1945

May 14. *Declaration of the Independence of Austria was broadcast by Radio Austria.*

Dr. Emil Hacha, Nazi puppet President of Czechoslovakia, was arrested.

Americans launched heavy air-raids on Central and Southern Japan.

May 15. *It was announced that all trade, industries, man-power and food resources in Germany were being mobilized to feed and equip occupying armies.*

British carrier-borne aircraft again struck at Sakishima Islands south of Japan.

May 16. *6th Army in Austria linked up with the Russians.*

It was announced that Doenitz, Goering, Kesselring, Rundstedt and other German leaders had been removed to selected places pending their trials.

Mr. Bevin announced that 750,000 men would be released from war services by the end of the year.

May 17. *Total of German prisoners in the West stated to be 5,000,000.*

It was announced that six new Campaign Stars and a Defence Medal had been instituted by the King.

British warships were in action in the Straits of Malacca, and a 10,000 ton Japanese cruiser was sunk.

May 18. *America expressed willingness to relinquish part of U.S. zone of occupation in Germany to France.*

In the Pacific the Australians in Tarakan broke down Japanese resistance and advanced ten miles to the East coast.

[*May* 18, 1945.

THE House will have learned this morning of the new distinctions which have been created by His Majesty for service in the war. It is now some fourteen months since we debated this subject, and hon. Members will have noticed, in that interval, one or two events which seem to call for recognition.

The new Campaign Stars are six in number—the Atlantic Star, the

Air Crew Europe Star, the Italy Star, the France and Germany Star, the Pacific Star, and the Burma Star. They will commemorate the feats of arms, the endurance and the courage of our Forces by sea, land and air and our Merchant Navy in the main theatres of war. Two new stars for operations in the East will also mark the service of those who have gone out, or go out in the future, to finish the war against the Japanese.

The ribbons are now being woven with full priority, and issues will begin within a very short time. The stars have not been struck, but I will with Mr. Speaker's permission put a case containing all the ribbons in the Tea Room if it is thought that that would be of interest to Members who would like to see them. The troops are particularly pleased to be able to mount them.

The currency of the 1939-43 Star has been prolonged until this month, and the award will be described for the present as the " 1939-45 Star," that is to meet the time involved. At the same time His Majesty the King has approved the award of this Star and the African Star to the same individual. Hitherto only one or the other could be worn. The maximum number of stars granted to any one recipient will be five.

His Majesty has also instituted a gilt rose emblem to be worn on the ribbon of the 1939-45 Star for air-crews of fighter aircraft engaged in the Battle of Britain between July and 31st October, 1940. The ribbons of these Stars will be coming out now, but I cannot promise a date for the actual stars to be struck. They have been most carefully considered so that every difficulty that we can foresee has been dealt with. The matters were of extreme complication, but we have tried to meet all objections. No doubt there will be some improvements which can be suggested later, and I do not say that anything is absolutely final in the sense that a reasonably hard case could not conceivably be considered.

The Defence Medal is intended to recognize the service here of Forces from the Dominions which stood by us in a time of the gravest need, and it will also be awarded subject to a three-years qualification, to those citizens of this country who, during the years of danger, served here in the Forces, the Home Guard, the National Fire Service, the Police and Civil Defence. This medal will touch about 7,000,000 people, and recognizes the struggle against the enemy's air and bomb attacks.

His Majesty has given much time to the subject and has considered and designed all these ribbons himself, but, of course, on all questions likely to involve controversy, I am the responsible Minister. If there are any complaints, they should be addressed to me, and I shall be very ready to deal with them. Many of the decisions that have to be taken will undoubtedly raise points of difference, as there are always border-line cases. A substantial and complicated White Paper, every word of which has been the result of prolonged discussion by an expert committee, sitting through all these months, and on which all the Services have been represented, is now in the Vote Office.

The Home Guard will come in to the new Defence Medal. The Atlantic Star is

"intended to commemorate the Battle of the Atlantic, and is designed primarily for Convoys and their Escorts and Anti-Submarine Forces, as well as for fast Merchant ships that sailed alone. The Atlantic Star is to be granted for six months' service afloat, in the Navy, in the Atlantic and Home waters, since the 3rd September, 1939, and until the 8th May, 1945, the date of the end of active hostilities in Europe and the Atlantic."

It can be worn in addition to the 1939–45 Star.

Questioned regarding the services eligible for the Defence Medal, the Prime Minister said :

Among the services eligible are the following : Warden Service, Rescue Service, Decontamination Service, Report and Control Service, Messenger Service, Ambulance Service, First-Aid Service, Rest Centre Service, Emergency Food Service, Canteen Service, Emergency Information Service, Mortuary Service.

Questioned regarding the Women's Voluntary Services, the Prime Minister said :

Under head (p), will be seen

"Women's Voluntary Services for Civil Defence. Members of the W.V.S. may qualify if (a) they are enrolled in an eligible local authority Civil Defence Service, (b) they perform duties analogous to those of one of the eligible local authority Civil Defence Services, and the section of the W.V.S. to which they belong is one which functions operationally during or immediately after enemy attacks."

* * * * *

I think a matter which ought to be considered is the appointing of certain days when persons entitled to wear medals should wear them on their civilian clothes, certain days of ceremony and holiday ; otherwise in the case of those who have not uniforms it will hardly ever be known what they were. We must never forget that these medals are the poor man's escutcheon.

SYRIA AND LEBANON

A Statement to the House of Commons
June 5, 1945

May 19.	*Marshal Tito rejected the Anglo-American demand for his forces to leave Trieste.*
	Chinese recaptured port of Foochow.
May 20.	*Japanese installations on Formosa were bombed for the sixth successive day.*
	Yugoslav forces in Austria began to withdraw behind the Austrian-Yugoslav border.
May 21.	*U.S. First Army, under the command of General Hodges, began to leave Europe on its way to the Pacific.*
	Syria requested the Allies to evacuate their troops from Syria.
May 22.	*Field-Marshal Alexander and General Mark Clark arrived in Trieste. Field-Marshal Montgomery was appointed Commander in Chief of British Occupation Forces in Germany.*
May 23.	*Himmler committed suicide after being captured by the British Second Army.*
	Doenitz and others of the so-called " Flensburg Government " together with German High Command officers were arrested by orders of the Allied Supreme Commander.
	Admiral General von Friedeburg, who signed the German surrender to Montgomery, committed suicide.
	Julius Streicher, most notorious of Jew-baiters, was captured by the Americans.
	Super-fortresses dropped several thousand tons of incendiary bombs on Tokio.
	It was announced that Parliament would be dissolved on June 15, and that polling for the General Election would take place on July 5.
May 24.	*Field-Marshal Alexander established a military government in British-occupied Austria.*
	Bassein, a port 88 miles west of Rangoon, was reached by the 14th Army.
	It was announced that there was widespread devastation in Tokio following recent heavy raids.
May 25.	*Two American columns linked up on the Island of Mindanao, cutting the Island in two.*
	Switzerland decided to expel German Legation and Consular officials.

May 26. American super-fortresses continued their heavy raids on Tokio.

May 27. Chinese recaptured Nanning, a port on the Yu-Kiang river.

Dispute between French and the Syrians and Lebanese caused state of tension in Levant.

Field-Marshal Ritter von Greim, former head of Luftwaffe, committed suicide.

May 28. Japanese in Southern Okinawa made new withdrawals from Shuri. Yokohama, Japan's chief port, was bombed by 500 super-fortresses.

William Joyce (Lord Haw Haw), the radio traitor, was captured by the British in Germany.

Fighting broke out between Syrians and French troops.

May 29. U.S. troops occupied most of Naha, capital of Okinawa.

Mr. Eden, the Foreign Secretary, declared that the Syrian situation was dangerous.

May 30. Fighting between Syrians and French spread to Damascus.

It was announced that the Duke of Gloucester's Red Cross Fund had reached 50 millions and was to be closed.

May 31. British Government intervened in the Franco-Syrian dispute, and General de Gaulle was requested to withdraw all French troops.

It was announced that Britain's zone in occupied Germany would comprise Schleswig-Holstein, Hanover, Westphalia and the Rhine.

United Nations War Crimes Commission held its opening session in London.

June 1. President Truman announced that the U.S. Army in the Pacific would be doubled.

The S.E. Asia Command became all-British with the withdrawal of the American Air Force to other parts of the campaign against Japan.

A new British Army—the 12th Army—was formed based on Rangoon.

Fighting ceased in Damascus.

June 2. General de Gaulle alleged that Britain had stirred up trouble in Syria.

Japanese suffered another heavy defeat on the Irrawaddy in Burma.

June 3. 45 Japanese planes were shot down in attacks on Okinawa.

June 4. U.S. Marines made new landings on Okinawa and Australians began new drive in Southern Bougainville.

General Lindemann, German Commander-in-Chief in Denmark, was captured by the British.

June 5. General Eisenhower, Field-Marshal Montgomery, Marshal Zhukov and General de Lattre de Tassigny met in Berlin and issued a joint statement on the defeat of Germany and assumption of supreme authority.

Kobe, leading Japanese port, was attacked by superfortresses.

[*June 5, 1945.*

W HEN regrettable incidents like those in Syria occur between nations so firmly attached to one another as are the French and the British, and whose fortunes are so closely interwoven, it is nearly always a case of " the less said the better." On the other hand, I am assured that harm would be done by leaving some of the statements in General de Gaulle's speech to the Press of June 2 unanswered by His Majesty's Government ; and I feel also that the House of Commons would expect to be authoritatively informed.

The sense of General de Gaulle's speech was to suggest that the whole trouble in the Levant was due to British interference. I think the Foreign Secretary has already made it clear that so far from stirring up agitation in the Levant States our whole influence has been used in precisely the other direction.

The most strenuous and, I think, successful efforts have been made by His Majesty's Minister in Beirut to produce a calmer atmosphere in which negotiations could be conducted for a settlement of outstanding questions between France and the Levant States. I myself impressed upon the President of Syria most strongly the need for a peaceful settlement when I saw him in Cairo in February. We were successful in persuading the Levant States to open negotiations, which they had previously been unwilling to do. They asked the French for their proposals. That was last February. While General Beynet was still in Paris awaiting his instructions, it became known in the Levant in April that the French intended to send reinforcements. The Syrian and Lebanese Governments were greatly disturbed by the delay in receiving the French proposals, and also by the prospect of reinforcements arriving. We had already represented to the French Government that the arrival of reinforcements, however small, was bound to be misunderstood as a means of pressure in these negotiations and to have serious repercussions, but our representations did not meet with success.

On May 4, at the suggestion of the Foreign Secretary, I sent a friendly personal message to General de Gaulle, who had expressed to our Ambassador his concern as to our ultimate intentions in the Levant States. I explained, as I have done on many occasions, that we had absolutely no ambitions there of any kind. We want only to be treated just as any other country would be treated. We seek no territory or any kind of advantage there that is not given to all the other nations of the world. I also explained that we had recognized France's special position in the Levant. That does not mean that we undertake to enforce that special position. We shall be no obstacle to it, either at the council table or in any other way. But, I explained, our commitments and duties extended throughout the Middle East, where our main task was to ensure that Allied war communications were kept secure from interruption and disturbance. We could not, therefore, disregard events in the Levant States. His Majesty's Government had no designs against French interests in Syria and Lebanon and I was willing, I told General de Gaulle, to order a withdrawal of all British troops from Syria and the Lebanon the moment a treaty had been concluded and was in operation between the French Government and the Syrian and Lebanese Governments.

From this point of view, I expressed the opinion that it would be a great pity if the sending-in of reinforcements above those which were needed as replacements were to cause unrest or a rise of temperature. I urged that the reinforcing of French troops at this moment when the Levant States had been waiting for treaty proposals would give the impression that the French were preparing a settlement to be concluded under duress, and thus poison the atmosphere for the negotiations which were about to begin. General de Gaulle replied that General Beynet, the French Delegate-General, was returning with instructions to open negotiations, but made no reference to the question of French reinforcements. When these arrived, the effect was as we had feared and as we had warned him would be the case.

On May 12, General Beynet returned to Beirut and started his discussions with the Syrian and Lebanese Governments. They informed him that they were prepared to negotiate, but not if reinforcements arrived. In spite of this and of our representations—I might almost have said entreaties, because it would have been no exaggeration —French Forces began to arrive on May 17, and on account of that and because the Levant States considered that the French proposals went farther than they were prepared to discuss, the Syrian and Lebanese Governments broke off negotiations.

The internal situation became very tense. In the towns of Damascus, Beirut and Tripoli the bazaars and shops were closed on May 19, and there were demonstrations in Damascus involving some firing from the grounds of the French hospital. About a dozen people were injured, but none were killed. On the next day, May 20, a serious

British Official

Mr. Churchill views the ruins of Berlin. Accompanied by his daughter
Mary, he stands on the steps of the shattered Chancellery. A Russian officer
points out the landmarks

British Official

Mr. Churchill, across the Rhine, congratulates men of the 79th Armoured Division
on their fine work

British Official

On VE-Day Mr. Churchill addresses the vast crowd in Whitehall from a balcony
of the Ministry of Health.   On his right may be seen Mr. Bevin and Mr. Oliver
Lyttelton

riot took place at Aleppo. Three French soldiers were killed and some injured. French armoured cars entered the town and cleared the streets after a good deal of firing. It was estimated that at least ten civilians were killed and thirty injured. In all the main towns in Syria the bazaars remained closed for some days, and in Aleppo both the Syrian gendarmerie and the French troops patrolled the town. In the Lebanon the towns of Beirut and Tripoli re-opened their shops on May 23, after an appeal by the Lebanese Government to the population to carry on their business and to leave it to the Government to defend Lebanese independence.

Throughout these events we constantly counselled patience on both sides, and we were endeavouring to arrange diplomatic consultations in which the whole situation produced by the breakdown of negotiations could be discussed and if possible settled. The Syrian Government appealed earnestly to us to supply further arms for the gendarmerie to enable them to keep order in spite of the popular excitement. They could, they said, retain control of the situation provided the population were not unduly excited by too ostentatious French military precautions, and provided that the gendarmerie, who were becoming tired, were reinforced. Nevertheless the French authorities persisted in their objection to our supplying any further arms to the Syrian gendarmerie for their reinforcements, presumably because they were afraid they might be used against themselves. By May 24 the French had had to evacuate their troops from the citadel in Aleppo, but disorder was feared in the process, and the French General threatened to shell the town if any shot were fired.

On May 25 His Majesty's Minister was instructed by the Foreign Office to represent to the Syrian Government at once that it was essential that they should maintain control of the situation, especially at Homs and Hama, where great tension had developed. Strong representations were also made in Paris and to the French Embassy in London drawing attention to the extremely tense local situation, and urging that the French Government should suspend the dispatch of the contemplated further reinforcements. It was pointed out that French armoured-car and lorry patrols continued in the streets of Aleppo and Damascus, that aircraft were flying low over the mosques during the hour of prayer, and machine guns were prominently placed on the roofs of buildings. This naturally excited the population. We represented very strongly the unfortunate consequences which further disturbances might have in the Middle East as a whole, which incidentally would affect the communications of the war with Japan.

Serious fighting broke out in Hama on May 27. The gendarmerie, under the orders of the Syrian Government, at first protected the railway station from being interfered with, but were eventually overpowered. This was disappointing, as only the day before the British political officer had been able to arrange a meeting between the various parties, and a diminution of tension had ensued. I need not detail the spread of disorders, but on May 28 the Syrian Minister for Foreign Affairs informed His Majesty's Minister that events had overtaken him and he could no longer be responsible for internal security. At Homs and Hama there was shelling by the French, and the situation got quite out of hand. Disorders spread to Damascus, where French shelling began on the evening of May 29—into this open and crowded city—and continued off and on until the morning of May 31. The official casualty figures for Damascus are : Killed, gendarmes 80 ; civilians 400 ; seriously wounded, 500 ; injured 1,000. Those are, of course, approximate. The Foreign Secretary has already explained to the House how these very unfortunate events overtook our proposals for international discussion of the position, and how a tense situation was created throughout the Middle East, which made it inevitable for us to intervene to restore a situation which had got out of hand and might spread almost without limit.

I should like here to express my regret that the message to General de Gaulle informing him of our intervention reached him some three quarters of an hour after the Foreign Secretary had made his statement in the House. I need hardly say that no discourtesy was intended. I should also like to say that it was a pity that General de Gaulle did not see fit to inform His Majesty's Government of the instructions which, I understand, he has said were sent to General Beynet late on May 30 to cease fire. At the moment when we took our decision we had no reason to suppose that that was the case, and the shelling of Damascus was certainly continued on the morning of May 31.

I hope it will be clear from the information which has been given to the House that it is not true, as has been suggested, that we have endeavoured to stir up agitation, but that the very opposite is the truth. We have done our utmost to preserve calm, to prevent mis-understandings, and to bring the two sides together. My promise to General de Gaulle to withdraw all our troops as soon as satisfactory arrangements were made which would prevent disorder in Syria and the Lebanon was a serious step in policy, and ought completely to have removed from the French mind the idea that we wished to supplant them or steal their influence. We do not intend to steal the property of anybody in this war, though a caveat may be necessary in respect of foreign enemies, and that not for our own benefit. General de Gaulle also suggested that after the recent breakdown of negotiations disturbances were caused by bands armed with British weapons attacking isolated French posts. As the House has been informed by the Foreign Secretary, the Syrian gendarmerie and police were last year supplied, by agreement with the French, with some modern rifles and equipment.

I wish to make it clear here and now that until we had to intervene no arms were issued by us to the Syrians or Lebanese except by agreement with the French, although in the opinion of our military authorities the Syrian Government would have been better able to maintain order if more arms had been issued to their gendarmerie. For the sake of maintaining order we are now doing that. We have now issued some arms. It is unfortunately true that some 200 men of the 16th Arab Battalion of the Palestine Regiment were involved in minor disturbances in Beirut, the capital of Lebanon, on VE Day, which is a long time ago compared with these events, and the day after. There were a number of other disturbances in Beirut at that time, and it would be absurd to suggest that these incidents had the smallest connection with the subsequent serious disturbances in Syria. An immediate inquiry was held, and the unit concerned was withdrawn from the Levant States at once. There is no evidence at all to support the allegation that the men carried a Swastika flag.

Finally, I feel that I must answer the insinuation that the Member for Carlisle [Sir E. Spears] was recalled from his post as His Majesty's Minister at Beirut at the request of General de Gaulle. The reason for which he wished to relinquish his post, namely, to return to his Parliamentary duties before the General Election, was fully explained in communiqués issued at the time, and the suggestion that he was recalled to please General de Gaulle is entirely unfounded. I may say that he was selected by me a long time ago for this appointment in the Lebanon because, among other qualifications, he wears five wound stripes gained in his work as liaison officer between the French and British Armies during the last war. He is the last person on whom General de Gaulle should cast reflections, because he personally secured General de Gaulle's escape to England from Bordeaux in his motor car and airplane on June 18, 1940.

Our acceptance of the idea that there should be a conference between the British, United States and French Governments still stands, and we hope that it will not be cast aside. I have seen it stated that it should be a five-Power conference bringing in Russia and China. That would certainly cause a great deal of delay and require very careful consideration on many grounds. If there is anything to tell the House while it is in being, I shall certainly take advantage of any opportunity I may be given.

NEGOTIATIONS WITH VICHY

A Statement to the House of Commons
June 12, 1945

[*June* 12, 1945.

I RUN great risks, I am sure, in asking the indulgence of the House to make a statement, but this statement is on a question which, so far as I know, has nothing to do with controversial policy. Yet it is important that it should be answered in a way which will bring it to notice abroad in a manner which is desirable. This statement is made in answer to a Question in the name of the Member for Berwick and Haddington [Captain McEwen]:

> " To ask the Prime Minister if he will now make a statement on the negotiations which took place in 1940 between His Majesty's Government and the Vichy Government."

I think that it would be useful for me to give the House a brief account of the facts, in order to correct any misunderstandings which may have been caused by the very inaccurate reports which have been published on this subject. After the withdrawal of the French Ambassador from London in 1940, His Majesty's Government sought to maintain contact with Marshal Pétain and his Ministers through less direct channels, in the hope of encouraging them to keep up a maximum of passive resistance to the enemy. To this end a series of messages were exchanged with the Vichy Administration during the autumn of 1940, through the British and French representatives at a neutral capital.

The object of the exchanges was to obtain assurances from Vichy that they would not surrender the French Fleet to the Germans, nor allow the Germans to obtain control of French overseas territory, nor themselves attack the French Colonies which had rallied to General de Gaulle. We explained that, if such assurances were forthcoming, we should be prepared to negotiate a *modus vivendi* whereby limited trade would be permitted through the blockade between Metropolitan France and the African territories under Vichy control. In the event nothing came of these proposals. The replies to our approaches were unsatisfactory, and it soon became clear that Vichy was too much under German duress to be able to give adequate assurances on the points in question, or to carry them out if given.

In October, 1940, an emissary from Vichy, who represented himself

NEGOTIATIONS WITH VICHY, JUNE 12, 1945

as acting on the personal instructions of Marshal Pétain, got in touch with the British authorities, and was brought to London, where he saw me and the then Foreign Secretary, Lord Halifax. This emissary did not, however, come with any specific mission, and the object of his visit seems primarily to have been to gauge the state of opinion in this country and the prospects of our continued resistance to the enemy. He brought with him no proposals for an agreement, and no agreement was in fact ever concluded with the Vichy Administration, either through this emissary or through any other channel. This reply which I have made has a reference to proceedings which are taking place in France against certain individuals.

Americans who have reached our shores and dwelt a considerable time among us. We honour him very much for his invariable consideration of the British point of view, for his impartial treatment of all the officers under his command. I know he will tell you when he rises that he never gave an order to a British officer which he could not immediately obey.

We also have made our contribution to the battles on the Continent, and I am quite sure that the influence he will wield in the world will be one always of bringing our countries together in the much more difficult task of peace, in the same way as he brought them together in the grim and awful cataclysm of war. I have had personal acquaintance with him now for three years. It is not much, but three years of this sort may seem five-and-twenty. I feel we have here a great creative, constructive and combining genius, one from our sister nation across the ocean, one who will never speak evil but will always cherish his contact with the British people, and to whom I feel we should at this moment give the most cordial testimony in our power of our admiration, of our affection, and of our heartfelt good wishes for everything that may happen to him in the future.

ANSWERS IN THE HOUSE OF COMMONS

APRIL, MAY, JUNE

WOMEN'S LAND ARMY

Questioned regarding the decision not to pay war gratuities to the
Women's Land Army and also about the shortage of agricultural workers,
the Prime Minister said on April 10 :

THE request for more women's labour, which is very necessary on
the land, should be accompanied by conditions governing the
future and not necessarily by gratuities or rewards which have relation
to the past.   With regard to the 135 Members who have put down their
names on this question, nothing would be easier, and, if I were so base,
nothing more tempting, than to offer large and unconsidered concessions
at the public expense.

I have looked around carefully for something that would be suitable
and would not open too wide a door, but one must be very careful, in
a Parliament which is in its closing phase, not to embark on a com-
petition for winning popularity for any party, without due regard to
the public and financial consequences.

The principle of division is that the Women's Land Army fell into
the general industrial sphere.   We may be wrong, but we have taken
it up.   One hundred Members have put their names to a statement
that we are wrong, but probably we have a majority which thinks
we are right.   I do not know.   But naturally the future is a separate
topic from the past.   In the future, if women are needed on the land
the necessary attractions must be offered to secure their supply.

EVACUATED LONDONERS

Asked to give advice to evacuees from Greater London living in the
country and looking forward to returning home, the Prime Minister
said on April 12 :

My earnest and urgent advice is that all the half-million Londoners
who are now accommodated in the reception areas under the Government Evacuation Scheme should stay where they are for the present.
As soon as the time is ripe, they will be told of the Government's
organized arrangements for their return in comfort and with all due
speed.   In view of the great number of bomb-damaged houses in the
London area which have still to be made habitable, these arrangements

157

will provide that evacuees who have no proper home to go ba
should remain in the reception areas until they can be rehoused.
confident that the kindly hosts and hostesses of the reception
will readily continue, even after V.E. day, to give hospitality to
less mothers and children, aged, and infirm from our invincible Lo

Asked whether " V.E. Day " was " basic English " for " Vic
Europe," Mr. Churchill said :

It is a term that has crept in, without careful consideration
exact origin, and also without any precise or accurate definit
what it will imply or when it will come.

GERMAN SURRENDER

When an M.P. drew attention to a statement by General Eis
to the effect that it was probable there would never be a clean cut
surrender of the German forces, and that V-Day would come a
proclamation, and that this meant that the policy of unconditional s
was unworkable, the Prime Mini ter said on April 12 :

The policy of unconditional surrender does not exclude uncond
surrender piecemeal. It does not necessarily apply wholesale.

CONCENTRATION CAMPS

Asked to make a statement regarding the German prison ca
Prime Minister said on April 19 :

No words can express the horror which is felt by His M
Government and their principal Allies at the proofs of these fr
crimes now daily coming into view.

I have this morning received an informal message from
Eisenhower saying that the new discoveries, particularly at W
far surpass anything previously exposed. He invites me to
body of Members of Parliament at once to his Headquarters i
that they may themselves have ocular and first-hand proof o
atrocities.

The matter is one of urgency, as of course it is not possible t
the processes of decay in many cases. In view of this urgency,
come to the conclusion that eight Members of this House a
Members of the House of Lords, should form a Parliamentary
tion, and should travel out at once to the Supreme Headquarters
General Eisenhower will make all the necessary arrangements f
inspection of the scenes, whether in American or British
Members who volunteer for this extremely unpleasant but n
less necessary duty should give their names to their Party W

order that a body representative of all Parties may be selected by the usual methods during this afternoon. I should propose that they should start to-morrow.

I hope that the House will approve of the somewhat rapid decision I have taken.

CARE OF PRISONERS

Asked to confirm that the Allied warning to Germany about the care of prisoners extended to all prisoners in Nazi hands of whatever race or origin, and in particular Stateless Jews and German and Austrian political prisoners, the Prime Minister said on April 26 :

The Allied warning to Germany about the care of prisoners is not in principle limited to Allied prisoners of war, internees and deported citizens of the United Nations. Its scope extends to all prisoners in Nazi hands, of whatever race, origin or religion, including Stateless Jews and German and Austrian political prisoners who have suffered as a result of sympathy with or activities on behalf of the cause for which the United Nations are fighting. His Majesty's Government, in common with other Governments of the United Nations, have repeatedly declared their intention to hold enemy authorities responsible for the maltreatment of persons who have been imprisoned on grounds of race and religion.

I must add that in framing this answer I have not had time to consult other Allied Governments upon its actual terms. But I cannot conceive there is the slightest difference between us on the main principles.

V.E. CELEBRATIONS

Asked whether it would not be wrong to celebrate the forthcoming victory over Germany when fighting was still going on in Burma, the Prime Minister said on April 26 :

It would be very foolish to have any celebrations or speeches made or joy-bells rung about the defeat of Germany—after all, a considerable event—without at the same time public men of every party making it perfectly clear that our war with Japan goes forward.

ROCKET ATTACKS

On April 26 the Prime Minister was asked whether he was now able to make any statement with regard to the enemy rocket attacks, and he replied :

Yes, Sir. They have ceased.

When the questioner then asked whether there was any prospect of their resumption, Mr. Churchill said :

It is my duty to record facts rather than indulge in prophecy, but I have recorded certain facts with a very considerable air of optimism, which I trust will not be brought into mockery by events.

When another member suggested that congratulations should be offered to the R.A.F. for stopping these bombs, Mr. Churchill said :

We must offer them to the Royal Air Force for what they did, we must offer them to the Anti-aircraft gunners for what they did, but we must not forget it was the British Armies that took the sites.

LIBERATED POLES

Asked to ensure that no liberated Polish prisoners would be returned to their country against their will, the Prime Minister said on May 1 :

The large numbers of Polish prisoners liberated by the advance of the Allied armies are being given shelter and maintenance under the authority of the Supreme Commander-in-Chief at various centres set up for their reception. They will continue to be cared for in this way so long as conditions make it impracticable or undesirable for them to be repatriated or otherwise provided for. The matter is one for inter-Allied discussion, but I cannot conceive that Poles in danger of reprisals would be sent back to Poland against their will. I trust, however, that the conditions which will be created in Poland as the result of the inevitable further discussion on this subject between the Great Allies will be such that the numbers failing to return to their native land may be very few.

GERMANS IN CIVILIAN CLOTHES

Asked why the German delegates who signed the unconditional surrender in Italy were permitted to sign in civilian clothes, the Prime Minister said on May 10 :

The German officers who signed the surrender of the 22 German Divisions and six Italian Fascist Divisions in Italy had to travel through Switzerland, and therefore had to be dressed as civilians.

A member then asked " Does not the right hon. Gentleman consider the transfer of the major part of the German population from uniformed activity to civilian work in civilian clothing one of the major objectives of the war ? " and the Prime Minister replied :

It might be one of the indirect results, but it certainly was not presented to the public here as a major objective.

The spectacles which are witnessed in Germany of the frightful destruction of all the towns and cities and so on should be in themselves considerable arguments to the German people in favour of the fact that they have suffered some military reverses.

T.U.C. AT SAN FRANCISCO

Asked to define the exact status of the Trades Union Congress delegation at San Francisco, the Prime Minister said on May 2:

The Trades Union Congress has no official status at the Conference, which is between representatives of Governments. The United Kingdom delegation, which includes representatives of the political Labour movement in this country, will of course take advantage of the presence of British Trade Union leaders in San Francisco to consult them as and when necessary on Labour matters that may arise during the Conference.

We have all got along pretty well together in this hard war ; we owe an immense debt to the Trade Unions, and never can this country forget how they have stood by and helped. At the same time, I personally do not feel that we should, without very much careful Parliamentary consideration, set up other bodies besides the official bodies which are based upon Ministries responsible to the House of Commons.

I earnestly hope that the closest consultation will be maintained, but to give official status is quite different. I stand on the basis of a universal suffrage electorate, and a House of Commons elected by them.

T.U.C. AT SAN FRANSCISO (2)

Asked whether the same principles of consultation as those enjoyed by the T.U.C. would be enjoyed by representatives of employers, the Prime Minister said :

No, Sir. I think the cases are different.

I should be sorry to have to embark upon an argument, but I do not consider that a world-wide employers' organization would stand on the same footing as an organization which has to consider maintaining all the necessary rights and interests of the labouring masses throughout the world.

THOSE WHO DESERTED

Asked to review and remit some of the long sentences being served by Servicemen for offences committed while serving abroad, the Prime Minister said on May 15 :

No, Sir, I do not think this is the time to reconsider punishments inflicted upon people who deserted their comrades and forced their places to be taken in battle, and danger and losses to be sustained, by gallant men who did not flinch.

POPULARITY-HUNTING

Asked if the Government intended to revise the regulations governing Service disability or dependants' pensions prior to the General Election, the Prime Minister said on May 15 :

Sir, I trust there will be no popularity-hunting at the public expense on this or kindred subjects. War Pensions were comprehensively reviewed in July, 1943, when a number of major improvements both as to the scope and amounts were made. From time to time since then other changes have been made, and the system will continue to be adjusted as and when required.

TASKS AHEAD

Asked if he proposed to hold formal victory parades before the end of the Japanese war, the Prime Minister said on May 15 :

No, Sir. Our brief rejoicings and celebrations are over, and we must now turn again to many difficult and unpleasant tasks, including, especially, the defeat of Japan.

ADMINISTRATION OF GERMANY

Asked to ensure that Germans would be entrusted only with regional government and not central government in Germany, the Prime Minister said on May 16 :

I am not sure whether any machinery of government, whether central or regional, can be said to exist at present in Germany, and in any case I should prefer, in replying to this Question, to speak of administration rather than government. In general it is our aim that Germans should administer their country in obedience to Allied directions. We have no intention of undertaking the burden of administering Germany ourselves.

WAR CRIMINALS TRIALS

About to make a statement regarding the trials of war criminals, the Prime Minister circulated the following with the Official Report, May 29, 1945 :

Under the terms of the Moscow Declaration on German Atrocities, published on 1st November, 1943, those major war criminals whose crimes have no particular geographical localization will be punished by a joint decision of the Governments of the Allies, and discussions are at present in active progress with a view to deciding on the best procedure.

As regards criminals who are accused of having taken part in specific war crimes against Allied nationals, the Moscow Declaration laid down that they should be sent back to the countries in which their offences were committed, in order that they might be judged and punished there by the Governments concerned. So far as regards those who have been guilty of crimes against British subjects, the procedure is that the charges brought against them are examined by the United Kingdom National Office, of which the Treasury Solicitor is the head, and submitted by him to the War Crimes Commission. The Judge-Advocate-General will be responsible for the collection of evidence against these criminals and their prosecution before military courts. The Attorney-General exercises a supervisory role in matters relating to war crimes which concern His Majesty's Government, and, in particular, in prosecutions against persons who have committed alleged war crimes against British subjects. His fiat is required for any such prosecutions. In addition, he has been appointed as the United Kingdom representative for the prosecution of such war criminals as may be brought before the proposed Inter-Allied Military Tribunal.

The functions of the United Nations War Crimes Commission were described by the Lord Chancellor in his speech in another place on 7th October, 1942, when he proposed the establishment of this body. The Commission is principally concerned with the drawing-up of lists of persons alleged to have committed war crimes, on the basis of material which is normally submitted to it by the various National Offices of the Allies represented upon it. Arrangements are being made for these lists to be forwarded to Allied commanders in the field, and the lists will, I am sure, prove of very considerable use to them in ensuring that all these criminals are detained as a preliminary to their appropriate disposal.

The Allied Control Commission will, when established, be generally responsible for the administration of justice in Germany, but it is not at present envisaged that Control Commission courts will deal with war crimes against British subjects.

HANOVER

Asked whether, as other members of the United Nations were taking steps to ensure strategic control of the approaches to their countries, consideration would be given to the safeguarding of the United Kingdom by retaking the former Kingdom of Hanover, the Prime Minister said on May 29 :

No, Sir. We are not seeking to enlarge our bounds as a result of this war. We have fought it for great principles, and in the satisfaction of those principles we shall find our reward.

EMPIRE CASUALTIES

Asked to state the total British casualties during the war compared with those suffered in the 1914–1918 war, the Prime Minister said on May 29 :

The total casualties suffered by the Armed Forces of the British Commonwealth and Empire in the present war, as reported from 3rd September, 1939, to the end of February, 1945, a total of 66 months, were 1,128,315, of which 307,201 were deaths. In the first Great War the total casualties suffered by the British Commonwealth and Empire Forces in 52 months were 3,286,090 of which 996,230 were deaths. It should, however, be borne in mind that in this present war the following additional losses have been inflicted upon the civil population of Great Britain by the enemy bombardment, namely : killed, 60,585 ; seriously injured, 86,175. I cannot give the precise figures for the slightly injured, but they are upwards of 150,000.

WAR MEDALS

Asked to extend the award of the 1939–45 Star to Anti-Aircraft personnel who were operationally engaged in the defence of Britain, the Prime Minister said on May 30 :

No, Sir, the Defence Medal is to be granted in recognition of such service in the United Kingdom.

When the questioner said there should be a distinction between A.A. men and members of the civilian services, Mr. Churchill said :

The losses in the Fire Service were many times higher than those in Anti-Aircraft Command. I do not think this is a case for making particular trouble. I should have liked very much to make some particular distinction for Anti-Aircraft Command, but that, as I have said before, involves bringing in enormous other numbers. Whatever Anti-Aircraft Command gets, the air ground staffs, running into 700,000, require, and before you know where you are the number has reached a million. We have tried to cater for all these millions by the Defence Medal. If we now pick out any special honour for Anti-Aircraft Command, that will open the whole question again. I only wish that we could meet the case, perhaps by more small badges and so forth, but I am very much afraid of opening again the floodgates, and having to begin again from where we started.

TANKS ON VIEW

Asked to arrange for an inspection by M.P.s of German, American and British tanks, the Prime Minister said on May 31 :

Yes, Sir. The exhibition will be ready in ten days or a fortnight. The Tiger and the Panther could be shown. There is only one Royal

Tiger at present in the country, and it has been damaged. In various respects it is not complete. It is doubtful whether it can be made a showpiece. The following British and American tanks could be shown : Sherman ; Sherman 17-pounder ; Churchill A. 22 ; Cromwell A. 27 ; Comte ; a Centurion A. 41 could also be shown. It is on the secret list, but it is not likely to be used in the immediate future. I have asked the War Office to make special efforts to exhibit the Royal Tiger.

EUROPEAN RELIEF

Asked to establish an Allied Committee composed of Ministers of Cabinet rank empowered to co-ordinate the activities of the various organizations, national and international, concerned with relief measures in Europe, the Prime Minister said on May 31 :

The United Nations Relief and Rehabilitation Administration is already charged, under the terms of the Agreement signed at Washington on 9th November, 1943, by all the United Nations, with the duty of co-ordinating relief measures, though its power to do so is of course subject to the consent of the member Governments concerned. The Council which controls the policy of this international body consists of representatives of the United Nations, most of whom are of rank corresponding to that of Cabinet Ministers. It is the Committee of the Council for Europe which meets in London which is specially concerned with relief measures in Europe. The administration maintains close touch with the Allied military authorities, and endeavours to combine its relief measures with theirs. No useful purpose would appear to be served by attempting to set up another Allied Committee for the same purpose.

Another member asked what Government Departments were concerned with European relief and what were the arrangements for ensuring co-ordination with other countries, Mr. Churchill replied :

The principal responsibility in these matters lies with the Foreign Office, the War Office and the Ministry of Production. Their action and that of other Departments concerned is co-ordinated in the normal way, by means of Cabinet Committees and otherwise. The combined organizations include the Combined Boards, the United Nations Relief and Rehabilitation Administration, the Provisional Executive for European Inland Transport, the United Nations Maritime Authority, the European Coal Organization, and the Emergency Economic Committee for Europe. The Emergency Economic Committee for Europe, which held its first meeting on 28th May, will also, where appropriate, concert the action of specialist organizations in the European field.

ENERGETIC IMAGINATION

When, at the end of a series of questions about the policy of the Control Commission for German industry, Mr. Ernest Bevin asked whether one remark by the Prime Minister was a suggestion that his late colleagues who had left his Government had shown private papers to persons outside. Mr. Churchill replied on June 5 :

I cannot conceive, even by the most energetic exercise of my imagination, how any such train of thought could have arisen in my right hon. Friend's mind.

WARSHIPS FOR RUSSIA

Asked to give information as to the transfer of vessels from the British Navy to the Red Fleet, the Prime Minister said on June 5 :

After the Italian Fleet had surrendered, the Soviet Government raised with the Governments of the United Kingdom and the United States the question of handing over to the Soviet Government a number of Italian warships and merchant ships. The Soviet Government represented that they had waged war against Italy in alliance with His Majesty's Government and the United States Government, and that the Soviet Navy would make good use of any ships so handed over for prosecuting the war against the principal enemy, Nazi Germany.

The ships for which the Soviet Government asked were :

1 Battleship
1 Cruiser
8 Destroyers
4 Submarines
40,000 tons of merchant shipping.

These ships the United Kingdom and United States Governments agreed, at the Teheran Conference, should be made available to the Soviet Navy.

His Majesty's Government later pointed out however that the Italian ships were built to sail in the temperate waters of the Mediterranean, and were unsuitable for immediate service in the severe climate of the Northern Seas where the Soviet Government proposed to employ them. It had moreover to be borne in mind that the Italian Navy had sailed forth from their ports to join the Allies in defiance of German orders, that they were pursued by aircraft and suffered losses in vessels and personnel, including one modern capital ship. Their surrender was received by Admiral Sir Andrew Cunningham in Malta harbour, and must be considered an honourable naval event. The accession of the Italian Fleet to the naval forces of the Allies was, at that time, definitely helpful. Some served in the Mediterranean as warships, others as warship transports, and a good deal of valuable work was done by them. They also served in the Indian Ocean and on anti-blockade runner patrols in the Atlantic. Their dockyards rendered important service.

The question then arose of how to meet the very reasonable and natural request of Soviet Russia. His Majesty's Government did not wish to see Italy, at that moment, deprived of its Navy, which was an essential part of the national life we were resolved to preserve. We therefore proposed that the request of Soviet Russia for this share of the Italian Navy should be met by the United States and Great Britain. Accordingly it was further agreed that the Italian ships should, for the time being, continue to serve the Allied cause, which they had done with discipline and vigour, and that an equivalent number of British or American warships and merchant ships should be delivered to the Soviet Navy on temporary loan. This leaves the issue of the disposition of the Italian Navy to the Peace Conference, which I hope will take place some time or other, it being quite usual that wars should be followed by Peace Conferences.

The following action was therefore taken. Half the merchant shipping and all the warships, with the exception of the United States cruiser *Milwaukee*, were provided by His Majesty's Government. The British warships handed over to the Soviets were the battleship *Royal Sovereign*, eight ex-American (" Town " Class) destroyers and four modern submarines. A further non-operational " Town " Class destroyer was made available to provide spare parts.

The Russian sailors came to the United Kingdom in the spring of 1944, and spent some weeks here working-up the ships preparatory to taking them to North Russia. When this important Fleet of 13 vessels sailed into the Russian harbour of Murmansk, a good impression was made upon our Soviet ally, and I received a message of thanks from Marshal Stalin himself. I feel bound to state that I take full responsibility for this transaction. The units of the Royal Navy have since then been operating as part of the Red Fleet. The destroyer *Churchill* and submarine *Sunfish* have been lost on active service, and the remaining ships will continue on loan to the Soviet Government until otherwise agreed between the two Governments.

These would not be vessels that we should use in the war against Japan. Admittedly, they are of an older type, and we send to the other side of the world only the best and newest ships, because the cost and difficulties of maintaining them there make it worth while to send only the best and newest, and the Americans would not thank us if we brought older vessels. On the other hand, I could not think of anything so ungracious at this moment as to suggest to the Soviet

Government by withdrawing these vessels that we had any objection whatever to their having a fleet and training their men for a powerful fleet and an adequate mercantile marine free to traverse all the oceans of the world.

All the actions which I have taken are War Cabinet decisions, and when I was ill at Marrakesh I telegraphed this project home to my colleagues and they all accepted the proposal; but as I was the principal inaugurator of it, and as it seemed to be coming under question, I thought I would say that I would take responsibility on account of my prominence in the matter. But my colleagues are equally bound with me in this, which was a very serious step, involving the transfer of so many of His Majesty's ships; and as the House has taken it so well, I invite former colleagues on the opposite Bench to share the credit.

The following are the details of the ships transferred:

Battleship—
H.M.S. Royal Sovereign .. .. 29,150 tons
Destroyers—
H.M.S. Brighton .. .. ..
,, Chelsea .. .. ..
,, Churchill .. .. ..
,, Georgetown .. .. Town class
,, Leamington .. .. 1,090 tons
,, Richmond .. .. ..
,, Rosborough .. ..
,, St. Albans .. .. ..
Destroyer—
(non-operational)
H.M.S. Lincoln
Submarines—
H.M.S. Sunfish .. .. .. 768 tons
,, Unbroken .. .. ..
,, Unison .. .. .. } 646 tons
,, Ursula .. .. ..

In addition to the warships, 20,000 tons of merchant shipping was also transferred.

SCOTTISH CASUALTIES

Asked the number of Scottish casualties since 3rd September, 1939, the Prime Minister said on June 5:

A great deal of time and trouble would be required to make an exact analysis of the Scottish casualties. They served in many regiments and divisions besides those of their own countrymen, and many Scottish regiments contained a large proportion of English. We have not got a foundation list of soldiers by birth, but only by residence. Surely it is enough to say that no more splendid record exists than that of the Scottish nation in this war, although one might sometimes have a word for London and a few other places in England, Wales and Northern Ireland.

I should be the last to wish to keep under a leaf the glories of Scotland, but I cannot undertake, without careful consideration, to attempt to make these very difficult analyses of race. Suffice it to say that they have been the first, or among the first, in every famous engagement.

SHORT OF—TIME

When a member suggested that a White Paper should be issued to give an account of the work of our forces in North-West Germany, as the public was anxious to know what was being done there, the Prime Minister said on June 7:

We were for a very long period short of white paper, and now we are very short of time.

COMPASSIONATE RELEASES

Asked to modify the regulations whereby serving personnel granted compassionate temporary release were made to extend their subsequent service beyond their normal release date, the Prime Minister said on June 7:

No, Sir. Where a man has private troubles, or important business affairs, and is sent back and has special leave, while so many others who have been out longer than he has are longing to get home, I do not see why that specially advanced and specially cherished additional emergency compassionate leave should be deducted from the total time which the man has to serve.

SECRET AGREEMENTS

Asked to assure the House of Commons that no secret engagements were entered into at Yalta or Teheran, the Prime Minister said on June 7:

I cannot give a guarantee that the newspaper reporters were there all the time.

Certainly there were no secret engagements entered into there at all, except that we kept secret the addition of two members of Russia, Byelo-Russia and the Ukraine. That was kept secret at the desire of the United States, so that the President could get home and make the necessary arrangements on the spot. Otherwise, there were no secret engagements, but the conversations, of course, proceeded in a very intimate manner, and I am not prepared to say that everything discussed at Yalta could be made the subject of a verbatim report.

I do not accept the view that it is absolutely necessary that there should never be on any occasion a secret clause in some arrangement, provided that is reported to a wide Cabinet. It may very often be necessary to do so. It would hamper very much the whole proceedings if no understanding could be made which had not to be immediately published. I should not approve of that myself, although I know that a lot of claptrap is talked about it.

MESSAGES

APRIL, MAY, JUNE, JULY

THE ALLIED LINK-UP

A message on the occasion of the meeting in Germany of the Allied
Forces from East and West. April 27, 1945.

After long journeys, toils, and victories across the lands and oceans,
across so many deadly battlefields, the armies of the great Allies have
traversed Germany and have joined hands together. Now their task
will be the destruction of all remnants of German military resistance,
the rooting-out of the Nazi power, and the subjugation of Hitler's
Reich. For these purposes ample forces are available, and we meet
in true and victorious comradeship and with inflexible resolve to
fulfil our purpose and our duty. Let all march forward upon the foe.

LIBERATION OF ITALY

A message to Signor Bonomi, the Prime Minister of Italy. May 3,
1945.

On the occasion of the surrender of the German armed forces in
Italy, I send your Excellency, on behalf of His Majesty's Government
in the United Kingdom, a message of warm congratulation on the
final liberation of Italian territory from our common enemy, and in
particular on the part played by the Italian regular forces and patriots
behind the lines.

The knowledge that they have contributed to this unprecedented
victory and have materially accelerated the cleansing of their country's
soil will, I trust, be a source of strength to the Italian people in the
no less strenuous days which lie ahead. It is a matter for great
satisfaction to His Majesty's Government, as it will undoubtedly be to
your Excellency's Government, that the defeat of the German armies
in North Italy should have been accomplished with so little human
suffering, and with relatively little damage to the material resources of
that part of your country.

I extend to your Excellency the good wishes of His Majesty's Government for the great work of reconstruction which now faces the Italian
Government and people.

I look forward to the time, which cannot be long delayed, when
Italy, whose forces have co-operated in war with those of the United
Nations, will work with the United Nations in the more fruitful labours
of peace.

VICTORY

THE BURMA STAR

A message to Admiral Lord Louis Mountbatten, Supreme Allied Commander, South-East Asia, on the victory in Burma. May 10, 1945.

I send you my most heartfelt congratulations upon the culminating victory at Rangoon of your Burma campaigns.

The hard fighting at Imphal and Kohima in 1944 prepared the way for the brilliant operations conducted over a vast range of territory which have crowned the exertions of the South-East Asia Command in 1945.

When these matters were considered at Quebec last September, it was thought both by your High Command and by the combined Chiefs of Staffs, reporting to the President and me, that about six British and British Indian divisions, together with much shipping and landing-vessels, all of which and more were asked for by you, would be required for enterprises less far-reaching than those you and your gallant forces and allies have in fact accomplished. The prolongation of the German war made it impossible to send the British and British Indian divisions which you needed, and a good many other units on which you were counting had to be retained in the decisive European theatre.

In spite of this diminution and disappointment, you and your men have done all and more than your directive required. Pray convey to everyone under your command or associated with you the sense of admiration and gratitude felt by all at home at the splendid close of the Burma campaign.

In honour of these great deeds of S.E.A.C. His Majesty the King has commanded that a special decoration, the Burma Star, should be struck, and the ribbons will be flown out to you at the earliest moment.

VICTORY MESSAGES

Reply to a message from President Truman on the victorious conclusion of the war in Europe. May 10, 1945.

Your message is cherished by the British nation, and will be regarded as if it were a battle honour by all His Majesty's Armed Forces of all the races in all the lands. Particularly will this be true throughout the great armies which have fought together in France and Germany under General of the Army Eisenhower and in Italy under Field-Marshal Alexander.

In all theatres the men of our two countries were brothers-in-arms, and this was also true in the air, on the oceans, and in the narrow seas. In all our victorious armies in Europe we have fought as one. Looking at the staffs of General Eisenhower and Field-Marshal

172

Alexander, anyone would suppose that they were the organization of one country, and certainly a band of men with one high purpose. Field-Marshal Montgomery's 21st Army Group, with its gallant Canadian Army, has played its part both in our glorious landing last June and in all the battles which it has fought, either as the hinge on which supreme operations turned or in guarding the Northern flank, or advancing northward at the climax. All were together heart and soul.

You sent a few days ago your message to Field-Marshal Alexander, under whom, in command of the army front in Italy, is serving your doughty general, Mark Clark. Let me tell you what General Eisenhower has meant to us. In him we have had a man who set the unity of the Allied Armies above all nationalistic thoughts. In his headquarters unity and strategy were the only reigning spirits. The unity reached such a point that British and American troops could be mixed in the line of battle, and that large masses could be transferred from one command to the other without the slightest difficulty. At no time has the principle of alliance between noble races been carried and maintained at so high a pitch. In the name of the British Empire and Commonwealth, I express to you our admiration of the firm, far-sighted, and illuminating character and qualities of General of the Army Eisenhower.

I must also give expression to our British sentiments about all the valiant and magnanimous deeds of the United States of America, under the leadership of President Roosevelt, so steadfastly carried forward by you, Mr. President, since his death in action. They will for ever stir the hearts of Britons in all quarters of the world in which they dwell, and will, I am certain, lead to even closer affections and ties than those that have been created by the two world wars through which we have passed with harmony and elevation of mind.

Other messages sent by the Prime Minister at the end of the war in Europe included the following :

To General de Gaulle :

I thank you for your cordial message. Although we have had our ups and downs, I have never forgotten that day at Tours when I passed you amid the sorrowful crowd and said, in the hearing of several : " There is the man of destiny." I see you now at the head of France, representing more than any other man known to the world her will to live and her resolve to recover her greatness.

France declared war on Hitler's tyranny at a moment when, like Britain, she was far from sure of her military strength or of her power to dominate the deadly foe. Since then, mighty powers have come into the line of battle. Now after all that has happened we stand together in victory. As you have often heard me say, Great Britain desires that France shall stand in the van of the nations, and that the French Army shall by its strength and quality bear forward the martial glories of the past, even of those parts of the past in which our countries have not always been in the closest agreement. Vive la France !

To the British Civil Service :

This war, which brought us to the brink of disaster, called forth from the people of this country a response unsurpassed in our history. Behind the great achievements of the nation now issuing in victory stands a proud record of determined endeavour and unflagging toil, knit together by sound organization and united in purpose.

In all this the Civil Service has played its part, unobtrusive and unspectacular may be, but alert and indispensable, while bearing its full share of the hardships and strains of war.

To all is due a word of praise and commendation, to those who have served in depots, dockyards and offices in London, in the country, or abroad, to those who have chosen the Civil Service as their career, and to those who have joined the Government Service for the war, putting their special skill and experience at the disposal of the State. Men and women, young and old, all in the service have given of their best in these tremendous years.

To-day we rejoice in the hour of victory. To-morrow we brace ourselves to the task before us of restoring, and where need be re-building, our dwellings and our life. In this task I know that the Civil Service, sterling in character and steady of purpose, will not be found wanting.

To Air Chief Marshal Sir Arthur Harris, Chief of R.A.F. Bomber Command :

Now that Nazi Germany is defeated, I wish to express to you on behalf of His Majesty's Government the deep sense of gratitude which is felt by all the nation for the glorious part which has been played by Bomber Command in forging the victory.

For over two years Bomber Command alone carried the war to the heart of Germany, bringing hope to the peoples of occupied Europe, and to the enemy a foretaste of the mighty power which was rising against him.

As the Command expanded, in partnership with the Air Forces of our American ally, the weight of the attacks was increased, dealing destruction on an unparalleled scale to the German military, industrial and economical system.

Your Command also gave powerful support to the Allied Armies in Europe and made a vital contribution to the war at sea. You destroyed or damaged many of the enemy's ships of war and much of his U-boat organization.

By a prolonged series of mining operations you sank or damaged large quantities of his merchant shipping.

All your operations were planned with great care and skill. They were executed in the face of desperate opposition and appalling hazards. They made a decisive contribution to Germany's final defeat.

The conduct of these operations demonstrated the fiery gallant spirit which animated your air crews, and the high sense of duty of all ranks under your command.

I believe that the massive achievements of Bomber Command will long be remembered as an example of duty nobly done.

To Air Marshal Sir Arthur Coningham, Chief of the Second Tactical Air Force:

The great deeds of the Second Tactical Air Force bear eloquent testimony to the high morale which has sustained your air crews, and to the devotion with which their efforts have been supported by their comrades on the ground.

UNITY FOR PEACE TALKS

A message to Lieutenant-Commander Bell, Conservative and National Government candidate in Newport by-election. May 11, 1945.

In this hour of triumph, reached at last after $5\frac{1}{2}$ years of grim struggle, Newport is given an opportunity to record its opinion of the Government which has organized our victory. One part of our task has been achieved, but the enemy in the Far East is still unconquered, and the extermination of Hitler and his accomplices has not wiped out the evil they have wrought.

Tremendous problems await solution. Our victory has to be made secure at home and abroad. Our representatives at San Francisco need the assurance that they have behind them a Government supported by a nation united for the tasks of peace as of war.

The Government which I lead has already given ample evidence of its zeal and ability to plan wisely for the future. I claim the right to ask the electors of Newport to register their confidence in me and in His Majesty's Government by returning you to Parliament.

You have youth, keenness, and political experience on your side, and you have done splendid service in the Navy since the early days of the war. I wish you success.

NORWAY CONSTITUTION DAY

A message to the Norwegian people. May 17, 1945.

On this anniversary of Norway's Constitution Day, which follows so closely upon the liberation of Norway from the German yoke, I wish to send you a message on behalf of the British people. Throughout this long and arduous war, we in Britain have watched with the deepest admiration the steadfast and indomitable fortitude with which you have resisted the enemy, and we now join in your rejoicings that the collapse of his armed might in your country has been accomplished so speedily and without adding to the grievous burdens and losses which the Norwegian people has already sustained during this war.

You and we and the other United Nations stand at the victorious goal towards which we have all struggled so hard during five long years. By our exertions we have saved from extinction those precious human freedoms which are the fruit of centuries of civilization, and among the first of which are numbered the ideals and liberties which your forefathers enshrined at Eidsvold in the Norwegian Constitution of 1814. Nothing could more clearly demonstrate the living power of these human freedoms than the fact that, over 130 years after it was first conceived, the Eidsvold Constitution has had the power to unite the whole Norwegian people in unyielding defence of the inalienable rights which it asserts.

To-day the Norwegian people are at last able to celebrate once more on May 17 as citizens of a sovereign, independent and democratic Norway; and they can with confidence aver that by May 17 next year they will have so laboured and wrought that the ravages of five years of occupation will be reduced to the slightest of scars on the face of their liberated country. The burden of my message to you is that, in the future triumphs of reconstruction as throughout the past trials of occupation, you may depend on the sincere support and friendship of the whole British people, based upon our ancient ties and our common heritage, and forged into an enduring bond by our comradeship in war.

CRISIS IN THE LEVANT

A message to General de Gaulle. May 30, 1945.

In view of the grave situation which has arisen between your troops and the Levant State and the severe fighting which has broken out, we have, with profound regret, ordered the Commander-in-Chief, Middle East, to intervene to prevent a further effusion of blood in the interests of the security of the whole Middle East, which involves communications for the war against Japan. In order to avoid collision between British and French forces we request you immediately to order the French troops to cease fire and to withdraw to their barracks. Once firing has ceased and order has been restored, we shall be prepared to begin tripartite talks here in London.

A NAVAL ACTION

A message to the Commanding Officer of the destroyer *Kelvin*. June 13, 1945.

Please convey my warm thanks to all those stokers under your command who sent me the delightful flowers and kind message on the anniversary of my trip in H.M.S. *Kelvin* to the Normandy beaches. This was the only time I have been in action in one of His Majesty's ships.

OKINAWA VICTORY

A message to President Truman. June 22, 1945.

The strength of the will-power, devotion and technical resources applied by the United States to this task, joined with the death struggle of the enemy, of whom 90,000 are reported to have been killed, places this battle among the most intense and famous of military history.

It is in profound admiration of American valour and resolve to conquer at whatever cost might be necessary that I send this tribute from your faithful Ally.

SAN FRANCISCO CONFERENCE

A message to Lord Halifax, British Ambassador to the United States, at the conclusion of the Conference. June 26, 1945.

Now that the San Francisco conference has brought its deliberations to such a satisfactory conclusion, I send you, Lord Cranborne, and all the members of the United Kingdom delegation my warm congratulations on the success of their labours and on the quality of the results which have been achieved. By wisdom in counsel and sincerity of conviction the United Kingdom delegates did much to secure the unity of views without which a world organization can have no reality. You have made an invaluable contribution to the re-establishment of a hopeful basis for the future of peace, understanding, and good will among the nations.

ST. MARY'S HOSPITAL

An appeal for funds. June 27, 1945.

In the future health services of this country, greatly increased demands will inevitably be made on St. Mary's as one of our vital medical teaching centres. No hospital has a finer record of work and achievement.

The discovery of penicillin at St. Mary's by Sir Alexander Fleming has placed the whole world in its debt.

Let us therefore be quite sure that its work is in no way hampered by lack of proper accommodation and modern equipment.

I most heartily commend this appeal to all men of good will throughout this country and our Dominions, and also to our very great friends in the United States. No cause could be more worthy.

TO MR. EDWARD STETTINIUS

On his relinquishing his post of United States Secretary of State to become American representative on the United Nations Security Council. July 2, 1945.

Please accept my warm congratulations on your appointment as United States representative on the United Nations Security Council and chairman of the United States delegation to the General Assembly. This indeed gives you a noble opportunity. Your friendship and great help as Lend-Lease Administrator and Secretary of State will always be remembered with gratitude by the Government and people of this country. This is also true of your father's work, with which I was brought into such close contact during the first world war against German tyranny.

TO MR. JAMES BYRNES

On his appointment as United States Secretary of State. July 2, 1945.

I send you my heartiest congratulations on your appointment to the great office of Secretary of State for the United States. I recall with pleasure our various meetings at the White House and in the Crimea, and I look forward to seeing you again in the near future.

CHINA'S NINTH YEAR OF WAR

A message to Generalissimo Chiang Kai-shek. July 8, 1945.

At the beginning of the ninth year of China's war of resistance, I should like to convey to your Excellency, to the Chinese Government, and to the Chinese people a message of cordial greeting.

Hostilities in Europe have been brought to a successful conclusion.

But the world-wide war against the aggressors has still to be completed. This country w.ll now concentrate its efforts upon the achievement, in co-operation with its allies, of final victory over the common enemy in the Far East.

It is my earnest belief that the day is not far distant when the invader will have been driven from Chinese territory, and when, after its long years of sacrifice and suffering, the Chinese nation will be free to engage with the other peace-loving peoples in the tasks of world reconstruction, on the basis of our common ideals of democracy, international harmony, and good will.

THE U-BOAT WARFARE

MONTHLY STATEMENTS ISSUED JOINTLY BY THE PRIME MINISTER AND
THE PRESIDENT OF THE UNITED STATES

JANUARY

The German U-Boat warfare flared into renewed activity during
December. This is but another index that the European war is far
from over.

Increased losses in Allied merchant craft have been officially recorded
as a result of the U-Boats' spurt last month.

In spite of these, the United Nations regularly continue to supply
their expanding armies over the world, enabling them to resist the
attackers or drive back the foe. The Allies continue to sink the enemy
under-sea craft in widely separated parts of the Atlantic.

The announcement of the recent landing of enemy agents from a
U-Boat on the Maine coast is yet another indication that the menace
of Germany's under-sea fleet is real and continuing.

FEBRUARY

Throughout January the enemy's U-Boat activity was slightly
greater than in December, but losses of merchant shipping were not
substantially different.

The U-Boats, making use of their new devices, penetrated farther
into focal areas of shipping close inshore. The results of our counter-
measures have been encouraging.

MARCH

During the month of February a moderate number of Allied merchant
vessels fell victim to U-Boat activity. However, the anti-submarine
forces were successful in destroying more enemy submarines this past
month than in January.

In spite of satisfactory results now being obtained in the war on
under-sea raiders, our forces must maintain unceasing vigilance, because
an enemy with a large number of submarines always possesses a
potential threat.

APRIL

During March the U-Boat effort continued to increase, but fewer
successes were obtained against our shipping than in February.
Casualties inflicted on U-Boats were again severe, and the prolonged

and extensive bombing and mine-laying policy of the Allies has undoubtedly delayed the introduction of the new type of U-Boats. In
a similar manner the capture of Danzig by the Soviet Armies helps to
cut off the evil at its source.

JUNE

With the surrender of Germany the Battle of the Atlantic has ended ;
German U-Boats have ceased to operate and are now proceeding under
Allied orders.

Beginning in September, 1939, it has been a long and relentless
struggle ; a struggle demanding not only the utmost courage, daring,
and endurance, but also the highest scientific and technical skill.

Germany's object was to cut the Allied sea communications, upon
which the maintenance of the Allied war effort depended. This included the movements and supply of armies and air forces during
successful campaigns in four continents.

Losses have been heavy both in lives and material ; at the peak in
1941 and 1942 the issue of the struggle hung in the balance. On the
other hand, over 700 U-Boats have been sunk, and many others have
been destroyed by the Germans themselves in the final stage. Most
of these successes have been achieved by the combined Allied naval and
air forces working in the closest co-operation ; others are due to mines
laid from aircraft and ships ; others to bombing in harbour, and a few
U-Boats were lost by marine dangers.

But success was achieved. Thanks to the sailors and airmen, the
scientists and technicians, the shipbuilders and the factory workers,
the convoys reached their destination, and enabled the soldiers and
the airmen to fulfil their tasks.

We, President and Prime Minister, in this our last joint statement
on the U-Boat war, can now report that the Allies have finished the job.

THE GENERAL ELECTION

THE COALITION BREAKS UP

On May 18, 1945, the Prime Minister sent the following letter to Mr. Attlee, the Leader of the Labour Party

My dear Attlee,—From the talks I have had with you and your principal Labour colleagues I have gathered the impression that the Labour Party, instead of leaving the Government on the defeat of Germany, would be willing to continue the Coalition until the autumn.

I have given the most careful and anxious thought to this suggestion, and I regret to say that in its present form I cannot feel it would be in the public interest. A union of parties like that which now exists should come together and work together, not for a particular date without regard to world events, but for the achievement of some great national purpose transcending all party differences. For the last five or six months our Ministerial and Parliamentary affairs have been increasingly affected by the assumed approach of a General Election at the end of the German war. This has not conduced to the national interest so far as domestic affairs are concerned.

I therefore make you the following proposal, which I earnestly hope you will not readily reject—namely, that we should fix upon another object for our joint endeavours and adjourn the question of our separation until it is gained. The First Lord of the Admiralty has already expressed in his speech in the City of London his regret that a General Election should be held before the Japanese war was finished. It would give me great relief if you and your friends were found resolved to carry on with us until a decisive victory has been gained over Japan. In the meanwhile we would together do our utmost to implement the proposals for social security and full employment contained in the White Papers which we have laid before Parliament. On this basis we could work together with all the energy and comradeship which has marked our long and honourable association.

I am conscious, however, in the highest degree of our duty to strengthen ourselves by a direct expression of the nation's will. If you should decide to stand on with us, all united together until the Japanese surrender is compelled, let us discuss means of taking the nation's opinion, for example, a referendum, on the issue whether in these conditions the life of this Parliament should be further prolonged.

I am sending letters in similar terms to Sir Archibald Sinclair and to Mr. Ernest Brown.

Yours sincerely,

Winston S. Churchill.

To this letter Mr. Attlee replied rejecting the Prime Minister's proposal for the continuation of the Coalition, and Mr. Churchill then sent a second letter to the Leader of the Labour Party as follows :

My dear Attlee,—I am sorry to receive your letter of May 21, in which you reject my proposal that we should work together until the defeat of Japan is achieved and the job is finished.

In this letter you tell me that our only course is to prolong the present Coalition till a General Election in October. This would mean that from now until October, outside the Government, and even within it, we should be continually preparing for an election. We have already suffered several months of this electioneering atmosphere, which, I am sure, is already affecting administrative efficiency and might soon weaken the country before the world at a time when, above all others, it should be strongest.

I agree with what you say in your letter that it is " on the problems of the reconstruction of the economic life of the country that party differences are most acute." " What is required," you say, " is decisive action. This can only be forthcoming from a Government united on principle and policy." I agree also with your statement, " My colleagues and I do not believe that it would be possible to lay aside political controversy now that the expectation of an election has engaged the attention of the country." For my part, I am sure that a continuance of uncertainty and agitation would be harmful to the whole process of the recovery of our trade and the change-over in industry. It is not good for any country, and it is impossible for any Coalition, to live for so long a time under the spell of an approaching General Election. Least of all is this possible in a world where events are so tumultuous and dangerous as now.

Opinions are much divided as to how party advantage may lie between a July and an October election, and I regret the aspersions with which you have darkened this correspondence. I have concerned myself solely with trying to create tolerable conditions under which we could work together. It is clear from the tone of your letter and the feelings of your party that these no longer exist, and it is odd that you should accompany so many unjust allegations with an earnest request that we should go on bickering till the autumn. Such a process would not be a decent way of carrying on a British Government.

I regret that you should speak of " rushing " an election. Foreseeing what might arise at the close of the German war, we discussed, as you will remember, the whole question of procedure in detail in the War Cabinet. The normal period between a Dissolution and the poll is seventeen days, and it was you and your colleagues who proposed that there should be at least a three weeks' additional interval, in view of the special circumstances prevailing.

We gladly accepted this reasonable request, and the unanimous decision of the Cabinet was made known by you on January 17 when you announced in the House of Commons that the King had been graciously willing for this occasion to announce his intention to dissolve Parliament at least three weeks beforehand.

Yours very sincerely,
WINSTON S. CHURCHILL.

MESSAGE TO THE ELECTORS

Mr. Churchill sent the following message to electors throughout the country asking them to support the Government candidates:

On September 3rd, 1939, we began an heroic crusade for right and freedom. Our hard task is not yet finished. We have still to beat the Japanese, to work with our Allies to ensure that victory leads to a durable peace, to put this land of ours on its feet again.

Believing that these tasks call for continued national unity, I invited the leaders of the Labour and opposition Liberal Parties to stay in the Government to help us to finish the job. They refused.

Men of good will of other parties and of no party have accepted the invitation. Together we shall tackle the pressing military and political problems that lie ahead.

When those problems have been solved, and Britain is a going concern again, there will be plenty of time to argue about whether we want to discard our whole system of society in favour of strange ideas which are quite out of accord with our hard-won individual liberty.

" VOTE NATIONAL, NOT PARTY "

I AM sorry to have lost so many good friends who served with me in the five years' Coalition. It was impossible to go on in a state of " electionitis " all through the summer and autumn. This election will last quite long enough for all who are concerned in it, and I expect many of the general public will be sick and tired of it before we get to polling day.

My sincere hope was that we could have held together until the war against Japan was finished. On the other hand, there was a high duty to consult the people after all these years. I could only be relieved of that duty by the full agreement of the three parties, further fortified, perhaps, by a kind of official Gallup Poll, which I am sure would have resulted in an overwhelming request that we should go on to the end and finish the job. That would have enabled me to say at once, " There will be no election for a year," or words to that effect.

I know that many of my Labour colleagues would have been glad to carry on. On the other hand, the Socialist Party as a whole had been for some time eager to set out upon the political warpath, and when large numbers of people feel like that it is not good for their health to deny them the fight they want. We will therefore give it to them to the best of our ability.

Party, my friends, has always played a great part in our affairs. Party ties have been considered honourable bonds, and no one could doubt that when the German war was over and the immediate danger to this country, which had led to the Coalition, had ceased, conflicting loyalties would arise. Our Socialist and Liberal friends felt themselves forced, therefore, to put party before country. They have departed, and we have been left to carry the nation's burden.

I have therefore formed, exactly as I said I would two years ago, another form of National Government, resting no longer on the agreement of the three official party machines, but on the Conservative Party, together with all the men of good will of any party or no party who have been ready to give their services. I claim the support of all throughout the country who sincerely put the nation first in their thoughts. This is a National Government. I shall stand myself as a Conservative and National candidate. Others may choose to call themselves National or National Liberal, and those who give us their support should vote National rather than Party on polling day.

Why do I claim the right to call this Government National ? First of all, because those who have left us have left us on party grounds alone. Secondly, because the Conservative Party, which has for many years been the strongest party in this country, has been willing to abandon party feeling to such an extent that more than one-third of the members of Cabinet rank in this new Government are not members of the Conservative Party. Many of these very able men, without whose aid we could not have got through the war, would prefer not to call themselves Conservative in a party sense. They prefer to call themselves National. And many Conservatives who might have looked forward to high office have accepted cheerfully the interruption of their political careers in order to aid the nation in its time of trouble.

Particularly do I regret the conduct of the Liberal Party. Between us and the orthodox Socialists there is a great doctrinal gulf, which yawns and gapes. Of this continental conception of human society called Socialism, or in its more violent form Communism, I shall say more later. There is no such gulf between the Conservative and National Government I have formed and the Liberals. There is scarcely a Liberal sentiment which animated the great Liberal leaders of the past which we do not inherit and defend. Above all, there is our championship of freedom at home and abroad. All the guiding principles of the British Constitution are proclaimed and enforced by us in their highest degree.

When could any Liberal Party in the past have been offered a political programme of social reform so massive, so warm, so adventurous as that which is contained in our Four Years' Plan ? Indeed, I feel that Mr. Gladstone would have recoiled from a great deal of it. He would have thought it was going too far. But we still have a Rosebery and a Lloyd-George to carry forward the flags of their fathers.

Why, then, should the Liberal Party spurn us ? Why then should they leave the fighting line ? Why could not they, at any rate, stay with us till we have beaten down the cruel domination of Japan and until we have set on foot some tolerable way of life for agonized Europe ? I am sorry to tell you that they have yielded to the tactical temptation, natural to politicians, to acquire more seats in the House of Commons, if they can, at all costs. It is also obvious that the more equally the two large parties can be brought together at the polls, the greater will be the Liberal bargaining power. That is, no doubt, why all the criticisms of the Sinclair-Beveridge Liberals, who have been very active against us, are directed upon us. It is us they abuse.

I am sorry, indeed, to see such a line developed by men and women who are my friends, by a party many of whose ideals I cherish and will always strive to achieve or guard to the best of my strength. I do not wonder at all that a very large part of the Liberal Party have chosen the national course and still remain in office with us, bearing the heavy burden.

But I appeal to Liberals in all parts of the land, and I call upon them to search their hearts as to whether their differences with a British Government which will put through the Four Years' Plan, a Government which is animated by the love of freedom, which is vowed to that harmonious medium of justice and generosity so befitting to the conqueror, has not more claim on their ancestral loyalties than has a Socialist Party administration, whose principles are the absolute denial of traditional Liberalism. Let them think it out carefully in the light of the speeches of the famous Liberal leaders of the past. Let them think it out carefully in the warmth which may come to the weary Liberal combatant when he sees his ideas increasingly accepted by enlightened peoples and victorious nations.

My friends, I must tell you that a Socialist policy is abhorrent to the British ideas of freedom. Although it is now put forward in the main by people who have a good grounding in the Liberalism and Radicalism of the early part of this century, there can be no doubt that Socialism is inseparably interwoven with Totalitarianism and the abject worship of the State. It is not alone that property, in all its forms, is struck at, but that liberty, in all its forms, is challenged by the fundamental conceptions of Socialism.

Look how even to-day they hunger for controls of every kind, as if these were delectable foods instead of war-time inflictions and monstrosities. There is to be one State to which all are to be obedient in every act of their lives. This State is to be the arch-employer, the arch-planner, the arch-administrator and ruler, and the arch-caucus-boss.

How is an ordinary citizen or subject of the King to stand up against this formidable machine, which, once it is in power, will prescribe for every one of them where they are to work; what they are to work at; where they may go and what they may say; what views they are to hold and within what limits they may express them; where their wives are to go to queue-up for the State ration; and what education their children are to receive to mould their views of human liberty and conduct in the future?

A Socialist State once thoroughly completed in all its details and its aspects—and that is what I am speaking of—could not afford to suffer opposition. Here in old England, in Great Britain, of which old England forms no inconspicuous part, in this glorious Island, the cradle and citadel of free democracy throughout the world, we do not like to be regimented and ordered about and have every action of our lives prescribed for us. In fact we punish criminals by sending them to Wormwood Scrubs and Dartmoor, where they get full employment, and whatever board and lodging is appointed by the Home Secretary.

Socialism is, in its essence, an attack not only upon British enterprise, but upon the right of the ordinary man or woman to breathe freely without having a harsh, clumsy, tyrannical hand clapped across their mouths and nostrils. A Free Parliament—look at that—a Free Parliament is odious to the Socialist doctrinaire. Have we not heard Mr. Herbert Morrison descant upon his plans to curtail Parliamentary procedure and pass laws simply by resolutions of broad principle in the House of Commons, afterwards to be left by Parliament to the executive and to the bureaucrats to elaborate and enforce by departmental regulations ? As for Sir Stafford Cripps on " Parliament in the Socialist State," I have not time to read you what he said, but perhaps it will meet the public eye during the election campaign.

But I will go farther. I declare to you, from the bottom of my heart, that no Socialist system can be established without a political police. Many of those who are advocating Socialism or voting Socialist to-day will be horrified at this idea. That is because they are short-sighted, that is because they do not see where their theories are leading them.

No Socialist Government conducting the entire life and industry of the country could afford to allow free, sharp, or violently-worded expressions of public discontent. They would have to fall back on some form of *Gestapo*, no doubt very humanely directed in the first instance. And this would nip opinion in the bud ; it would stop criticism as it reared its head, and it would gather all the power to the supreme party and the party leaders, rising like stately pinnacles above their vast bureaucracies of Civil servants, no longer servants and no longer civil. And where would the ordinary simple folk—the common people, as they like to call them in America—where would they be, once this mighty organism had got them in its grip ?

I stand for the sovereign freedom of the individual within the laws which freely elected Parliaments have freely passed. I stand for the rights of the ordinary man to say what he thinks of the Government of the day, however powerful, and to turn them out, neck and crop, if he thinks he can better his temper or his home thereby, and if he can persuade enough others to vote with him.

But, you will say, look at what has been done in the war. Have not many of those evils which you have depicted been the constant companions of our daily life ? It is quite true that the horrors of war do not end with the fighting-line. They spread far away to the base and the homeland, and everywhere people give up their rights and liberties for the common cause. But this is because the life of their country is in mortal peril, or for the sake of the cause of freedom in some other land. They give them freely as a sacrifice. It is quite true that the conditions of Socialism play a great part in war-time. We all submit to being ordered about to save our country. But when the war is over and the imminent danger to our existence is removed, we cast off these shackles and burdens which we imposed upon ourselves in times of dire and mortal peril, and quit the gloomy caverns of war and march out into the breezy fields, where the sun is shining and where all may walk joyfully in its warm and golden rays.

Our present opponents or assailants would be, I am sure, knowing many of them, shocked to see where they are going, and where they are trying to lead us. So they adopt temporary expedients. They say, let us just nationalize anything we can get hold of according to the size of our majority and get the Bank of England into the hands of trustworthy Socialist politicians, and we will go ahead and see what happens next. Indeed you would see what happens next.

But let me tell you that, once a Socialist Government begins monkeying with the credit of Britain and trying, without regard to facts, figures, or confidence, to manipulate it to Socialist requirements, there is no man or woman in this country who has, by thrift or toil, accumulated a nest-egg, however small, who will not run the risk of seeing it shrivel before their eyes.

Mr. Greenwood said two years ago—and I rebuked him for it then—" Pounds, shillings and pence are meaningless symbols." All this " meaningless symbol " talk is very dangerous, and would enable a Socialist Government which had got control of the Bank of England to issue notes that would destroy the value of any scrap of savings or nest-egg that anyone had accumulated in this country.

The new National Government stands decisively for the maintenance of the purchasing power of the pound sterling, and we would rather place upon all classes, rich and poor alike, the heaviest burden of taxation they can bear than slide into the delirium of inflation.

I warn you that if you vote for me and those who are acting with me, we give no guarantee of lush and easy times ahead. On the other hand, you need not expect pounds, shillings and pence to become a " meaningless symbol." On the contrary, our resolve will be that what has been earned by sweat, toil, and skill or saved by self-denial shall command the power to buy the products of peace at an equal value in sweat, toil, and skill. We will also take good care against unfair rake-offs and monopolies, and we will protect the common man by law against them by controlling monopolies whose operations are any restraint on trade or oppressive to the smaller producer or distributor.

My friends, I have been forced into a discussion between the Socialist and individualist theories of life and government. That is because for the first time the challenge has been made, in all formality, " Socialism versus the rest." But now I must come back to the job which stands in front of us. What have we got to do ? What have we got to do now ?

We have to bring home the soldiers who have borne the brunt of the war, and make sure, by every scrap of strength and brains we possess, that they find waiting for them food, homes, and work. The Demobilization Scheme has been drawn up with all the advantages of seeing what mistakes were made last time. Mr. Bevin has worked out a scheme which aims at being fair and square between one soldier and another, besides avoiding undue complications. But what a terrific business he has left us to carry through !

And then you have to add to it that out of this demobilizing army has got to be formed at the same time a new army to go out and finish off, at the side of our American brothers, the Japanese tyrants at the other side of the world. Here is a tremendous task.

And then come along serious people who say that we have got to get our mills going to provide new clothes and articles of all kinds for home and for our export trade. And what about our food, of which we grow only about two-thirds, even under war-time pressure ? We have got anyhow to buy food and raw materials oversea, and how are we going to pay for these ? We gave our foreign investments largely to the common cause. We sold every asset we could lay hands on in that year, that memorable, grim year, when we stood alone against the might of Hitler, with Mussolini at his tail. We gave all and we have given all to the prosecution of this war, and we have reached one of the great victorious halting-posts.

Then we have our Four-Year Plan, with all its hopes and benefits, and with all the patient work that it means to pass it into law and bring it into action. All these are definite, practical, gigantic tasks. They will take every scrap of strength, good management, and, above all, good comradeship that we can possibly screw out of ourselves.

What a mad thing it would be to slash across this whole great business of resettlement and reorganization with these inflaming controversies of Socialistic agitation ! How foolish to plunge us into the bitter political and party fighting which must accompany the attempt to impose a vast revolutionary change on the whole daily life and structure of Britain ! Surely at least we can wait till another Election ? The world is not coming to an end in the next few weeks or years. The progress of free discussion can show whose fears or whose hopes are well founded. Can we not get Europe settled up, and Britain settled down? Before we plunge out on this hateful internal struggle, let us concentrate on practical and immediate action, and make sure that in gazing at the stars we do not fail in our duty to our fellow-mortals.

On with the forward march! Leave these Socialist dreamers to their Utopias or their nightmares. Let us be content to do the heavy job that is right on top of us. And let us make sure that the cottage home to which the warrior will return is blessed with modest but solid prosperity, well fenced and guarded against misfortune, and that Britons remain free to plan their lives for themselves and for those they love.

A HEALTHIER NATION

THE SECOND ELECTION BROADCAST
JUNE 13, 1945

[June 13, 1945.

NEARLY ten days have passed since I last addressed you, and of course, as you would expect in an election fight, the relations between the parties have distinctly worsened. With others, I regret that this break in national unity should be exposed to all the nations of the world, many of whom do not at all understand the way we manage our affairs, or the deep underlying comradeship which is the foundation of our island life.

Until the election has been decided, we are bound to be weakened in the world for all purposes. We are not, my friends, so numerous a people that we could afford indefinitely to disparage and belittle each other while we aspire to be the heart-centre of the British Empire and Commonwealth. We must show ourselves united in all the main essentials, and thus alone can we walk side by side with mighty entities like the United States and Soviet Russia.

Some powerful organized and integrated force must be found in this Island which will have the right and the authority to speak for the United Kingdom of Great Britain and Northern Ireland. We shall sink very rapidly in the world's regard if, as the result of this election, we fall into an epoch of party strife ; and if party passions, doctrines, and ambitions were to dominate our life for any lengthy period, the Great Powers of the world, one of which is steel-knitted, heroic Russia, and the other of whom has a strong President with a three and a half years' tenure and purpose before him, would proceed on their way, settling affairs without the British voice being heard, except in terms of meek compromise abroad or raucous brawl at home.

Therefore I am glad that the election strife, though twice its usual length, will not be drawn out until the autumn. In a few weeks we shall have a verdict from the British people which will make matters plain, and in one way or the other give the authority of proved popular support to whatever Government may then be charged with our affairs.

I believe that the new National Government which I have formed is the one best suited to carry out the tasks which lie ahead. But it is for you to decide. Consider, however, before you do so the gravity of these tasks.

For instance, and first of all, we have to do our duty to the utmost in the war against Japan.

Secondly, and as a part of this, we must remodel the armies so that a great measure of demobilization can accompany the further discharge of our task in Europe, and so that we may at the same time reshape our armies for the great war in which we are engaged on the other side of the globe.

Thirdly, we have to use modern science, organization, and enterprise to get our industries started again so as to supply the necessities of life to our people and, so far as we can, to our friends and allies in Europe.

Fourthly, we must rebuild as far as possible our export trade. Without that all our post-war efforts would be vain.

Our fifth task must be to carry into law and put into execution the far-reaching proposals of the Four-Years Plan. I announced this to the nation two years ago under the simple watchword of food, work, and homes. Of this extensive plan as yet only education and family allowances stand on the Statute-book, and they have yet to be carried into full effect. But we have left social insurance, industrial injuries insurance, and the national health service to be shaped by Parliament and made to play a dynamic part in the life and security of every family and home. In this Four-Years Plan also there was, and I hope there still is, a wide measure of agreement between the Conservative and National Government on the one hand and the parties which are against them at the polls.

Both at home and abroad there is a full four years' work for all to do. That is the reason why I have censured in the most severe terms the Socialist effort to drag their long-term fads and wavy Utopias across the practical path of need and duty. I denounce the scheme of the making of a Socialist Britain at this time while we are in such difficulties, and in danger of losing much that we have gained at so great a cost.

The public control of the means of production, distribution, and exchange is one of the Socialist Party tenets, and is published as being part of their constitution. In December last, the Labour Party Conference in London passed a resolution in favour of the transfer to public ownership of the land, of large-scale building, of heavy industry, and all forms of banking, transport, and fuel and power.

It is true that these revolutionary aims have been somewhat watered down in the last few days, to make them less repulsive to the electorate. For instance, Mr. Attlee, in his broadcast a week ago, made no reference whatever to the long-proclaimed, and also recently-proclaimed, Socialist intention of nationalizing the Bank of England; and yet it was upon this point I had challenged his party only the day before. Many of the Socialist leaders seek to present themselves as no more than harmless and well-meaning philanthropists and progressives.

Nevertheless, however their appearance may fit their desires, their ultimate policy cannot be disguised. And I am entitled to say that men like Sir Stafford Cripps and Mr. Herbert Morrison have shown by their public statements that they would use any majority they might obtain to stifle or greatly curtail the rights of Parliament to criticize such vast transformations of our British life. If and when the plans to which they are publicly and irrevocably committed came into force in their entirety, and we had a complete Socialist system, all effective and healthy opposition and the natural change of parties in office from time to time would necessarily come to an end, and a political police would be required to enforce an absolute and permanent system upon the nation.

I am as much opposed to the creation of a complete Socialist system as I am in favour of the immense social reforms, in many of which a free British nation has long led the world. There could never be a worse time to raise these academic Socialist arguments than now, when all the practical tasks which stare us in the face, and upon which we are engaged, would be delayed, confused, interrupted, and perhaps stricken to the ground. Our place in the world would be lost, and ruin instead of glory would be the recompense of Britain after all her trials and triumphs.

And here we may take some long-term views, on which we may find ourselves united. No one who cares about the continuing greatness of our country should avert his eyes from the future of our population. Statistics of future population are one of the new forms of prophecy. But they are a form of prophecy which rests on mathematics and therefore can be trusted. Already in 1945 we have many fewer young people under 20 than we had at the end of the last war. We are assured as a matter of practical certainty that this Island will contain in 30 years' time a far larger number of people over 65—that is to say, the old. And if the married people of this country do not have larger families in the future than they were having before this war, there will be in 30 years' time a smaller proportion of children under 15, and a far smaller number of men and women in their prime who have to bear the main burden in industry, in agriculture, and in defence.

Our Dominions are now in many cases anxious to receive as immigrants considerable numbers of the best people we have. We cannot meet this desire on a falling birth-rate. Our future as a nation, our future as the centre of a great Empire, alike depend upon our ability to change the present trend in our population statistics. This is no party question. It should be the aim of all parties to increase the number of British homes and the size of the families brought up in them. Radical measures will be required to achieve this.

As you will find in the manifesto I have put forward in the name of the National Government, we have laid the greatest stress upon all that surrounds the life of the home, the bringing into the world under satisfactory conditions of the largest number of children, and the making sure, so far as possible, that the arrival of a baby is regarded as a joy and not as a new burden beyond the strength of the married couple or of the household to maintain.

In my old age, I naturally look ahead. The whole theme of motherhood and family life, with those sweet affections which illuminate it, must be the fountain spring alike of present happiness and future survival. We have the immortal bard of Scotland, Robbie Burns—

> To mak' a happy fireside clime
> To weans and wife,
> That's the true pathos and sublime
> Of human life.

If our wealth and enterprise are not cracked and spoiled by the fetters of authoritarian Socialism, there lie open vast possibilities of social endeavour in this vital sphere. We must encourage by every means the number of births.

Over all spreads Disraeli's celebrated maxim, ever I trust to be the guide of the Tory Party, of which he was so proud, " Health and the laws of health." Our new health policy, framed by the late Government, which we shall carry through, will alleviate the mother's burden in child-bearing. War is a hard teacher, but we all learn much under her rod. We have set out in our Conservative and National manifesto much of what we have learned.

There is also a very good tale to be told about the milk. Have you heard about our national milk scheme ? In summer and in winter, whether milk is scarce or plentiful, every expectant mother, and every baby or child under five years of age, can get a pint of milk a day at a specially reduced price. The very poor can get it free. Nursing mothers can get a further pint guaranteed to them at the ordinary price if they want it.

During the war years we have been making this provision for the future of our race, and the results have more than justified our hopes. In spite of the restrictions of war-time diet, the death rate of mothers and of babies has fallen to the lowest figure we have ever known in this country. So has the rate of still-birth. In March, 1943, I said in my broadcast to you : " There is no finer investment for any community than putting milk into babies." To-night I say to you that the new National Government is determined that this good work, begun by its forerunner, shall go on.

But our war-time fight for a healthy and well-nourished race of citizens has not been confined to the babies. It has also been waged in defence of the schoolchildren. Milk in schools was known before the war, and had made some headway as a practice. As we announced in the White Paper on Social Insurance, we intend to make school milk a free family allowance to every child attending a primary or secondary school.

We have also carried out during the war an immense expansion in the provision of school meals. Whereas before there used to be about a quarter of a million meals served daily in elementary and secondary schools, to-day, in spite of all the difficulties of labour shortage and food shortage, of bombed school premises and other handicaps, the total is not less than one and three-quarter million.

The National Government realizes that the true wealth of this nation is in its fit and healthy men and women, and we are determined to secure the nation's future by seeing that from birth, and even before birth, every British infant is well nourished and given a chance to grow up sturdy and strong.

The British people are good all through. You can test them as you would put a bucket into the sea, and always find it salt. The genius of our people springs from every class and from every part of the land. You cannot tell where you will not find a wonder. The hero, the fighter, the poet, the master of science, the organizer, the artist, the engineer, the administrator, or the jurist—he may spring into fame. Equal opportunity for all, under free institutions and equal laws—there is the banner for which we will do battle against all rubber-stamp bureaucracies or dictatorships.

I am the oldest living champion of Insurance in the House of Commons. It was 34 years ago that I carried the first Unemployment Insurance Bill, being guided at the Board of Trade by the far-seeing wisdom and efficiency of Sir Hubert Llewellyn-Smith. The foundation of Unemployment Insurance is, of course, the Labour or, as it is now called, Employment Exchange. In 1909 I obtained the power to spread a network of these exchanges over the whole of Great Britain and Ireland. For that purpose we brought into the public service Mr. Beveridge, a young man much recommended to me by Mr. and Mrs. Sydney Webb, and he learned much from Sir Hubert Llewellyn-Smith about State insurance for unemployment.

At the same time my friend Mr. Lloyd-George was busy with Old Age Pensions and Health Insurance. All this stood us in good stead in the confusion and frightful unemployment that followed the last war, when no one had experience of what follows in the sullen aftermath of victory. Unemployment Insurance was made universal, at enormous cost to the State. It saved us from catastrophe during some terrible years. I have always been fascinated with this idea of what I once called " bringing the magic of averages to the rescue of the millions."

Presently, when in changed circumstances I rejoined the Conservative Party and became Chancellor of the Exchequer, I devised, drove forward and placed upon the Statute-book another, and perhaps the largest, measure of insurance, in 1925. This made old-age pensions contributory, but brought the age down from 70 to 65, and thus substantially increased the contribution of the State, and also instituted that insurance for widows and orphans without which no national scheme could be complete.

Here was involved a capital liability estimated at £750,000,000. Here in a land where the great majority had little or nothing to leave behind them, it gave to a man of 30 with a wife and two children, a not uncommon case, should he die, what was virtually a power of bequest actuarially valued at over £450 sterling.

By this great series of insurance measures, carried by the Conservative Party, joined with those of Mr. Asquith's Liberal administration, was formed the foundation of the universal, national, compulsory insurance scheme which our famous Coalition Government, over which I have had the honour to preside, have designed and laid before Parliament. Mr. Beveridge, now Sir William, after a long absence from this field, having been called upon by the late National Government to head an official committee upon this subject, gave a valuable impulse to this crowning measure at a time when most of the men in power had their main thoughts concentrated upon the war.

But this culminating measure of national insurance, combining all other schemes I have referred to and adding much to them, has still to be passed into law, and thereafter to be put into execution. I regard it as the first in magnitude of the great measures embodied in the Four Years Plan announced by me in March, 1943. But what is the worth of it till it is working ? It is now no more than a pious aspiration to which leading men in all parties are pledged.

For the care of this vast policy a separate Department has been created, the Minister for which, if we should be returned to power, will have the tremendous task and honour of carrying out our mighty plan from thought to action, and from paper to reality. I have urged upon him the importance of humanizing this scheme in the interests of all those who will receive its great benefits, and so as to take better care of the scores of thousands of insurance agents who served the great approved societies, and who, when they come home from the fronts where many of them have been for so long, should not find themselves forgotten.

I shall also require of any Government of which I am the head that the public contributors receive, so far as possible, the same measure of courtesy and consideration from the State officials as they used to do when all these beneficent societies sprang up under private enterprise.

I have kept till the last the most urgent of our domestic tasks: the rebuilding of our shattered dwellings, and the great increase on normal building needed on account of the 68 months of war paralysis. This confronts us with the need of exceptional effort.

Private enterprise had carried the construction of houses up to a pitch of over 350,000 a year in the years before the war, and in the 21 years between the two wars, during 18 of which Conservative or National Governments ruled, the number of houses was increased from 9,000,000 to 13,500,000, 300,000 unworthy houses being replaced by new ones. That was a magnificent achievement, for which the Conservative Party may claim credit.

Had it not been for the war, we should by now in all probability have rid the land of what are called slums. We have now greater difficulties to face than the pre-war Governments, because of the devastation caused by German bombing, and also because this war has exceeded the last war by 17 months.

I shall not hesitate to use war-time expedients to repair war-time injuries and the inevitable war-time lag.

It is on the provision of homes that all the other plans which I have mentioned turn. Every method, public or private, for houses, permanent or temporary, will be employed, and all obstructions, from whatever quarter they come, be they price-rings, monopoly, or any other form of obstacle, will be dealt with by the whole power of Parliament and the nation.

A THREAT TO FREEDOM

THE THIRD ELECTION BROADCAST
JUNE 21, 1945

[June 21, 1945.

MANY voices sound to you amid the clatter and hum of this election, and you have got to decide as well as you can which are right and true, and which will bring our country into happier and better times.

We have been through a cruel ordeal lasting for nearly six years. We have yet another struggle against Japan before us, which must be wound up and finished off before peace returns to this tortured world. The Americans have stood by us, and we must stand by them. Quite apart from this, we have our own possessions, conquered and ravaged by the Japanese, from which there comes an additional call of honour for their clearance and redemption.

The Socialists tell us very loudly that the only way to save Great Britain and the future is to put them in power, with a mandate to transform our island life as fast as possible into that of a Socialist community under their authority. From many sides we hear their war-cries, and from many sides we hear the promises that all the evils and miseries of mankind will be cured by the plans they will make for us and by the rules they will make us obey.

In order to prove that their policies are right and will lead us out of our troubles, they pour out their abuse and condemnation of the world in which we have hitherto lived, and they assert that none of the evils that happened after the last war or before it, or even now in the few weeks since they left the Government, would have befallen us if only their system had been in force.

Sir Stafford Cripps addressed you last night about how we had suffered between the two wars. There certainly was great distress between those two shattering and terrific earthquakes, and we know much more now than we did then; but on the other hand there was much less suffering in Great Britain in this period than in any other war-stricken State in Europe, and great advances were made even in those circumstances of difficulty. The British nation that entered the new war on September 3, 1939, was a far stronger, healthier, better bred, better fed, better housed, and better educated race than the bygone heroes who drew the sword on August the 4th, 1914.

But now we are told that the existing structure must be swept away. There is to be made as a result of this Election a Socialist world, a Socialist Britain where all the means of production, distribution, and exchange are to be owned by the State, and worked by the State through public departments with their officials in Whitehall, or wherever convenient. Moreover the central Government is to plan for all our lives and tell us exactly where we are to go and what we are to do, and any resistance to their commands will be punished. This is of course their ultimate goal, and how long they take to reach it must assuredly depend on you.

Sir Stafford Cripps has made it clear that he and his kind must give the orders to us all, and that if Parliament says no, or even asks awkward questions, it will be controlled or swept out of the way and its rights of debate curtailed. On the very first day, according to him, an Emergency Powers Bill must be passed, leaving the majority leaders the power to act without restraint by the courts of law.

He and some of the Socialist leaders, though others repudiate them I am glad to see, talk of violence to be used upon us, if necessary, to make us conform sharply and promptly to the benevolent ideas of these autocratic philanthropists who aspire to change the human heart as if by magic and make themselves our rulers at the same time.

I have given you my warnings in the past, and they were not listened to. I do sincerely believe that I can help you, in this critical future which is rushing towards us, in as good a way as anyone else, and as long as my faculties and your confidence last I will strive to do so.

But do not let it be put about, as I have heard it is in some quarters, that I would ever associate myself with plans to impose the yoke of Socialism upon the necks of the free British people. Such an attempt would lead us into a period of disorder and party strife and of Parliamentary eclipse such as has never been seen in the long, steady, developing history of our country.

This they will do, if you give them power, at a moment when the whole of our strength should be concentrated upon solving practical problems, those practical problems which present themselves grimly every morning on the doorstep, demanding attention and demanding reply—to bring the armies home ; to build the houses which could not be built in the war or were blasted by the enemy ; to make up the new armies and fleets and air forces which must advance against Japan ; to get our trade working both at home and abroad ; to carry through Parliament and put into operation the enormous social programme comprised in the Four Years Plan, upon which so large a measure of agreement exists. Why cannot we concentrate on these realities without being at the same time forced to argue about the acceptance of an entirely new system of society ?

These piercing discussions into the roots of human society are new to many who will cast what may be a decisive vote at this election. When they make their cross on the corner of the ballot paper, they may not, because of the hard times and the hard service which we have endured, realize the perils which may spring from a wrong decision.

I told you the other day that the violent imposition of the socialistic system, such as has now emerged as a demand from the extreme and potentially dominant forces of the Socialist Party, would involve the restriction of Parliamentary Government as we have known it, and the denial of the rights of effectual opposition as hitherto practised in this country.

But how would it affect the ordinary wage-earner ? Let me tell you that it would rob him of his personal freedom to an extent unknown. I will go so far as to say a rather odd thing, about which no doubt there will be several opinions. It might well be in the interest of the factory workers, or indeed of the wage-earners generally, not to have too strong an employer over them. I should like to feel that he would be strong in the sense of being capable and efficient as a producer or competitor in the world markets. But it is abhorrent to our idea of freedom that the employer should have undue power over his employees.

Now under our present democratic system the wage-earner can of course appeal to his trade union, and also the sacred right of collective bargaining, largely promoted in bygone days by the Conservative Party, comes into play. Then there is Parliament, while it is free, in which the behaviour of all employers of labour, either generally or in individual cases, can be brought out and discussed in the full light of day.

But none of this would be possible in a Socialist State, where the central executive authority could not allow itself to be challenged or defeated at any time in any form of Parliament they might allow to exist. And I declare to you that the freedom of the wage-earner to choose or change his employment, or to use collective bargaining by all means, including the right to strike, runs absolutely counter to the Socialist doctrine and theory of the State.

I have read great complaints about our calling ourselves a National Government, and I gave you, in my first broadcast, several reasons why we had a right to do so.

But what about the Socialist Party calling themselves the Labour Party ? Of course, every one can call himself anything he likes in a free country, but what about the Labour Party as a title ? Are they the only people who labour in this country ? Are they the only people who have fought in the war ? Are they the only people who have hearts pure from all selfish interest ? Are they the only ones who join the trade unions and take effective action with them ?

Why, my friends, millions of trade unionists are Conservatives, and several other millions are going to vote for the National Government for patriotic reasons, they are going to give their vote for the National Government on account of the dangers amid which we stand at the present time. The Socialist Party have far less right to call themselves the Labour Party than Mr. Attlee has to call himself their leader.

Look what has happened in the last week, and ponder gravely upon where we are and what you ought to do.

When I proposed to my Socialist and Liberal colleagues in the late Coalition that we should march on in good comradeship and loyal co-operation until the Japanese war was victoriously concluded, one of the matters which weighed most heavily and anxiously upon my mind was the need to maintain our direction of foreign affairs upon a steady course through the careful and intimate negotiations which must take place between the defeat of Nazi Germany and the defeat of Japan.

My hopes that the coalition of all parties would continue were disappointed. I tried hard to get the next best thing. I recalled the fruitful and cordial meeting of minds which had existed on all the main issues of foreign policy between the Socialist Ministers of the coalition and all the other Ministers of that Government. It appeared to me, therefore, as the best solution in the changed circumstances, to invite Mr. Attlee, the titular Socialist leader, to accompany Mr. Eden and myself to the forthcoming Conference with President Truman and Marshal Stalin.

It was my conception that I should enjoy Mr. Attlee's counsel at every stage of the discussions, and that what he said and agreed to he would naturally stand by. And from what I knew of him and his views over these last five years I did not expect there would arise in foreign affairs a single issue which could not be reconciled in an agreeable manner. In accepting my invitation Mr. Attlee showed that he shared this hopeful opinion.

However, a new figure has leaped into notoriety. The situation has now been complicated and darkened by the repeated intervention by Professor Laski, chairman of the Socialist Party Executive. He has reminded all of us, including Mr. Attlee, that the final determination on all questions of foreign policy rests, so far as the Socialist Party is concerned, with this dominating Socialist Executive.

Professor Laski has declared on several occasions, three at least, that there is no identity of purpose between the coalition foreign policy of the last five years, as continued by the present National Government, and the foreign policy of the powerful backroom organizations, over one of which he presides.

My friends, the British people have always hitherto wanted to have their affairs conducted by men they know, and that the men should work under the scrutiny and with the approval of the House of Commons. Now it seems we must refer to an obscure committee and be governed by unrepresentative persons, and that they will share the secrets and give the orders to the so-called responsible Ministers of the Crown, who will appear on the front Socialist bench of Parliament if they are returned and deliver orations upon which they have been instructed not from their own heart and conscience, not even from their constituencies, but from these dim conclaves below.

I confidently believe that the British democracy, with their long-trained common sense and innate love of independence, even while they are still struggling forward out of the exhaustion and sacrifices inseparable from hard-won victory, will ward off these dangers and make their way steadfastly towards something that can justly be called " hearth and home " in the land of hope and glory.

ELECTION ADDRESS

I HAVE served you for nearly twenty-two years, and this is the fifth time I ask for a renewal of your confidence.

I can say with heartfelt gratitude that without your unswerving support during the eleven years I was in the political wilderness I should not have been in a position to be called up to assume the supreme responsibility for guiding our country at the moment of its mortal danger.

Moreover, I should not have been able to give in Parliament those warnings which, when the moment came, were recognized to have been true by the whole British nation and Empire.

Both in the old constituency and the new you have been through very hard and long trials.

Not only did your manhood go to the wars, and share in every theatre upon land, upon the seas and in the air, the glory of the British Arms, but here at home, where their wives and children were dwelling, there fell an unusually prolonged and heavy bombardment from the enemy; finishing up with the flying-bomb and rocket attacks, in which you were one of the most hard-hit constituencies in the land.

During all this ordeal, under the continued fire of the enemy, you conducted yourselves with that fortitude, composure and constancy for which the British race has always been renowned.

You have suffered in silence and in secrecy, making no complaint, with every man, woman and child going about their duties honestly and diligently as they were required. Your men abroad will be as proud of you when they return as you have always been of them.

At my age, having already passed the allotted span, I might well have claimed relief from the burden which victory has not lightened.

I feel, however, that my faculties and energies are as good as they have ever been, and therefore, unless relieved by the nation, I cannot shrink from the tasks which have devolved upon me.

The war itself is not finished. The causes for which we drew the sword, not yet fully won, are not yet safe.

I still hope to take my share in a peace which shall be both world-wide and lasting, out of which will come victories in social progress not less than those in battle for which we are already well spoken-of throughout the world.

THE VOTER'S CHOICE

THE FOURTH ELECTION BROADCAST
JUNE 30, 1945

THIS strange, unnatural election, tearing asunder so many ties of mutual comprehension and comradeship which had grown up in our political life, is now, to everybody's relief, drawing to its close.

Under the ordinary working of the British Constitution the Coalition Government, which had rescued our country from ruin and carried it to victory in war, and had moreover a full and widening field of social activities and progress to open to a new Parliament, should have presented itself to the nation as a united body and asked for a renewal of their confidence.

Although this would have been the true interest and would have been also the wish of the nation and of the Empire, it was brushed aside by the overwhelmingly strong opinion of the Socialist party.

At the Labour Party Conference as far back as June, 1943, Mr. Attlee declared : " The Executive is absolutely opposed to a coupon election." " No coupon election " was the cry, and we all too tamely, I must admit, bowed to this view. Had we appealed to the country as a united Government, we should have been spared what we are going through now, and some things what we may have to go through in the near future.

One must make allowances for the banked-up impatience of party extremists who have not been able to take any useful part in the war. There is always the natural desire of minority parties to improve their representation in the House of Commons.

Above all, there was the need of refreshing the Parliament by an electoral stir-up in the constituencies, and resuming direct contact with the electorate after more than nine years.

The Coalition Ministers on both sides nourished the idea that when the German war was finished there could be a polite, friendly election— as the National Executive of the Labour Party put it—the great partnership should be dissolved with dignity and good feeling.

But all this has turned out to be an illusion. When it comes to a blunt, prosaic question of several hundred pairs of gentlemen wishing to sit on single seats, no compromise is possible, and a flood of violent altercation and extreme bitterness has broken loose.

This flood has caused much disturbance in political circles, but it has not affected to any serious extent the spirit of co-operation among the broad masses of the people for the main objects and causes we are pursuing.

The people liked the late Coalition Government, and would have been well pleased to give it a vote of confidence. They are puzzled and to some extent distressed by finding themselves in the midst of a wordy storm while so many grave matters enter into their lives or lie ahead in the world.

They do not seek violent political change at the present time. Their loyalties remain unshaken.

During my five days of touring among multitudes and addressing immense concourses, I have been profoundly moved by the kindness and confidence with which I was everywhere received.

It was wonderful to see the beauty of so many human faces lighting up often in a flash with welcome and joy, and this continued day after day along hundreds of miles through crowded towns and cities and also along high roads, where there were arrayed every few hundred yards groups and often large parties of men, women and children displaying the national flags and flags of other nations, and showering down their blessings and acclamations.

When I reflect on all the hardships and privations which the Government over which I have presided has found it necessary to enforce upon the nation, the heavy sacrifices they have demanded from them, affecting every home and every form of comfort ; and on the blood that has been shed and lives laid down by their dear ones, not to speak of the constant toil and faithful discharge of duty in all circumstances, often under fire, and among so many mistakes which have no doubt been made—when I reflect on all this, I cannot help feeling uplifted by the noble, generous, and dauntless character of the British people.

I was deeply struck by the appearance of our children who, in vast numbers, with bright eyes and vigorous voices, assembled by the roadside, or ran, some for great distances, beside the car.

Here is the hope of the future. We must all be thankful that, in spite of all the pressures of war, they at least have not suffered lack of wholesome food. What can I say to you of the girls and women, whose beauty charmed the eye, or of the old ladies, who were brought up in chairs or waved encouraging flags from high-perched windows ? All this I saw as I passed through the English countryside, the Midlands, Cheshire, Lancashire and Yorkshire, and no less dazzling were the spectacles which Scotland in all her splendour, presented.

My sorrow is that time did not allow me to visit many other counties in England, and to visit especially the principality of Wales, in order to give the Welshmen my thanks for the heroic services which they have rendered in the winning of the war.

What a magnificent part our women have played in this total war, into which we plunged for honour, though ill-armed; a war in which mingled so vividly the terrible with the sublime—in the homes, where often another family had to be received; in the factories, without which our munitions could not have been produced; on the land, where perhaps some are disappointed in their recognition; in the three Services, with the women looking so sprightly in their uniforms, in the hospitals like merciful angels, in the batteries, with nothing but a tin helmet night after night between them and the blitz, and setting men free for mobile service at the front! Who can measure their gifts to Britannia in her years of pain and glory?

A Royal Commission is now sitting on equal pay for equal work between men and women. The Commission must carefully consider where the true, permanent and lasting advantage to women in particular occupations lies in this matter. But I trust the new Parliament will establish, in an effective manner, the principle of the complete equality of women in industry, in all walks of life, and before the law, and that this will be achieved without any diminution in the chivalry and the protection of the strong right arm of the male warrior or toiler.

This is the last of the broadcasts of this election. It ends the series which the B.B.C. have placed at the disposal of the politicians, and it may be the last time that I shall so address you through this medium as Prime Minister. That rests with you. I am convinced that I can help you through the dangers and difficulties of the next few years with more advantage than would fall to others, and I am ready, if desired, to try my best.

I await your answer. It must be Aye or No. I await it not with pride or thirst for power—for what have I to gain or lose after all that has happened, and all you have done for me? But I await your answer with confidence. I have high confidence in the answer you will give.

Soldiers, sailors and airmen abroad in Germany, in Italy, in India and Burma or on the seas and oceans, I have a message which, though it applies everywhere, applies especially to you who are far from home. Here is the message:

Beware that you are not deceived about the workings of our political system at this Election. There is no truth in stories now being put about that you can vote for my political opponents at this election, whether they be Labour or Liberal, without at the same time voting for my dismissal from power. This you should not hesitate to do if you think it right and best for the country. All that I ask is that you should do it with your eyes open.

The Labour Party have formally declared and pledged themselves in their Conference on May 24 of this very year, 1945, not to make any coalition with the Conservatives after the election, and Mr. Laski, replying as chairman for the National Executive upon the discussion, gave the following pledge : " Delegates can be wholly assured that there is no possibility of Labour joining in a coalition with the Conservatives."

The delegates unanimously approved the National Executive's declaration of policy. Now that is a perfectly legitimate position for the Socialist Party to take up, if they feel that way. But it is also clear that it would be impossible for me to serve in a Labour Party Government when that party is wedded to policies which I regard as ruinous to the future of this country. If you wish me to continue to discharge the task of national leadership, there is only one way, and that is to vote for the candidates who support me and give me their confidence. I gravely deplore the unfair tactics adopted by those who have kept on trying to deceive you on this point after my repeated denials and the Labour Executive's published explicit declaration which I have read to you. If a Socialist Government is returned, it must come into power under its own leaders, and they must bear the responsibility, in so far as they are allowed to by the constitution of their party.

And here I must make a digression into what may be called " The Laski episode." It was a revelation to me when I, in all goodwill, invited Mr. Attlee to come with me to Berlin in July, in order to keep the flag of unity flying, that this hitherto almost unknown person, Professor Laski, who has never sought to face the electors and sits at the head of what is called " the National Executive Committee," of which the larger part are not even members of Parliament, that he should have the right—I can but call it the presumption—to lay down the law to the publicly-proclaimed leader of the Labour Party and tell him that he could only go to the Conference in the capacity of an observer, and that no continuity in our foreign policy could be undertaken.

Many days have passed since this happened. Mr. Laski has in no way withdrawn his instructions to the Labour Party leader. On the contrary, he has shown himself the master of forces too strong for Mr. Attlee to challenge by any effective counter-action.

Mr. Laski still remains chairman of the Socialist Executive. No vote of suspension, censure, or even deprecation has been passed upon him.

It appears that this Socialist Executive Committee possesses power over Socialist Ministers of a most far-reaching character ; that it could decide the action a Socialist Government would take in particular questions ; and that it could require the submission of Ministers to its will.

This means, for instance, that in foreign affairs, when there had to be discussion on some difficult question, secrets might have to be divulged to this committee of 27 members, very few of whom are Privy Councillors, and, though I am sure very great care would be taken, difficulties might arise.

It also means that the Socialist Ministers filling all the high offices of State would not be primarily responsible to the Crown and to Parliament, but would have to refer back to an utterly unconstitutional and undemocratic body lying in the background, whose names until the recent trouble have not been known to the public.

Such arrangements are abhorrent to the methods hitherto pursued in British public life. They strike at the root of our Parliamentary institutions, and, if they continue unabated, they will be one of the gravest changes in the constitutional history of England and of Britain.

There is another alternative we must bear in mind. In the event of the Socialists not having a working majority, but becoming the largest party in the House of Commons, they would have of course to rely on the support of that section of the Liberal Party—the Sinclair Liberals as they are called—which is hostile to the National Government.

A weak, unstable Government of that kind, based on unhealthy compromise between men who differ on fundamentals, and without any overpowering aim, except to hold office, would not be the sort of Government that we need at a time like this, when the country is faced with such enormous labours and grievous responsibilities.

We may well ask why the Sinclair Liberals pursue the present Conservative and National Government with such unrelenting abuse and opposition. There is nothing in the policy of the National Government, as announced in our manifesto, with which they do not agree. Sir Archibald Sinclair has been a party to the framing of the Four Years Plan, and thought it a fine thing while he was in office. I have never known that there was any difference between us on the broad essentials of foreign policy. On the other hand, the differences between Liberalism and Socialism are the most extreme and decisive that can be imagined. Yet it is the National Government which alone they attack by speech, by their newspapers and in the constituencies. They have done everything in their power to do us harm, and yet they can advance no claim of principle justifying their hostile action. That is a matter upon which all Liberals should question themselves.

I will now sum up in the simplest terms the issues which are at stake. Many anxious eyes are turned towards us. A failure by Great Britain to produce a strong, coherent, resolute Government, supported by a substantial and solid majority in Parliament, would alter the entire balance, not only of tortured Europe but of the whole world, now struggling to rise again and bring order out of chaos.

If our country dissolves into faction and party politics, we shall cease to fill the place won for us by our policy and our victories afloat and ashore, we shall cease to fill that place in the councils of the nations which so much blood and sacrifice has gained.

Without our effective aid, the world itself might go once again astray. Without our influence upon other nations, now so high, we should lose the confidence we have won during the war from the self-governing Dominions of our Empire and Commonwealth. In an incredibly short space of time we might then by our own folly fall to the rank of a secondary Power.

I have an invincible confidence in the genius of Britain. I believe in the instinctive wisdom of our well-tried democracy. I am sure they will speak now in ringing tones, and that their decision will vindicate the hopes of our friends in every land and will enable us to march in the vanguard of the United Nations in majestic enjoyment of our fame and power.

LETTER TO MR. ATTLEE

On June 15 the Prime Minister sent this letter to Mr. Clement Attlee,
leader of the Parliamentary Labour Party :

My Dear Attlee—I now send you a formal invitation to come with
us to the forthcoming tripartite Conference in the near future.

Since I announced this intention to Parliament, I observe that a
statement was made last night by Professor Harold Laski, the chairman of the Labour Party, in which he said, " It is, of course, essential
that if Mr. Attlee attends this gathering, he shall do so in the role of
an observer only."

His Majesty's Government must, of course, bear the responsibility
for all decisions. But my idea was that you should come as a friend
and counsellor, and help us on all the subjects on which we have been so
long agreed, and have been known to be agreed by public declaration.
In practice, I thought the British delegation would work just as they
did at San Francisco, except that, as I have already stated, you would
not have official responsibility to the Crown otherwise than as a Privy
Councillor.

Merely to come as a mute observer would, I think, be derogatory to
your position as the Leader of your party, and I should not have a
right to throw this burden upon you in such circumstances.

I hope, however, I may have your assurance that you accept my
invitation.

Yours very sincerely,
WINSTON S. CHURCHILL.

[Mr. Attlee accepted the invitation in a letter in which he said he had consulted his principal colleagues in the House of Commons, and that they
agreed the Prime Minister's offer should be accepted on the basis set out in
his letter. Mr. Attlee added that there was never any suggestion that he
should go as a mere observer.]

THE NATION'S VERDICT

A Statement issued by Mr. Winston Churchill from No. 10, Downing Street, after the declaration of the result of the General Election
July 26, 1945

THE decision of the British people has been recorded in the votes counted to-day. I have therefore laid down the charge which was placed upon me in darker times. I regret that I have not been permitted to finish the work against Japan. For this, however, all plans and preparations have been made, and the results may come much quicker than we have hitherto been entitled to expect. Immense responsibilities abroad and at home fall upon the new Government, and we must all hope that they will be successful in bearing them.

It only remains for me to express to the British people, for whom I have acted in these perilous years, my profound gratitude for the unflinching, unswerving support which they have given me during my task, and for the many expressions of kindness which they have shown towards their servant.

THE WAR

" DEAR DESERT RATS "

A SPEECH AT THE OPENING OF "THE WINSTON CLUB" FOR BRITISH
TROOPS IN BERLIN FOLLOWING A PARADE BY THE 7TH ARMOURED
DIVISION ("THE DESERT RATS")
JULY 21, 1945

June 13.   *President Truman announced that the time and place of the meeting between himself and Mr. Churchill and Marshal Stalin had been decided.*

June 14.   *It was stated that the trials of war criminals would begin within three weeks.*

June 15.   *It was revealed by Mr. Attlee that the meeting of the Big Three would be held in Berlin.*

     Admiral Mountbatten reviewed a ceremonial victory parade in Rangoon.

June 16.   *William Joyce (Lord Haw Haw, radio propagandist) arrived in London and was charged under the Treason Act at Bow Street.*

     Truk Atoll, the Gibraltar of Japan, was heavily attacked by sea and air.

June 17.   *General Buckner, U.S. Commanding Officer in Okinawa, was killed.*

June 18.   *German treasure hoard valued at £1,000,000,000 was found at Regensburg.*

June 19.   *Japanese industrial areas were heavily bombed by Superfortresses. U.S. submarine sank 11 Japanese ships.*

     British and Indian troops maintained progress in East Burma towards Siam.

     Four million New Yorkers welcomed General Eisenhower on his return to America.

June 20.   *U.S. carrier-based planes raided Wake Island in North Pacific and bombed other targets in Japan.*

June 21.   *Battle of Okinawa officially declared ended. Enemy losses in 82 days stated to be 100,000. General Stilwell was appointed to command U.S. 10th Army in Okinawa.*

     General Okulicki, former C-in-C Polish Home Army, was sentenced in Moscow to ten years for sabotage behind Red

Army front. Ten other Poles were sentenced on similar charges.

June 22. Sarawak was invaded by the Australians. Mr. Stettinius, U.S. Secretary of State, announced that 14 executive committee members of the United Nations would meet in London to plan the first conference of the new World Security Organization.

Super-fortresses dropped three thousand tons of high explosives on Japanese war industries.

June 23. Japanese planes and ships were destroyed in an assault on Sumatra by British carrier-based aircraft.

June 24. Australians advanced from Brunei Bay, Borneo, and seized the oil town of Seria.

June 25. 14th Army patrols cleared Japanese out of seven Burma villages South of Prome.

Darnand, former Vichy Minister of Interior, was arrested.

June 26. 50 delegates of the United Nations signed World Security Charter at San Francisco.

June 27. Japanese announced that the Allies had landed on the island of Kume, 50 miles West of Okinawa.

June 28. The entire island of Luzon in the Philippines was freed from the Japanese.

June 29. American bombers kept up heavy air attacks on Japanese sea ports.

June 30. 50 Allied ships and transports arrived off Balik Papan, oil port on the East coast of Borneo.

Australian forces landed near Balik Papan.

July 1. Russians began to move up to the Western borders of their occupation zone in Germany.

July 2. 600 U.S. Super-fortresses dropped record of 4,000 tons of incendiary bombs on Japanese cities.

British submarines sank a 10,000 ton Japanese cruiser.

July 3. It was reported that the Japanese had ordered civilians to evacuate Java.

British advance party arrived in Berlin.

July 4. Balik Papan almost encircled by Australian troops.

July 5. Japanese made small scale attacks against British positions on Sittang River 25 miles from Pegu.

July 6. The Union Jack was hoisted over Berlin when the British occupied their allotted zone.

Australian troops continued to make good progress in Borneo and captured an air-strip.

July 7. Mr. Churchill left England to spend a holiday in the South of France.

July 8. *American bombers from Iwojima attacked airfields on the Japanese mainland for the fourth day running. Tokio and Yokohama were also bombed.*

British cleared Japanese from more villages in Burma.

July 10. Two thousand Allied planes attacked Tokio.

July 12. Planes from British aircraft carriers attacked Sabang, off Sumatra.

July 13. SHAEF (Supreme Headquarters Allied Expeditionary Force) closed down.

Ten thousand British troops took part in a victory parade in Berlin.

July 14. Warships bombarded the port of Kamaishi on the Japanese mainland. Italy declared war on Japan.

July 15. Japanese strongpoint of Mount Batochampar, in Balik Papan area of Borneo, fell to the Australians.

July 16. Chiefs of Staff held a preliminary meeting before the opening of the Conference between the Prime Minister, President Truman and Generalissimo Stalin.

July 17. First meeting of the Big Three in Potsdam.

Allied battleships and bombers continued their attacks on the main islands of Japan.

July 18. Japanese were reported to be pulling out of the Sittang river bridgehead of Burma.

July 20. It was revealed that practically the entire British battle fleet had been moved into the war against Japan.

July 21. A United States broadcast called upon the Japanese to surrender.

In Burma the Japanese launched an attack on the British on the Sittang River.

[*July* 21, 1945.

I AM delighted to be able to open this club. I shall always consider it an honour to have it named after me.

This morning's parade brings back to my mind a great many moving incidents of these last long, fierce years. Now you are here in Berlin, and I find you established in this great centre which, as a volcano, erupted smoke and fire all over Europe. Twice in our generation as in bygone times the German fury has been unleashed on her neighbours.

Now it is we who take our place in the occupation of this country.

I think I may go so far as to ask Field-Marshal Montgomery to signalize the happy event of this great victory parade to-day by giving all the troops in Berlin a whole-day holiday. I hope, Field-Marshal, you can accommodate this operation.

"Dear Desert Rats," July 21, 1945

I have only one more word to say to the Desert Rats. You were the first to begin.

The 11th Hussars were in action in the Desert in 1940, and ever since you have kept marching steadily forward on the long road to Victory : through so many countries and changing scenes you have marched and fought your way.

I am unable to speak without emotion. Dear Desert Rats, may your glory ever shine. May your laurels never fade. May the memory of this glorious pilgrimage which you have made from Alamein to the Baltic and Berlin never die. A march—as far as my reading of history leads me to believe—unsurpassed in the whole story of war.

May fathers long tell their children the tale. May you all feel that through following your great ancestors you have accomplished something which has done good to the whole world, which has raised the honour of your country and of which every man has the right to feel proud.

TERMS FOR JAPAN

An Ultimatum issued by Mr. Churchill, President Truman and Generalissimo Chiang Kai-shek
July 26, 1945

July 22.   *Japanese battleship* Nagato *was bombed by Allied carrier planes at Yokosuka and twelve other enemy ships were sunk.*

July 24.   *1,000 planes of the Third U.S. fleet attacked enemy naval bases.*

July 25.   *Mr. Churchill, Mr. Eden and Mr. Attlee returned to London by air from Potsdam for the result of the General Election.*

    It was revealed that Admiral Mountbatten, Supreme Allied Commander South East Asia, had taken part in the Potsdam talks.

July 26.   *The Labour Party gained an overwhelming victory in the British General Election. Mr. Churchill resigned and Mr. Attlee became Prime Minister.*

    Britain, the United States and China addressed an ultimatum to the Japanese calling for immediate unconditional surrender, or complete destruction.

[July 26, 1945.

1. We, the President of the United States, the President of the National Government of the Republic of China, and the Prime Minister of Great Britain, representing the hundreds of millions of our countrymen, have conferred and agree that Japan shall be given an opportunity to end the war.

2. The prodigious land, sea, and air forces of the United States, the British Empire, and China, many times reinforced by their armies and air fleets from the West, are poised to strike the final blows upon Japan. This military power is sustained and inspired by the determination of all the Allied nations to prosecute the war against Japan until she ceases to resist.

3. The result of the futile and senseless German resistance to the might of the aroused free peoples of the world stands forth in awful clarity as an example to the people of Japan.

The might that now converges on Japan is immeasurably greater than that which when applied to the resisting Nazis, necessarily laid waste the lands, the industry, and the method of life of the whole German people. The full application of our military power, backed by our resolve, will mean the inevitable and complete destruction of the Japanese forces, and just as inevitably the utter devastation of the Japanese homeland.

4. The time has come for Japan to decide whether she will continue to be controlled by those self-willed militaristic advisers whose unintelligent calculations have brought the Empire of Japan to the threshold of annihilation, or whether she will follow the path of reason.

5. The following are our terms. We shall not deviate from them. There are no alternatives. We shall brook no delay :—

6. There must be eliminated for all time the authority and influence of those who have deceived and misled the people of Japan into embarking on world conquest, for we insist that a new order of peace, security and justice will be impossible until irresponsible militarism is driven from the world.

7.—Until such a new order is established and until there is convincing proof that Japan's war-making power is destroyed, points in Japanese territory designated by the Allies will be occupied to secure the achievement of the basic objectives we are here setting forth.

8.—The terms of the Cairo declaration shall be carried out, and Japanese sovereignty shall be limited to the islands of Honshu, Hokkaido, Kyushu, Shikoku, and such minor islands as we determine.

9. The Japanese military forces after being completely disarmed shall be permitted to return to their homes with the opportunity of leading peaceful and productive lives.

10. We do not intend that the Japanese shall be enslaved as a race nor destroyed as a nation, but stern justice will be meted out to all war criminals, including those who have visited cruelties upon our prisoners. The Japanese Government shall remove all obstacles to the revival and strengthening of democratic tendencies among the Japanese people. Freedom of speech, of religion and of thought as well as respect for fundamental human rights shall be established.

11. Japan shall be permitted to maintain such industries as will sustain her economy and allow of the exaction of just reparations in kind, but not those industries which would enable her to re-arm for war.

To this end access to, as distinguished from control of, raw materials shall be permitted. Eventual Japanese participation in world trade relations shall be permitted.

12. The occupying forces of the Allies shall be withdrawn from Japan as soon as these objectives have been accomplished and there has been established, in accordance with the freely-expressed will of the Japanese people, a peacefully-inclined and responsible government.

13. We call upon the Government of Japan to proclaim now the unconditional surrender of all the Japanese armed forces, and to provide proper and adequate assurances of their good faith in such action. The alternative for Japan is complete and utter destruction.

THE ATOMIC BOMB

ON AUGUST 6, 1945, PRESIDENT TRUMAN ANNOUNCED THAT
BRITISH AND AMERICAN SCIENTISTS HAD PRODUCED THE ATOMIC
BOMB AND THAT THE FIRST HAD THAT DAY BEEN DROPPED ON
JAPAN. MR. ATTLEE THEN ISSUED FROM NO. 10, DOWNING
STREET, THE FOLLOWING STATEMENT, WRITTEN BY MR. CHURCHILL
BEFORE THE CHANGE OF GOVERNMENT:

July 28.   *Japan rejected the Allied demand for surrender.*
          *Populations of 11 Japanese cities were warned to leave as
great air attacks were coming.*

July 29.   *Incendiary bombs were dropped on six Japanese cities.*

July 30.   *Allied air forces continued to raid Japan in ever-increasing
strength.*

July 31.   *Laval arrived in Austria by plane from Spain and was
handed over to the French for trial.*

August 1.   *Laval was taken to Paris to give evidence against Marshal
Pétain and to await his trial.*

August 2.   *The King met President Truman at Plymouth.*
          *It was announced that the Australians had trapped 50,000
Japanese in Rabaul.*

August 3.   *Enemy dead in the Pegu area of Burma announced to have
numbered 8,600.*

August 5.   *General MacArthur stated that 4,740 Japanese had been
killed in the mopping-up operations in the Philippines.*

August 6.   *President Truman announced that the first atomic bomb had
been dropped on Hiroshima, big city on the main island of
Japan. It was also stated that Japan had been given 48 hours
in which to surrender.*

August 7.   *It was revealed that Hiroshima had been completely wiped out
by the atomic bomb, and that a cloud of dust and smoke reached
to a height of 40,000 feet.*

[August 6, 1945.

BY the year 1939 it had become widely recognized among scientists
of many nations that the release of energy by atomic fission
was a possibility. The problems which remained to be solved before
this possibility could be turned into practical achievement were, how-

ever, manifold and immense ; and few scientists would at that time have ventured to predict that an atomic bomb could be ready for use by 1945. Nevertheless, the potentialities of the project were so great that His Majesty's Government thought it right that research should be carried on in spite of the many competing claims on our scientific man-power. At this stage the research was carried out mainly in our Universities, principally Oxford, Cambridge, London (Imperial College), Liverpool, and Birmingham. At the time of the formation of the Coalition Government responsibility for co-ordinating the work and pressing it forward lay with the Ministry of Aircraft Production, advised by a committee of leading scientists presided over by Sir George Thomson.

At the same time, under the general arrangements then in force for the pooling of scientific information, there was a full interchange of ideas between the scientists carrying out this work in the United Kingdom and those in the United States.

Such progress was made that by the summer of 1941 Sir George Thomson's committee was able to report that, in their view, there was a reasonable chance that an atomic bomb could be produced before the end of the war. At the end of August, 1941, Lord Cherwell, whose duty it was to keep me informed on all these and other technical developments, reported the substantial progress which was being made. The general responsibility for the scientific research carried on under the various technical committees lay with the then Lord President of the Council, Sir John Anderson. In these circumstances (having in mind also the effect of ordinary high explosive, which we had recently experienced), I referred the matter on August 20, 1941, to the Chiefs of Staff Committee in the following minute :—

" General Ismay, for Chiefs of Staff Committee : Although personally I am quite content with the existing explosives, I feel we must not stand in the path of improvement, and I therefore think that action should be taken in the sense proposed by Lord Cherwell, and that the Cabinet Minister responsible should be Sir John Anderson. I shall be glad to know what the Chiefs of Staff Committee think."

The Chiefs of the Staff recommended immediate action with the maximum priority.

It was then decided to set up within the Department of Scientific and Industrial Research a special division to direct the work, and Imperial Chemical Industries Limited agreed to release Mr. W. A. Akers to take charge of this directorate, which we called, for purposes of secrecy, the Directorate of " Tube Alloys." After Sir John Anderson had ceased to be Lord President and became Chancellor of the Exchequer I asked him to continue to supervise this work, for which he has special qualifications. To advise him there was set up under his chairmanship a consultative council composed of the President of the Royal Society, the Chairman of the Scientific Advisory Committee of the Cabinet, the Secretary of the Department of Scientific and Industrial Research, and Lord Cherwell. The Minister of Aircraft Production, at that time Lord Brabazon, also served on this committee.

Under the chairmanship of Mr. Akers there was also a technical committee, on which sat the scientists who were directing the different sections of the work and some others. This committee were originally composed of Sir James Chadwick, Professor Peierls, and Drs. Halban, Simon and Slade. Later it was joined by Sir Charles Darwin and Professors Cockcroft, Oliphant, and Feather. Full use was also made of university and industrial laboratories.

On October 11, 1941, President Roosevelt sent me a letter suggesting that any extended efforts on this important matter might usefully be co-ordinated, or even jointly conducted. Accordingly, all British and American efforts were joined, and a number of British scientists concerned proceeded to the United States. Apart from these contacts, complete secrecy guarded all these activities, and no single person was informed whose work was not indispensable to progress.

By the summer of 1942 this expanded programme of research had confirmed with surer and broader foundations the promising forecasts which had been made a year earlier, and the time had come when a decision must be made whether or not to proceed with the construction of large-scale production plants. Meanwhile it had become apparent from the preliminary experiments that these plants would have to be on something like the vast scale described in the American statements which have been published to-day.

Great Britain at this period was fully extended in war production, and we could not afford such grave interference with the current munitions programmes on which our warlike operations depended. Moreover, Great Britain was within easy range of German bombers, and the risk of raiders from the sea or air could not be ignored. The United States, however, where parallel or similar progress had been made, was free from these dangers. The decision was therefore taken to build the full-scale production plants in America.

In the United States the erection of the immense plants was placed under the responsibility of Mr. Stimson, United States Secretary of War, and the American Army Administration, whose wonderful work and marvellous secrecy cannot be sufficiently admired. The main practical effort and virtually the whole of its prodigious cost now fell upon the United States authorities, who were assisted by a

number of British scientists. The relationship of the British
and American contributions was regulated by discussion between the
late President Roosevelt and myself, and a combined policy committee
was set up.

The Canadian Government, whose contribution was most valuable,
provided both indispensable raw material for the project as a whole
and also necessary facilities for the work on one section of the project,
which has been carried out in Canada by the three Governments in
partnership.

The smoothness with which the arrangements for co-operation
which were made in 1943 have been carried into effect is a happy
augury for our future relations, and reflects great credit on all concerned
—on the members of the combined policy committee which we set up ;
on the enthusiasm with which our scientists and technicians gave of
their best—particularly Sir James Chadwick, who gave up his work
at Liverpool to serve as technical adviser to the United Kingdom
members of the policy committee and spared no effort ; and, not
least, on the generous spirit with which the whole United States
organization welcomed our men and made it possible for them to make
their contribution.

By God's mercy British and American science outpaced all German
efforts. These were on a considerable scale, but far behind. The
possession of these powers by the Germans at any time might have
altered the result of the war, and profound anxiety was felt by those
who were informed. Every effort was made by our Intelligence
Service and by the Air Force to locate in Germany anything resembling
the plants which were being created in the United States. In the
winter of 1942–43 most gallant attacks were made in Norway on two
occasions by small parties of volunteers from the British Commandos
and Norwegian forces, at very heavy loss of life, upon stores of what is
called " heavy water," an element in one of the possible processes.
The second of these two attacks was completely successful.

The whole burden of execution, including the setting-up of the plants
and many technical processes connected therewith in the practical
sphere, constitutes one of the greatest triumphs of American—or indeed
human—genius of which there is record. Moreover, the decision to
make these enormous expenditures upon a project which, however
hopefully established by American and British research, remained
nevertheless a heart-shaking risk, stands to the everlasting honour of
President Roosevelt and his advisers.

It is now for Japan to realize, in the glare of the first atomic bomb
which has smitten her, what the consequences will be of an indefinite
continuance of this terrible means of maintaining a rule of law in
the world.

This revelation of the secrets of nature, long mercifully withheld from man, should arouse the most solemn reflections in the mind and conscience of every human being capable of comprehension. We must indeed pray that these awful agencies will be made to conduce to peace among the nations, and that instead of wreaking measureless havoc upon the entire globe they may become a perennial fountain of world prosperity.

THE TRUE GLORY

A Speech to the House of Commons on a Motion congratulating
the King on the surrender of Japan
August 15, 1945

August 8.   *Russia declared war on Japan.*

August 9.   *The second atomic bomb was dropped on Nagasaki.*

August 10. *The Japanese Government surrendered, announcing by
radio that it would accept the Allied ultimatum issued by
Mr. Churchill, President Truman and Generalissimo Chiang
Kai-shek on July 26 on the understanding that the prerogative
of the Emperor of Japan was not compromised.*

August 11. *The Governments of Britain, the United States and China
announced that they would accept the Japanese surrender
offer and allow Hirohito to remain Emperor provided that
he ruled under the orders of the Allied Supreme Commander.*

August 12. *Tokio was bombed by Allied aircraft while the nations
awaited the Japanese reply to the demand for surrender.*

August 14. *Japan agreed to complete and final surrender, and the end
of the war was officially announced simultaneously in
London, Washington, Moscow and Chungking.*

[August 15, 1945.

THIS crowning deliverance from the long and anxious years of
danger and carnage should rightly be celebrated by Parliament
in accordance with custom and tradition. The King is the embodi-
ment of the national will, and his public acts involve all the might and
power not only of the people of this famous Island but of the whole
British Commonwealth and Empire. The good cause for which His
Majesty has contended commanded the ardent fidelity of all his subjects
spread over one-fifth of the surface of the habitable globe. That cause
has now been carried to complete success. Total war has ended in
absolute victory.

Once again the British Commonwealth and Empire emerges safe,
undiminished and united from a mortal struggle. Monstrous tyrannies
which menaced our life have been beaten to the ground in ruin, and a
brighter radiance illumines the Imperial Crown than any which our
annals record. The light is brighter because it comes not only from

the fierce but fading glare of military achievement such as an endless succession of conquerors have known, but because there mingle with it in mellow splendour the hopes, joys, and blessings of almost all mankind. This is the true glory, and long will it gleam upon our forward path.

THE SUPREME TRIUMPH

[August 16, 1945.

OUR duty is to congratulate His Majesty's Government on the very great improvement in our prospects at home, which comes from the complete victory gained over Japan and the establishment of peace throughout the world. Only a month ago it was necessary to continue at full speed and at enormous cost all preparations for a long and bloody campaign in the Far East. In the first days of the Potsdam Conference President Truman and I approved the plans submitted to us by the combined Chiefs of Staff for a series of great battles and landings in Malaya, in the Netherlands East Indies, and in the homeland of Japan itself. These operations involved an effort not surpassed in Europe, and no one could measure the cost in British and American life and treasure they would require. Still less could it be known how long the stamping-out of the resistance of Japan in the many territories she had conquered, and especially in her homeland, would take. All the while the whole process of turning the world from war to peace would be hampered and delayed. Every form of peace activity was half strangled by the overriding priorities of war. No clear-cut decisions could be taken in the presence of this harsh dominating uncertainty.

During the last three months an element of baffling dualism has complicated every problem of policy and administration. We had to plan for peace and war at the same time. Immense armies were being demobilized; another powerful army was being prepared and dispatched to the other side of the globe. All the personal stresses among millions of men eager to return to civil life, and hundreds of thousands of men who would have to be sent to new and severe campaigns in the Far East, presented themselves with growing tension. This dualism affected also every aspect of our economic and financial life. How to set people free to use their activities in reviving the life of Britain, and at the same time to meet the stern demands of the war against Japan, constituted one of the most perplexing and distressing puzzles that in a long life-time of experience I have ever faced.

I confess it was with great anxiety that I surveyed this prospect a month ago. Since then I have been relieved of the burden. At the same time that burden, heavy though it still remains, has been immeasurably lightened. On 17th July there came to us at Potsdam the eagerly-awaited news of the trial of the atomic bomb in the Mexican desert. Success beyond all dreams crowned this sombre, magnificent venture of our American Allies. The detailed reports of the Mexican desert experiment, which were brought to us a few days later by air, could leave no doubt in the minds of the very few who were informed, that we were in the presence of a new factor in human affairs, and possessed of powers which were irresistible. Great Britain had a right to be consulted in accordance with Anglo-American agreements. The decision to use the atomic bomb was taken by President Truman and myself at Potsdam, and we approved the military plans to unchain the dread, pent-up forces.

From that moment our outlook on the future was transformed. In preparation for the results of this experiment, the statements of the President and of Mr. Stimson and my own statement, which by the courtesy of the Prime Minister was subsequently read out on the broadcast, were framed in common agreement. Marshal Stalin was informed by President Truman that we contemplated using an explosive of incomparable power against Japan, and action proceeded in the way we all now know. It is to this atomic bomb more than to any other factor that we may ascribe the sudden and speedy ending of the war against Japan.

Before using it, it was necessary first of all to send a message in the form of an ultimatum to the Japanese which would apprise them of what unconditional surrender meant. This document was published on 26th July—the same day that another event, differently viewed on each side of the House, occurred. [Note : The result of the General Election and the resignation of Mr. Churchill from the Premiership.] The assurances given to Japan about her future after her unconditional surrender had been made were generous in the extreme. When we remember the cruel and treacherous nature of the utterly unprovoked attack made by the Japanese war lords upon the United States and Great Britain, these assurances must be considered magnanimous in a high degree. In a nutshell, they implied " Japan for the Japanese," and even access to raw materials, apart from their control, was not denied to their densely-populated homeland. We felt that in view of the new and fearful agencies of war-power about to be employed, every inducement to surrender, compatible with our declared policy, should be set before them. This we owed to our consciences before using this awful weapon.

Secondly, by repeated warnings, emphasized by heavy bombing attacks, an endeavour was made to procure the general exodus of the civil population from the threatened cities. Thus everything in human power, prior to using the atomic bomb, was done to spare the civil population of Japan. There are voices which assert that the bomb should never have been used at all. I cannot associate myself with such ideas. Six years of total war have convinced most people that had the Germans or Japanese discovered this new weapon, they would have used it upon us to our complete destruction with the utmost alacrity. I am surprised that very worthy people, but people who in most cases had no intention of proceeding to the Japanese front themselves, should adopt the position that rather than throw this bomb, we should have sacrificed a million American, and a quarter of a million British lives in the desperate battles and massacres of an invasion of Japan. Future generations will judge these dire decisions, and I believe that if they find themselves dwelling in a happier world from which war has been banished, and where freedom reigns, they will not condemn those who struggled for their benefit amid the horrors and miseries of this gruesome and ferocious epoch.

The bomb brought peace, but men alone can keep that peace, and henceforward they will keep it under penalties which threaten the survival, not only of civilization but of humanity itself. I may say that I am in entire agreement with the President that the secrets of the atomic bomb should so far as possible not be imparted at the present time to any other country in the world. This is in no design or wish for arbitrary power, but for the common safety of the world. Nothing can stop the progress of research and experiment in every country, but although research will no doubt proceed in many places, the construction of the immense plants necessary to transform theory into action cannot be improvised in any country.

For this and many other reasons the United States stand at this moment at the summit of the world. I rejoice that this should be so. Let them act up to the level of their power and their responsibility, not for themselves but for others, for all men in all lands, and then a brighter day may dawn upon human history. So far as we know, there are at least three and perhaps four years before the concrete progress made in the United States can be overtaken. In these three years we must remould the relationships of all men, wherever they dwell, in all the nations. We must remould them in such a way that these men do not wish or dare to fall upon each other for the sake of vulgar and out-dated ambitions or for passionate differences in ideology, and that international bodies of supreme authority may give peace on earth and decree justice among men. Our pilgrimage has brought us to a sublime moment in the history of the world. From the least to the greatest, all must strive to be worthy of these supreme opportunities. There is not an hour to be wasted ; there is not a day to be lost.

It would in my opinion be a mistake to suggest that the Russian declaration of war upon Japan was hastened by the use of the atomic bomb. My understanding with Marshal Stalin in the talks which I had with him had been, for a considerable time past, that Russia would declare war upon Japan within three months of the surrender of the German armies. The reason for the delay of three months was, of course, the need to move over the trans-Siberian Railway the large reinforcements necessary to convert the Russian-Manchurian army from a defensive to an offensive strength. Three months was the time mentioned, and the fact that the German armies surrendered on 8th May, and the Russians declared war on Japan on 8th August, is no mere coincidence, but another example of the fidelity and punctuality with which Marshal Stalin and his valiant armies always keep their military engagements.

I now turn to the results of the Potsdam Conference so far as they have been made public in the agreed communiqué and in President Truman's very remarkable speech of a little more than a week ago. There has been general approval of the arrangements proposed for the administration of Germany by the Allied Control Commission during the provisional period of military government. This régime is both transitional and indefinite. The character of Hitler's Nazi party was such as to destroy almost all independent elements in the German people. The struggle was fought to the bitter end. The mass of the people were forced to drain the cup of defeat to the dregs. A headless Germany has fallen into the hands of the conquerors. It may be many years before any structure of German national life will be possible, and there will be plenty of time for the victors to consider how the interests of world peace are affected thereby.

In the meanwhile, it is in my view of the utmost importance that responsibility should be effectively assumed by German local bodies for carrying on under Allied supervision all the processes of production and of administration necessary to maintain the life of a vast population. It is not possible for the Allies to bear responsibility by themselves. We cannot have the German masses lying down upon our hands and expecting to be fed, organized and educated over a period of years by the Allies. We must do our best to help to avert the tragedy of famine. But it would be in vain for us in our small Island, which still needs to import half its food, to imagine that we can make any further appreciable contribution in that respect. The rationing of this country cannot be made more severe without endangering the life and physical strength of our people, all of which will be needed for the immense tasks we have to do. I, therefore, most strongly advise the encouragement of the assumption of responsibility by trustworthy German local bodies in proportion as they can be brought into existence.

The Council which was set up at Potsdam of the Foreign Secretaries of the three, four or five Powers, meeting in various combinations as occasion served, affords a new and flexible machinery for the continuous further study of the immense problems that lie before us in Europe and Asia. I am very glad that the request that I made to the Conference that the seat of the Council's permanent Secretariat should be London, was granted. I must say that the late Foreign Secretary (Mr. Anthony Eden), who has, over a long period, gained an increasing measure of confidence from the Foreign Secretaries of Russia and the United States, and who through the European Advisory Committee which is located in London has always gained the feeling that things could be settled in a friendly and easy way, deserves some of the credit for the fact that these great Powers willingly accorded us the seat in London of the permanent Secretariat. It is high time that the place of London, one of the controlling centres of international world affairs, should at last be recognized. It is the oldest, the largest, the most battered capital, the capital which was first in the war, and the time is certainly overdue when we should have our recognition.

I am glad also that a beginning is to be made with the evacuation of Persia by the British and Russian armed forces, in accordance with the triple treaty which we made with each other and with Persia in 1941. Although it does not appear in the communiqué, we have since seen it announced that the first stage in the process, namely the withdrawal of Russian and British troops from Teheran, has already begun or is about to begin. There are various other matters arising out of this Conference which should be noted as satisfactory. We should not, however, delude ourselves into supposing that the results of this first Conference of the victors were free from disappointment or anxiety, or that the most serious questions before us were brought to good solutions. Those which proved incapable of agreement at the Conference have been relegated to the Foreign Secretaries' Council, which, though most capable of relieving difficulties, is essentially one gifted with less far-reaching powers. Other grave questions are left for the final peace settlement, by which time many of them may have settled themselves, not necessarily in the best way.

It would be at once wrong and impossible to conceal the divergences of view which exist inevitably between the victors about the state of affairs in Eastern and Middle Europe. I do not at all blame the Prime Minister or the new Foreign Secretary, whose task it was to finish up the discussions which we had begun. I am sure they did their best. We have to realize that no one of the three leading Powers can impose its solutions upon others, and that the only solutions possible are those which are in the nature of compromise. We British have had very early and increasingly to recognize the limitations of our own power and influence, great though it be, in the gaunt world arising from the ruins of this hideous war. It is not in the power of any British Government to bring home solutions which would be regarded as perfect by the great majority of Members of this House, wherever they may sit. I must put on record my own opinion that the provisional Western Frontier agreed upon for Poland, running from Stettin on the Baltic, along the Oder and its tributary, the Western Neisse, comprising as it does one quarter of the arable land of all Germany, is not a good augury for the future map of Europe. We always had in the Coalition Government a desire that Poland should receive ample compensation in the West for the territory ceded to Russia East of the Curzon Line. But here I think a mistake has been made, in which the Provisional Government of Poland have been an ardent partner, by going far beyond what necessity or equity required. There are few virtues that the Poles do not possess—and there are few mistakes they have ever avoided.

I am particularly concerned, at this moment, with the reports reaching us of the conditions under which the expulsion and exodus of Germans from the new Poland are being carried out. Between eight and nine million persons dwelt in those regions before the war. The Polish Government say that there are still 1,500,000 of these, not yet expelled, within their new frontiers. Other millions must have taken refuge behind the British and American lines, thus increasing the food stringency in our sector. But enormous numbers are utterly unaccounted for. Where are they gone, and what has been their fate ? The same conditions may reproduce themselves in a modified form in the expulsion of great numbers of Sudeten and other Germans from Czechoslovakia. Sparse and guarded accounts of what has happened and is happening have filtered through, but it is not impossible that tragedy on a prodigious scale is unfolding itself behind the iron curtain which at the moment divides Europe in twain. I should welcome any statement which the Prime Minister can make which would relieve, or at least inform us upon this very anxious and grievous matter.

There is another sphere of anxiety. I remember that a fortnight or so before the last war, the Kaiser's friend Herr Ballin, the great shipping magnate, told me that he had heard Bismarck say towards the end of his life, " If there is ever another war in Europe, it will come out of some damned silly thing in the Balkans." The murder of the Archduke at Sarajevo in 1914 set the signal for the first world war. I cannot conceive that the elements for a new conflict do not exist in the Balkans to-day. I am not using the language of Bismarck, but nevertheless not many Members of the new House of Commons will be content with the new situation that prevails in those mountainous, turbulent, ill-organized and warlike regions. I do not intend to particularize. I am very glad to see the new Foreign Secretary (Mr. Ernest Bevin) sitting on the Front Bench opposite. I should like to say with what gratification I learned that he had taken on this high and most profoundly difficult office, and we are sure he will do his best to preserve the great causes for which we have so long pulled together. But as I say, not many Members will be content with the situation in that region to which I have referred, for almost everywhere Communist forces have obtained, or are in process of obtaining, dictatorial powers. It does not mean that the Communist system is everywhere being established, nor does it mean that Soviet Russia seeks to reduce all those independent States to provinces of the Soviet Union. Marshal Stalin is a very wise man, and I would set no limits to the immense contributions that he and his associates have to make to the future.

In those countries, torn and convulsed by war, there may be, for some months to come, the need of authoritarian government. The alternative would be anarchy. Therefore it would be unreasonable to ask or expect that liberal government—as spelt with a small " l "— and British or United States democratic conditions, should be instituted immediately. They take their politics very seriously in those countries. A friend of mine, an officer, was in Zagreb when the results of the late General Election came in. An old lady said to him, " Poor Mr. Churchill! I suppose now he will be shot." My friend was able to reassure her. He said the sentence might be mitigated to one of the various forms of hard labour which are always open to His Majesty's subjects. Nevertheless we must know where we stand, and we must make clear where we stand, in these affairs of the Balkans and of Eastern Europe, and indeed of any country which comes into this field. Our ideal is government of the people by the people, for the people—the people being free without duress to express, by secret ballot without intimidation, their deep-seated wish as to the form and conditions of the Government under which they are to live.

At the present time—I trust a very fleeting time—" police governments " rule over a great number of countries. It is a case of the odious 18B, carried to a horrible excess. The family is gathered round the fireside to enjoy the scanty fruits of their toil and to recruit their exhausted strength by the little food that they have been able to gather. There they sit. Suddenly there is a knock at the door, and a heavily armed policeman appears. He is not, of course, one who resembles in any way those functionaries whom we honour and obey in the London streets. It may be that the father or son, or a friend sitting in the cottage, is called out and taken off into the dark, and no one knows whether he will ever come back again, or what his fate has been. All they know is that they had better not inquire. There are millions of humble homes in Europe at the moment, in Poland, in Czechoslovakia, in Austria, in Hungary, in Yugoslavia, in Rumania, in Bulgaria— where this fear is the main preoccupation of the family life. President

Roosevelt laid down the four freedoms, and these are expressed in the Atlantic Charter which we agreed together. " Freedom from fear "— but this has been interpreted as if it were only freedom from fear of invasion from a foreign country. That is the least of the fears of the common man. His patriotism arms him to withstand invasion or go down fighting ; but that is not the fear of the ordinary family in Europe to-night. Their fear is of the policeman's knock. It is not fear for the country, for all men can unite in comradeship for the defence of their native soil. It is for the life and liberty of the individual, for the fundamental rights of man, now menaced and precarious in so many lands, that peoples tremble.

Surely we can agree in this new Parliament, or the great majority of us, wherever we sit—there are naturally and rightly differences and cleavages of thought—but surely we can agree in this new Parliament, which will either fail the world or once again play a part in saving it, that it is the will of the people freely expressed by secret ballot, in universal suffrage elections, as to the form of their government and as to the laws which shall prevail, which is the first solution and safeguard. Let us then march steadily along that plain and simple line. I avow my faith in Democracy, whatever course or view it may take with individuals and parties. They may make their mistakes, and they may profit from their mistakes. Democracy is now on trial as it never was before, and in these Islands we must uphold it, as we upheld it in the dark days of 1940 and 1941, with all our hearts, with all our vigilance, and with all our enduring and inexhaustible strength. While the war was on and all the Allies were fighting for victory, the word " Democracy," like many people, had to work overtime, but now that peace has come we must search for more precise definitions. Elections have been proposed in some of these Balkan countries where only one set of candidates is allowed to appear, and where, if other parties are to express their opinion, it has to be arranged beforehand that the governing party, armed with its political police and all its propaganda, is the only one which has the slightest chance. Chance, did I say ? It is a certainty.

Now is the time for Britons to speak out. It is odious to us that governments should seek to maintain their rule otherwise than by free unfettered elections by the mass of the people. Governments derive their just powers from the consent of the governed, says the Constitution of the United States. This must not evaporate in swindles and lies propped up by servitude and murder. In our foreign policy let us strike continually the notes of freedom and fair play as we understand them in these Islands. Then you will find there will be an overwhelming measure of agreement between us, and we shall in this House march forward on a honourable theme having within it all that invests human life with dignity and happiness. In saying all this, I have been trying to gather together and present in a direct form the things which, I believe, are dear to the great majority of us. I rejoiced to read them expressed in golden words by the President of the United States when he said :

" Our victory in Europe was more than a victory of arms. It was a victory of one way of life over another. It was a victory of an ideal founded on the right of the common man, on the dignity of the human being, and on the conception of the State as the servant, not the master, of its people."

I think there is not such great disagreement between us. Emphasis may be cast this way and that in particular incidents, but surely this is what the new Parliament on the whole means. This is what in our heart and conscience, in foreign affairs and world issues, we desire. Just as in the baleful glare of 1940, so now, when calmer lights shine, let us be united upon these resurgent principles and impulses of the good and generous hearts of men. Thus to all the material strength we possess and the honoured position we have acquired, we shall add those moral forces which glorify mankind and make even the weakest equals of the strong.

I now turn to the domestic sphere. I have already spoken of the enormous easement in their task which the new Government have obtained through the swift and sudden ending of the Japanese war. What thousands of millions of pounds sterling are saved from the waste of war, what scores and hundreds of thousands of lives are saved, what vast numbers of ships are set free to carry the soldiers home to all their lands, to carry about the world the food and raw materials vital to industry ! What noble opportunities have the new Government inherited ! Let them be worthy of their fortune, which is also the fortune of us all. To release and liberate the vital springs of British energy and inventiveness, to let the honest earnings of the nation fructify in the pockets of the people, to spread well-being and security against accident and misfortune throughout the whole nation, to plan, wherever State planning is imperative, and to guide into fertile and healthy channels the native British genius for comprehension and goodwill—all these are open to them, and all these ought to be open to all of us now. I hope we may go forward together, not only abroad but also at home, in all matters so far as we possibly can.

During the period of the " Caretaker Government," while we still had to contemplate eighteen months of strenuous war with Japan, we reviewed the plans for demobilization in such a way as to make a very great acceleration in the whole process of releasing men and women from the Armed Forces and from compulsory industrial employment. Now, all that is overtaken by the world-wide end of the war. I must say at once that the paragraph of the Gracious Speech

[The King's speech outlining the new Government's policy] referring to demobilization and to the plans which were made in the autumn
of 1944—with which I am in entire agreement in principle—gives a
somewhat chilling impression. Now that we have had this wonderful
windfall, I am surprised that any Government should imagine that
language of this kind is still appropriate or equal to the new situation.
I see that in the United States the President has said that all the
American troops that the American ships can carry home in the next
year will be brought home and set free. Are His Majesty's Government now able to make any statement of that kind about our Armed
Forces abroad ? Or what statement can they make ? I do not want
to harass them unduly, but perhaps some time next week some statement could be made. No doubt the Prime Minister will think of that.
Great hopes have been raised in the electoral campaign, and from those
hopes has sprung their great political victory. Time will show whether
those hopes are well founded, as we deeply trust they may be. But
many decisions can be taken now, in the completely altered circumstances in which we find ourselves. The duty of the Government is to
fix the minimum numbers who must be retained in the next six or
twelve months' period in all the foreign theatres, and to bring the rest
home with the utmost speed that our immensely expanded shipping
resources will permit.

Even more is this releasing process important in the demobilization
of the home establishment. I quite agree that the feeling of the
Class A men must ever be the dominant factor, but short of that the
most extreme efforts should be made to release people who are standing
about doing nothing. I hope the Public Expenditure Committee will
be at once reconstituted, and that they will travel about the country
examining home establishments and reporting frequently to the
House. Now that the war is over, there is no ground of military
secrecy which should prevent the publication of the exact numerical
ration strengths of our Army, Navy and Air Force in every theatre and
at home, and we should certainly have weekly, or at least monthly
figures of the progressive demobilization effected. It is an opportunity
for the new Government to win distinction. At the end of the last
war, when I was in charge of the Army and Air Force, I published
periodically very precise information. I agree with the words used
by the Foreign Secretary when he was Minister of Labour in my
Administration, namely, that the tremendous winding-up process of
the war must be followed by a methodical and regulated unwinding.
We agree that if the process is to be pressed forward with the utmost
speed it is necessary for the Government to wield exceptional powers
for the time being, and so long as they use those powers to achieve the
great administrative and executive tasks imposed upon them, we shall

not attack them. It is only if, and in so far as, those powers are used to bring about by a side-wind a state of controlled society agreeable to Socialist doctrinaires, but which we deem odious to British freedom, that we shall be forced to resist them. So long as the exceptional powers are used as part of the war emergency, His Majesty's Government may consider us as helpers and not as opponents, as friends and not as foes.

To say this in no way relieves the Government of their duty to set the nation free as soon as possible, to bring home the soldiers in accordance with the scheme with the utmost rapidity, and to enable the mass of the people to resume their normal lives and employment in the best, easiest and speediest manner. There ought not to be a long-dragged-out period of many months when hundreds of thousands of Service men and women are kept waiting about under discipline, doing useless tasks at the public expense, and other tens of thousands, more highly paid, finding them sterile work to do. What we desire is freedom ; what we need is abundance. Freedom and abundance—these must be our aims. The production of new wealth is far more beneficial, and on an incomparably larger scale, than class and party fights about the liquidation of old wealth. We must try to share blessings and not miseries.

The production of new wealth must precede common wealth, otherwise there will only be common poverty. I am sorry these simple truisms should excite the hon. Member opposite—whom I watched so often during the course of the last Parliament and whose many agreeable qualities I have often admired—as if they had some sense of novelty for him.

We do not propose to join issue immediately about the legislative proposals in the Gracious Speech. We do not know what is meant by the control of investment—but apparently it is a subject for mirth. Evidently, in war you may do one thing, and in peace perhaps another must be considered. Allowance must also be made for the transitional period through which we are passing. The Debate on the Address should probe and elicit the Government's intentions in this matter. The same is true of the proposal to nationalize the coal mines. If that is really the best way of securing a larger supply of coal at a cheaper price, and at an earlier moment than is now in view, I, for one, should approach the plan in a sympathetic spirit. It is by results that the Government will be judged, and it is by results that this policy must be judged. The national ownership of the Bank of England does not in my opinion raise any matter of principle. I give my opinion—anybody else may give his own. There are important examples in the United States and in our Dominions of central banking institutions, but what matters is the use to be made of this public ownership. On this we must await the detailed statement by the Chancellor of the Exchequer, who, I am glad to say, has pledged himself to resist inflation. Meanwhile it may be helpful for me to express the opinion, as Leader of the Opposition, that foreign countries need not be alarmed by the language of the Gracious Speech on this subject, and that British credit will be resolutely upheld.

Then there is the Trade Disputes Act. We are told that this is to be repealed. Personally, I feel that we owe an inestimable debt to the Trade Unions for all they have done for the country in the long struggle against the foreign foe. But they would surely be unwise to reinstitute the political levy on the old basis. It would also be very odd if they wished to regain full facilities for legalizing and organizing a general strike. It does not say much for the confidence with which the Trades Union Council view the brave new world, or for what they think about the progressive nationalization of our industries, that they should deem it necessary on what an hon. and gallant Gentleman called " the D-Day of the new Britain " to restore and sharpen the general strike weapon, at this particular time of all others. Apparently nationalization is not regarded by them as any security against conditions which would render a general strike imperative and justified in the interests of the workers. We are, I understand, after nationalizing the coalmines, to deal with the railways, electricity and transport. Yet at the same time the Trade Unions feel it necessary to be heavily re-armed against State Socialism. Apparently the new age is not to be so happy for the wage-earners as we have been asked to believe. At any rate, there seems to be a fundamental incongruity in these conceptions to which the attention of the Socialist intelligentsia should speedily be directed. Perhaps it may be said that these powers will only be needed if the Tories come into office. Surely these are early days to get frightened. I will ask the Prime Minister if he will just tell us broadly what is meant by the word " repeal."

I have offered these comments to the House, and I do not wish to end on a sombre or even slightly controversial note. As to the situation which exists to-day, it is evident that not only are the two Parties in the House agreed in the main essentials of foreign policy and in our moral outlook on world affairs, but we also have an immense programme, prepared by our joint exertions during the Coalition, which requires to be brought into law and made an inherent part of the life of the people. Here and there there may be differences of emphasis and view, but in the main no Parliament ever assembled with such a mass of agreed legislation as lies before us this afternoon. I have great hopes of this Parliament, and I shall do my utmost to make its work fruitful. It may heal the wounds of war, and turn to good account the new conceptions and powers which we have gathered amid the storm.   I do not underrate the difficult and intricate complications of the task which lies before us ; I know too much about it to cherish vain illusions ; but the morrow of such a victory as we have gained is a splendid moment both in our small lives and in our great history.   It is a time not only of rejoicing but even more of resolve.   When we look back on all the perils through which we have passed and at the mighty foes we have laid low and all the dark and deadly designs we have frustrated, why should we fear for our future ?   We have come safely through the worst.

> *" Home is the sailor, home from sea,*
> *And the hunter home from the hill."*